Global Dynamics of Social Policy

This open access series welcomes studies on the waves, ruptures and transformative periods of welfare state expansion and retrenchment globally, that is, across nation states and the world as well as across history since the inception of the modern Western welfare state in the nineteenth century. It takes a comprehensive and globalized perspective on social policy, and the approach will help to locate and explain episodes of retrenchment, austerity, and tendencies toward de-welfarization in particular countries, policy areas and/or social risk-groups by reference to prior, simultaneous or anticipated episodes of expansion or contraction in other countries, areas, and risks. One of the aims of this series is to address the different constellations that emerge between political and economic actors including international and intergovernmental organizations, political actors and bodies, and business enterprises. A better understanding of these dynamics improves the reader's grasp of social policy making, social policy outputs, and ultimately the outcomes of social policy.

Armando Barrientos

Social Protection in Latin America

Causality, Stratification and Outcomes

palgrave
macmillan

Armando Barrientos
Global Development Institute
The University of Manchester
Manchester, UK

ISSN 2661-8672 ISSN 2661-8680 (electronic)
Global Dynamics of Social Policy
ISBN 978-3-031-49794-0 ISBN 978-3-031-49795-7 (eBook)
https://doi.org/10.1007/978-3-031-49795-7

This Palgrave Macmillan imprint is published by the registered company Springer Nature Switzerland AG.
The registered company address is: Gewerbestrasse 11, 6330 Cham, Switzerland

Paper in this product is recyclable.

Preface and Acknowledgements

This book builds on research on social protection institutions in Latin America conducted throughout my academic career. Social protection is an essential component of public policy. Its successes or failures have direct implications for the welfare of our populations, especially less advantaged groups. Social protection institutions reflect, unlike many other institutions, advances or regressions in social justice. Studying Latin American social protection institutions opens a window on social justice in practice.

Reflecting on the dynamics of social protection in Latin America in the 'long century' reminded me of some personal experiences. My father was part of a group of municipal workers who, on behalf of their union, secured legal recognition for the Occupational Insurance Fund of Municipal Workers (*Caja de Empleados Municipales*) in Chile. Revisiting Chile in 1990, after being exiled in 1975, I was intrigued by blanket advertising from the individual retirement savings plans (AFPs or *Administradoras de Fondos de Pensiones*) with claims to retirement 'riches'. I remember observing first hand the rapid global spread of 'cash transfers' with colleagues at the Chronic Poverty Centre in Manchester in the early 2000s and tracing the expansion of 'social pensions' and conditional income transfers in Latin America. This book reflects personal and academic journeys.

I owe a debt of gratitude to many colleagues and students who over many years sparked my interest, and educated me, on the intellectual challenges associated with researching social protection institutions in Latin America. We have also shared many frustrations with the failings and inequality of these institutions. I have not listed them individually as I have cited their many works in the reference list. As will be apparent from the book, I have borrowed freely from the canonical work of Carmelo Mesa-Lago (stratification and causality), Evelyne Huber and John Stephens (class and democracy), Stephen Haggard and Robert R. Kaufman (critical realignments), and Ruth Berins Collier and David Collier (incorporation). I have also benefited from the excellent work of recent cohorts of scholars offering new and challenging perspectives on social protection in Latin America. It is pleasing that research on social protection and social policy in the region is in excellent health.

My colleagues at the Global Development Institute at the University of Manchester and the amazing doctoral students I have had the fortune of working with, all helped to keep my research going and growing. As one of a handful of staff with an interest in Latin America at the Institute, comparative work was hugely rewarding. The research focus of the Global Development Institute, and the World Poverty Institute which preceded it, on disadvantaged groups in Latin America, Africa, and Asia, was transformative.

In 2019, I was invited to become a Mercator Fellow in the Collaborative Research Centre 1342 'Global Dynamics of Social Policy' at the University of Bremen. Despite the intrusion of COVID-19, I benefited greatly from engaging with the broad scope of research undertaken under this important project. The ambitious focus of this research programme helped me shape the contours of this book. In particular, I thank the Editors of the Palgrave Series on 'Global Dynamics of Social Policy', Lorraine Frisina Doetter, Delia González de Reufels, Kerstin Martens, and Marianne Ulriksen for making the publication of this book possible.

I thank my partner Stephanie for her support and understanding during the process of writing this book. Our children Kim and Rici used to complain about our dinner conversations around research, but I have learned most of what I know about global production networks and agriculture from Stephanie.

Open access of this publication was made possible through funding by the Collaborative Research Centre (CRC) 1342 'Global Dynamics of Social Policy' at the University of Bremen, funded by the Deutsche Forschungsgemeinschaft (DFG, German research Foundation – Projektnummer 374666841 – SBF 1342 and Specialised Information Service Political Science—POLLUX).

Manchester, UK Armando Barrientos

Contents

About the Author

Armando Barrientos is Professor Emeritus of Poverty and Social Justice at the Global Development Institute at the University of Manchester in the United Kingdom. His research focuses on the linkages existing between welfare programmes and labour markets in developing countries and on policies addressing poverty, vulnerability, and population ageing. His work has been published widely, including articles in *World Development*, *Economy and Society*, *Journal of Latin American Studies*, and *Journal of Development Studies*. His most recent books are *Social Protection for the Poor and Poorest* (2008, edited with D. Hulme, Palgrave); *Just Give Money to the Poor* (2010, with J. Hanlon and D. Hulme, Kumarian Press); and *Social Assistance in Developing Countries* (2013, Cambridge University Press). A database of social assistance in low and middle-income countries is available at http://www.social-assistance.manchester.ac.uk/

List of Figures

List of Tables

1

Introduction

This book provides an account of social protection institutions in Latin America. It aims to develop a systematic understanding of the contribution of social protection institutions to shaping economic and social cooperation in the region. It is motivated by an acknowledgement that we lack a settled theory of social protection institutions in Latin America. Comparative study of social protection in the region has accelerated in recent decades. The availability of harmonised data on social protection programmes, their features, implementation, and outcomes has made this possible. Regular household survey data, attitudinal data, and programme evaluation data offer a range of tools to support the study social protection institutions. A substantive comparative research literature built on improving comparative data is making a significant contribution to our understanding of the role and scope of social protection in the region. This book contributes to advance research further towards the development of a theory of social protection in Latin America. By theory it is meant a systematic and comprehensive analysis of the contribution of social protection institutions to shaping social and economic cooperation.

A. Barrientos, *Social Protection in Latin America*, Global Dynamics of Social Policy ,
https://doi.org/10.1007/978-3-031-49795-7_1

The development of a theory of social protection in Latin America has been delayed by two approaches common in the literature.[1] Implicit in much of the literature on social protection in the region is the assumption that our institutions are on a slow march towards fully fledged European welfare states, taken as the inescapable point of destination. The implication flowing from this assumption is that social protection institutions in the region are best understood as underdeveloped welfare states. Researchers interested in social protection in Latin America have much to learn from theories and methods developed to study welfare states. They provide a wealth of knowledge and practice that constitute an essential toolbox for social protection researchers worldwide. However, a global perspective on social protection will confirm that welfare states are a special case of institutional development, far from an inescapable destination. A general theory of welfare institutions, global in its scope, will be delayed in its advance if its parameters are set by a special case.[2]

A theory of social protection in Latin America has also been delayed by 'excess normativity'. It is apparent to any student of social protection institutions in the region that they fall short of securing minimum living standards for the population. There is consensus among researchers and policy makers that access to social protection is inadequate for the population groups that need it most. Some social protection institutions may even contribute to raise income inequality. Social assistance does not reach all those in poverty and might be insufficient to lift those it reaches out of poverty. Social protection in Latin America is pro-old, gendered, and compensatory. There is a large, and important, literature comparing these outcomes to normative standards and proposing reforms to achieve them.[3] Recent basic income proposals are perhaps an extreme example of this approach. However, an understanding of the contribution of social

[1] A more detailed discussion on these points, and references, will be found later in the book.

[2] In fact, the most significant advance in our understanding of welfare states came from acknowledging their diversity. They include social democratic, liberal, and conservative welfare states (Esping-Andersen, 1990).

[3] See for example Mesa-Lago (2007).

protection institutions to social and economic cooperation is a necessary condition for a successful reform of these institutions. On its own, a normative approach is unlikely to succeed.[4]

1.1 Why Focus on Social Protection?

Social protection is a component of social policy. Social policy is understood as the collective provision of transfers and services to the population of a country in response to agreed social goals and financed from government revenues. It includes transfers in kind or public services and transfers in cash or income transfers. The provision of public services includes inter alia education, health care, housing and sanitation, and national security. They are transfers in kind.

Social protection consists of publicly supported programmes directed at ensuring minimum standards of living for workers and their dependants. It describes institutions and policies protecting citizens from life course and employment income risks, ensuring minimum living standards, supporting investment in their productive capacity, and facilitating political participation (Barrientos, 2013). Social protection programmes are mainly associated with income transfers and with regulations ensuring minimum income levels, such as minimum wage or job termination regulations.

Societies provide a range of income transfers in response to the needs of population groups. They include, *inter alia*, child and family transfers, maternity benefits, subsidies to low paid workers, and pension benefits for older groups and people with disabilities. For our purposes, they can be arranged in two main groups: insurance and assistance. Insurance transfers address the impact of a range of contingencies on income or employment. They are in the main financed by contributions from workers and employers and compensate affiliates when affected by pre-specified contingencies. Assistance transfers provide income subsidies to

[4] Normative standards are important. When subscribed to by the population of a country, directly or through their representatives, they provide social policy with the direction of change. They cannot replace a theory of social protection institutions.

low-income groups to supplement their consumption and support human capital investment. Assistance transfers are budget financed. Insurance transfers can be financed from a range of sources: payroll contributions to occupational funds, payroll taxes, or budget subsidies.

Analytically, social protection institutions can be arrayed on a continuum.[5] Social insurance is financed from mandated payroll taxes and covers the entire population. Occupational insurance is financed from payroll contributions and is restricted to contributing members only. Social assistance is financed from budget revenues and entitlements are based on need and residence. Insurance and assistance embed forms of social stratification specific to countries or regions. This is why the qualifying term 'institution' is essential. Institutions are best described as "rules and procedures (both formal and informal) that structure social interaction by constraining and enabling actors' behaviour" (Helmke & Levitsky, 2004, p. 727). Understanding social protection institutions necessitates some understanding of the stratification they embed.

As the review of the main literature below will underline, most studies focus on the broader field of social policy and examine social protection as a component. In this respect, research in the Latin American region is heavily influenced by the welfare state literature in which welfare states combined transfers in cash and in kind. However, this book focuses exclusively on social protection and leaves aside any detailed examination of public services. There are some gains and some losses from adopting this approach.

Basic services such as education and health care provide transfers in kind. At the micro-level they are essential to secure well-being, productivity, and full participation in society, same as social protection. Basic services have many complementarities with social protection. Take for example the influence of education on skills or the contribution of health care to labour productivity. Some income transfers support access to education and health, as in conditional income transfers. Some active labour market policies combine services and transfers to maximise the employability of people with disabilities, or the long term unemployed.

[5] This also contributes to explain why terminology in this area can be somewhat elusive at times.

There is a macro-level complementarity which can best studied when examining services and transfers together. Studies of social spending are often deployed to characterise government social policy effort and changes over time. Comparative studies of the evolution of welfare states among early industrialisers have been able to identify a specialisation on services, especially education, in the United States and a specialisation on income transfers in European countries (Lindert, 2004). Cross-welfare states comparisons resting on one component would fail to get the whole picture (Alesina et al., 2001).

In the context of Latin America, however, a focus on social protection is justified. Latin American countries have not constructed comprehensive welfare states and, aside from health insurance, they developed social protection institutions largely independently from public services. Education provision has been universalised across the region, health provision has more recently began to be extended to most of the population, but social protection has remained selective. Research on social spending has demonstrated that trends in service provision often diverge from trends in social protection. Researchers focused on the impact of democratisation or globalisation on social spending, for example, have concluded that service provision and social protection appear to have a different political logic (Avelino et al., 2005; Kaufman & Segura-Ubiergo, 2001). It makes sense therefore to tackle social protection on its own. The main argument developed in the book would suggest that the distinctiveness of social protection institutions is associated with their role as a stratification mechanism. This provides a strong justification for looking at social protection separately.

Furthermore, combining social protection with basic service provision in the Latin American context can be misleading. The unique place given to Costa Rica and Uruguay as exemplars of successful social policy provision in Latin America rely to an important extent in their provision of basic services. If the focus is relocated to social protection instead, these two countries would remain on the top half of the rankings but not at the very top.

1.2 Theories of Social Protection in Latin America

The analysis below takes existing accounts of social protection in the region as its point of departure. This section provides a brief introduction to the key literature.

Mesa-Lago (1978) offered an early account of emerging social security institutions in the region, including country developments. It also provided an early classification of countries according to the development of their institutions. It is a canonical text and will be referred to often in the discussion that follows. Two contributions to this book need underlining. Mesa-Lago makes it clear from the outset that the main feature of social security institutions in the region is the stratification they generate. As he puts it, " … is my contention that … a variety of pressure groups with divergent powers constitute the predominant factor in the historical inception of a 'stratified' social security system in Latin America and that the system generates significant inequalities in the distribution of its services" (Mesa-Lago, 1978, p. 4).[6] He identifies three main models in the emergence of social security institutions, one in which pressure groups influence state recognition of occupational funds; a second in which the state co-opts pressure groups by granting them social security protection; and a third in which a combination of pressure groups and political parties influence state provision of social security. The relevant point to underline here is the identification of causal path, indicated by arrows, capturing alternative stratification effects.

An important strand of literature studies the emergence and development of social protection and social policy in Latin America by reconstructing countries development paths and the conditions that enabled them.

Segura-Ubiergo (2007) researches the emergence and development of welfare institutions, welfare states in his designation, in Latin American countries. He focuses on three main theoretical approaches drawn from the welfare state literature: (i) a modernity approach that associates the

[6] Stratification is prominent in the title of Mesa-Lago's (1978) book 'Social Security in Latin America: Pressure Groups, Stratification, and Inequality'.

development of welfare institutions with economic development and especially industrialisation; (ii) an approach that associates welfare institutions with globalisation and economic openness; and (iii) the power resources theory that associates welfare states with the demands of the working class and left parties against a context of deepening democratisation. These three theoretical approaches are tested against institutional development paths of social policy in countries in Latin America.

He focuses on two periods: 1930–1970 and 1970–2003. Relying in Qualitative Comparative Analysis to interrogate data for the earlier period, Honduras, Panama, and Cuba are excluded due to missing data, he finds that the paths shown by welfare institutions can be used to group countries into two clusters: one cluster exhibiting strong economic development, low openness, and democracy or left parties; and another cluster exhibiting weak economic development, high openness, and limited democratisation. The first cluster includes Southern cone countries and Costa Rica. The second cluster includes Andean and Central American countries. His findings suggest that Latin American countries welfare development paths run counter to theories of welfare institutional development emphasising responses to the uncertainties associated with increasing openness. They provide some support for the industrialisation explanation and for the power resources theories. Countries in the first cluster "had a longer history of continuous democracy and stronger labor movements than the group of non-welfare state countries" (Segura-Ubiergo, 2007, p. 71).

Analysis of the second period 1970–2003 interrogates correlates of social spending. The main findings indicate that all three theories of welfare state development could apply in Latin America, but not in the direction predicted. According to Segura-Ubiergo, late and capital intensive industrialisation did not generate a 'critical mass of workers' in Latin American countries. The absence of democratic institutions meant that "demands for compensation were either not voiced by groups that may have suffered the consequences of trade openness or not heard because governments were not accountable to citizens for their actions in the public realm through regular elections"(Segura-Ubiergo, 2007, pp. 263–264). Whereas trade openness encouraged demand for social protection in early industrialisers, in Latin American countries welfare institutions developed against the context of protectionist policies.

Huber and Stephens (2012) extend power resources theory to include two dimensions with particular influence in Latin American countries: the role of veto players and that of international actors. Compared to early industrialisers, Latin American countries have a more diverse class structure explaining limited redistribution and a *sui generis* development path for welfare institutions. To cite, "…the class structure of Latin America is inhospitable to class organization and class political mobilization compared to that of Western Europe…the scope for union organization is much more limited in Latin America …These same features of the class structure have not been favourable to democracy, …weaken the density of civil society and thus the potential for autonomous (i.e. non-clientelistic) political mobilization of lower class groups" (Huber & Stephens, 2012, pp. 25–26). A more diversified class structure and the influence of international organisation explains the presence of weaker and segmented welfare institutions in Latin American compared with European welfare states.

Haggard and Kaufman's (2008) book is motivated by the ambition to develop a general theory of welfare institutions, with a global scope. It provides as analysis of the development path of welfare institutions across world regions. In their view, welfare institutions development paths can be studied by focusing on 'critical realignments' that is a "focus on discontinuities in patterns of political domination… the emergence of new ruling coalitions and political incorporation or exclusion of working class and peasant organizations" (Haggard & Kaufman, 2008, p. 7). Critical realignments help set in place welfare institutions in response to interest coalitions. The incorporation or co-optation of workers organisations to the political system facilitates the development of social protection institutions. "In Latin America, this process of accommodation resulted in the extension of social insurance coverage to some portion of the organized urban working class, programs that became the template for further expansion of entitlements…[but they were not AB] associated with new political opportunities for the rural poor" (Haggard & Kaufman, 2008, p. 346). They pay close attention to conditioning factors, particularly country differences in terms of democracy, economic growth, fiscal constraints, and development models, but these conditioning factors are mediated through the quality of the social contract in place for specific countries or sets of countries. "Latin America's stratified welfare system reflected the urban biases of the political coalitions that challenged oligarchic rule. These biases were reinforced by the turn toward import substitution" (Haggard & Kaufman, 2008, p. 79).

Cross-country comparative studies identifying similarities and differences in social policy and social protection institutions offer a complementary perspective to the study of development paths. Following the approach developed in Esping-Andersen's three worlds of welfare capitalism, this set of studies aims to cluster countries in Latin America according to key features of their social policy (Antía, 2018; Filgueira, 2005; Martínez Franzoni, 2008; Sátyro et al., 2021). This is a fertile area of research because the grouping of countries around their social policy and social protection institutions can help identify structural explanations of welfare institutions and provide evidence for the relevance of alternative theories of social protection.[7]

This brief review of some key contributions to the theory of social protection institutions in Latin America help introduce some of the tools and concepts to be applied in the analysis in this book. Mesa-Lago's early emphasis on the stratification effects of social protection as its key feature and the hint towards causal inference will be important building blocks for the argumentation in this book. Haggard and Kaufman's notion of critical realignments as an essential tool to separate qualitatively distinct periods in the evolution of social protection, and the substantive role of worker's political incorporation or exclusion, will provide an important dimension of the analysis. Huber and Stephens's emphasis on the role of class differentiation and democratisation in making sense of social protection in the more recent period will guide the discussion below. Comparative analysis identifying country clusters will be taken up and expanded. These insights are central to the analysis in this book.

1.3 Some New Departures...

The analysis in the book takes up many of the themes and findings from this literature. It also makes some new departures. This section will introduce them.

[7] Chapter 8 offers a detailed discussion and assessment of this literature.

1.3.1 Wage Earners Are the Object of Social Protection Institutions

The analysis in this book takes wage earners as the main object of social protection institutions and their theory. By wage earners, it is meant the population dependent on labour earnings. They are that section of the population whose wellbeing is largely dependent on the income they can generate from selling their labour. They are by far most of the population in the region, especially when their dependents are included. Wage earners as a population category include salaried workers, own account workers who are not employers, unpaid family workers, and their dependents. The justification for focusing on wage earners, a broad category, is that they are the object of social protection. No wage earners, no social protection.

Research on social protection is often focused on a subset of wage earners. The emergence of occupational insurance funds in Latin American countries is predicated on a growing urban industrial working class. The expansion of social assistance in the 2000s aimed to reach population groups on low and irregular incomes and often dependent on informal and precarious employment. Attempting a more comprehensive analysis of social protection requires incorporating these population groups within a broader category, wage earners.

There are some important implications from a broader focus. The more significant implication is to shift the conventional focus of the analysis away from inter-class differentiation and coalitions and replacing it with a focus on intra-class differentiation and coalitions.

In the existing literature on social protection in Latin America, especially the literature influenced by welfare state theory, it is conventional to segment wage earners into two 'classes' the 'working' class and the 'middle' class. In welfare state theory, the working class includes industrial blue-collar workers, while the 'middle class' includes white-collar office and services workers. This distinction is central to welfare state theory, in as much as the three ideal types of welfare states—social democratic, liberal, and conservative -, are explained by alternative forms of working- and middle-class coalitions (van Kersbergen & Vis, 2014). Classes have a central role of in this approach because they enable researchers to read social protection preferences directly from occupational data.

It is questionable whether this approach is appropriate in the Latin American social protection context.[8] As noted above, Huber and Stephens (2012) argue that class[9] is significantly less homogeneous in the Latin America context, and that in any case reading social protection preferences from occupational class membership is far from straightforward. Taking income as opposed to occupational affiliation as the metric of class membership indicates that 'working' and 'middle' classes are insufficiently distinct. Figure 1.1. below shows the centile distribution of income in Brazil. It is hard to eyeball the middle class in the Figure.[10]

The Figure shows the mean income of each percentile of the population in Brazil reported in WIID 2022 for 1999 and 2009 in 2017 PPP USD, estimated from household survey data.

This is not to suggest that the wage earner category is a homogeneous group. In fact, a central argument of the book contends that social protection institutions are a mechanism to stratify wage earners, to be discussed further below. The approach adopted here acknowledges contestation across occupational groups within wage earners. Intra-class differentiation is very real and have a longstanding influence on social protection institutions in the region. Intra-class differentiation and coalition building will be explored in some detail later in the book. The approach does not presume there is a homogenous set of distributional preferences within wage earners. Stark differences in distributional preferences across groups of workers are all too apparent in a region where welfare institutions are so markedly segmented. In the analysis that follows no presumption will be made that distributional preferences could

[8] There are other contexts in which the 'middle' class might be an appropriate category. In Latin America the middle class has a near mythical status in the context of economic development. Lopez-Calva and Ortiz-Juarez note that assessing the growth of the middle class is essential because of the "...large literature arguing that the size and composition of the middle class is critical for strengthening and stabilizing the democratic system and its institutions, for better economic performance, and for social cohesion" (López-Calva & Ortiz-Juarez, 2014, p. 40). They define the 'middle' class as population groups that have a (low) probability of falling into poverty.

[9] "We define class as a group of people who by virtue of their assets are compelled to engage in similar activities in the productive process...Assets include tangible property, intangible skills, and cultural traits"(Huber & Stephens, 2012, p. 22).

[10] Hsieh and Olken (2014) show that purposely imposed categorisation of firms in Mexico, and elsewhere, encouraged the claim that a missing middle in the distribution of firms acts as a significant brake on economic development. Their analysis has parallels with research on the 'middle class' in Latin America.

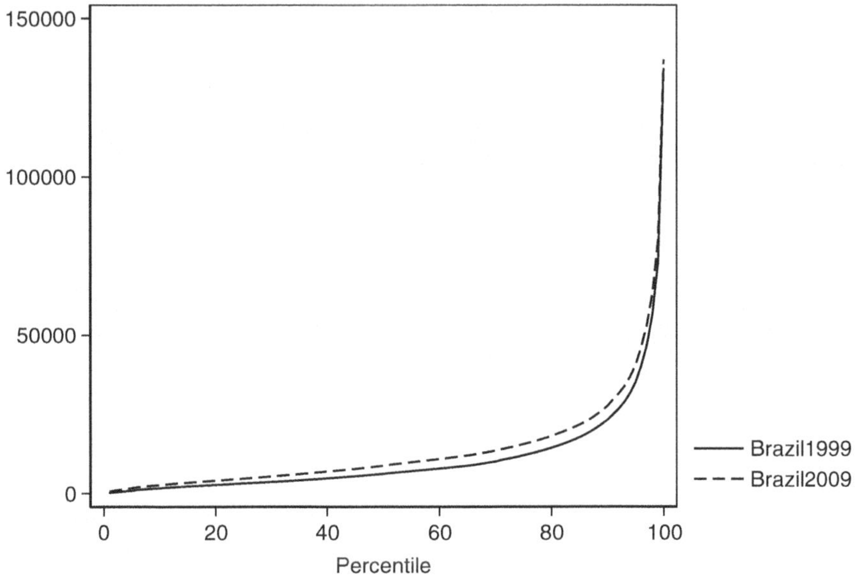

Fig. 1.1 Percentile distribution of income in Brazil. Data Source: WIID (UNU-WIDER, 2022)

be reliable read from the occupational or income position of groups of wage earners. The focus on wage earners shifts attention the focus away from inter-class differentiation and coalition and towards intra-class differentiation and coalition.

In the context of social protection in Latin America a further advantage of this approach is to include groups with low income and dependent on informal employment. They are a significant section of wage earners, around one half of workers in the region when measured as the proportion of workers not contributing to social protection schemes. Until the turn of this century, they only figured in social protection debates as an amorphous group devoid of agency and excluded from participation, lacking the capacity to mobilise and organise around social protection demands. Segura-Ubiergo claims that "the fragmentation and lack of collective identity of the poor themselves … leaves them without interests to be represented" (Segura-Ubiergo, 2007, p. 111). Haggard and Kaufman argue that the "… fate of the poor and vulnerable is therefore never in their hands alone but will depend on the self-interest of other social groups and the formation of cross-class coalitions with an interest in equity and social justice" (Haggard & Kaufman, 2008, p. 362). Huber and Stephens note a more recent shift: "…the poor were not organised and did not constitute an effective pressure group, least so under authoritarian regimes…Since democracy had been (re)installed, however, politicians began to pay more attention to the poor as potential voters" (Huber & Stephens, 2012, p. 171). Recent analyses of the politics of social protection and social policy reforms in the region emphasise the substantive role of low income workers and excluded groups (Garay, 2016; Kapiszewski et al., 2021; Silva & Rossi, 2017). This issue will be taken up in more detail below in connection with the expansion of social assistance.

In the study of social protection institutions, intra-class conflict and contestation constitutes a more reliable, flexible, and productive approach. It can accommodate a hard distinction between manual and intellectual work made by researchers studying industrialisation processes in the first half of the twentieth century. It can also accommodate the sectoral divisions among wage earners associated with fordism, and its weakness, in Latin America. It can also accommodate a blurring of this distinction associated with tertiarisation, global production networks, and job polarisation in the knowledge economy.

To repeat, the main justification for focusing on a broader category of wage earners is empirical, they are the main object of social protection institutions in Latin America.[11] Change and innovation in social protection institutions over time has direct effects on wage earner stratification, and on intra-class differentiation and coalition building.

[11] Focusing on wage earners would also be justified in a global comparative setting. Ranaldi and Milanovic (2020) study the concentration of factor income, income from labour and capital, across countries based on a cross-section of household survey data. They show that Latin American countries belong to a group of 'class societies' in the sense that the concentration of capital is such that most people in these societies rely in labour income and only a few are able combine income from labour and capital. This in contrast to countries in which income from capital is more widely spread out.

1.3.2 Social Protection Institutions Are Stratification Mechanisms

In the literature on social protection institutions in Latin America, and elsewhere, it is common to find that they are justified in terms of specific social goals. For example, to co-opt and control potential challenges to elites; or to protect labour power from globalization or industrialisation-caused social risk; or as a means to ensure productivity and economic growth. In this literature, social protection institutions are normatively assessed in terms of their adequacy and/or efficiency in securing these goals. However, establishing whether social protection meets normatively defined standards is not an explanation why particular institutions are in place or are missing. There are numerous strategies that policy makers could follow to address these goals, aside from social protection. Provision of a basic income, say equivalent to median labour earnings, to all residents in a country would help achieve many of the social goals listed above, without the need for social protection.

Social protection institutions are not engines of equality or poverty reduction, although they may secure these goals, but they are primarily engines of wage earner stratification. Capitalist production requires wage earners, that is independent workers able and willing to work for a wage.[12] Production in advanced forms of capitalism require workers with specific skills and motivation. Social protection institutions help ensure that wage earners are available in the quantity and quality needed to ensure capital accumulation. Social protection institutions support the stratification of wage earners under capitalism. Alternative types of social protection institutions generate different forms of stratification, as the analysis in the book will demonstrate. A comparative examination of social protection institutions will throw light on different forms of stratification.

The view that the primary contribution of social protection is wage earner stratification is well established in the literature. The analysis and evaluation of social protection systems focuses on their effects on the

[12] "I define capitalism in the fashion of Karl Marx and Max Weber, as the system where most production is carried out with privately owned means of production, capital hires legally free labor, and coordination is decentralized" (Milanovic, 2019, p. 12).

wellbeing of wage earners and on wage earners' incentives to work. Effective social protection systems support adequate living standards and maximise work incentives for distinct categories of workers. A central issue in the economics literature on social protection is precisely the 'incentive compatibility' features of social protection programmes and policies (Aizer et al., 2020; Barth & Greenberg, 1971; Lazear, 2018; Ravallion & Chen, 2015). The dominant research focus is on whether social protection interventions maximise labour supply and productivity incentives for categories of wage earners, skilled and unskilled workers for example. Interventions that mollify work incentives are perceived as problematic.

Research and policy perspectives on social protection underline the fact that wage earners are its object. Risk perspectives suggest that the role of social protection is to mitigate the effect of social risks on workers (prudential) (Rehm, 2011). Productivity perspectives suggest that the function of social protection is to improve the productivity of workers by facilitating adaptation to economic change (mobility) (Ippolito, 1997). Human capital accumulation perspectives focus on the role of social protection in encouraging skills acquisition and firm attachment (social investment) (Moffitt, 2002). Redistribution perspectives emphasise the need for social protection to ensure social trust and cohesion (equity) (Attanasio et al., 2009). Poverty and inclusion perspectives underline social protection effects on redressing disadvantage and exclusion (citizenship) (Barrientos, 2007; Garay, 2021). Acknowledgement that social protection is fundamentally directed at wage earners runs through all perspectives on the role of social protection.

An understanding that social protection is a mechanism for wage earner stratification is at the core of welfare state theory. For Esping Andersen and Myles, a "… quick historical glance at social reform will dispel of any notion that the welfare state was pursued for egalitarian reasons. Its foundations were typically laid by conservative reformers who, like Bismarck, sought primarily to reproduce, rather than to alter, prevailing social hierarchies. When the opportunity arose, socialists pushed for social policies that would better the conditions of workers, eliminate poverty, and equalize opportunities" (Esping-Andersen & Myles, 2012, p. 639). Some researchers claim that the evolution of welfare institutions is best explained as status preserving social mechanisms (Garcia-Fuente, 2021).

These examples demonstrate that the view that social protection is primarily a stratification device is well understood in the literature.

1.3.3 Social Protection Institutions and Dominant Forms of Stratification

The emergence and dynamics of the three main social protection institutions in place in Latin America—occupational insurance funds, individual retirement savings plans, and social assistance—reflect dominant forms of stratification. In the 'long century' (1900–2020) it is possible to distinguish four periods associated with significant social change with implications for social protection institutions

The first period includes the first wave of industrialisation (1880s–1930s) (Bénétrix et al., 2012; Williamson, 2011). This period is dominated by factor stratification leading to the emergence of an urban working class as an economic and political actor. Factor stratification describes the development of social groupings based on ownership of factors of production: capital, labour, land. This form of stratification precedes the emergence of large scale social protection institutions, but it is a necessary precondition. During this period early industrialising countries in the region saw the emergence of autonomous working class organizations with incipient mutual aid associations (Illanes, 2003). The antagonistic nature of state institutions precluded the development of publicly supported social protection institutions. Research has considered the extent to which factor stratification sets parameters for the development of social protection institutions that follow (Wibbels & Ahlquist, 2011).

The suspension of world trade associated with the two world wars put to an end the first wave of industrialisation in Latin America and encouraged a shift to import-substitution-industrialisation. In the more industrialised countries, the state took an active role in supporting industrialisation, described as State-led development (Astorga & Herraz-Loncán, 2020; Bértola & Ocampo, 2012). Sectoral stratification became central to the new political economy. Development strategies based on import-substitution-industrialisation were stratified by sector. State-led development was supported politically by a coalition of industrial and financial capital and the nascent urban industrial working class. The process leading to the growing participation of working class organisations in the political process has been described as a first incorporation (Collier & Collier, 1991). State support for selected economic sectors was replicated and reinforced by Bismarckian occupational insurance. This process is absent in Central American countries with a dominant agro-exporting economy, and Andean countries where industrialisation was incipient.

The exhaustion of state-led development import substitution policies in the 1980s signalled another critical realignment with implications for social protection. Export-led-growth policies rose to dominance, leading to extensive economic liberalisation. The opening of the relatively protected economies of the region involved far reaching structural adjustment, impacting more strongly on previously protected sectors, and placed considerable pressure on worker organizations and occupational insurance funds in these sectors. Skill stratification replaced sectoral stratification as the dominant form of stratification. Pension reforms and the introduction of individual retirement plans in some countries sought to remove the influence of worker organisations on social protection policies and institutions.

The commodity boom in the 2000s reinforced the dominance of skill stratification. It encapsulated a more gradual change in the domestic and global economy. Global production networks involved new forms of integration in the growing global economy. Technological change placed rising demands on the expansion of the pool of skilled workers, encapsulated in the 'knowledge economy' (Chorev & Ball, 2022; Gasparini et al., 2021; Iversen & Soskice, 2015). The emergence of conditional income transfers and old age transfers (social pensions) signalled a significant shift in social protection provision in the region. For the first time, a programmatic and rules-based set of social protection institutions reached low wage and informal population groups in all countries in the region (Barrientos, 2013; Cecchini & Madariaga, 2011; Villatoro & Cecchini, 2018). It embedded new political strategies for connecting these groups to social policy, described as a (second) incorporation (Collier, 2021; Roberts, 2021; Silva & Rossi, 2017).

The three dominant forms of social protection in Latin America: occupational insurance funds, individual retirement savings plans, and social assistance can be associated with critical realignments and with associated shifts in the dominant forms of stratification. The confluence of diachronic, synchronic, and analytical perspectives in the study of social protection institutions in Latin America will anchor and frame the discussion in the book. This will be examined in greater detail in Chap. 3 of the book.

Four main periods in Latin America's social protection (Table 1.1):

1.3.4 Methodologically, from Correlation to Causality

Researchers on social protection in Latin America have employed a variety of methodologies. Qualitative methods have been deployed to construct case studies and comparative cross-country studies. Data reduction methods have been employed to assess similarities and dissimilarities in social protection provision and institutions across countries (Martínez Franzoni, 2008; Pribble, 2011). QCA has also been employed to research institutional configurations and their path over time (Cruz-Martínez, 2014; Segura-Ubiergo, 2007). There has been growing interest in establishing the impact of social protection institutions, especially social assistance by interrogating quasi-experimental evaluation data and household survey dataset (Molina Millán et al., 2019; Saavedra & Garcia, 2017). Attitudinal data has been used to throw light upon the political effects of social assistance programmes (Araújo, 2021). Quantitative studies using time-series cross-section and panel data have been favoured by researchers investigating the correlates of social protection development (Haggard & Kaufman, 2008; Segura-Ubiergo, 2007) and the impact of globalisation and democracy in social spending (Avelino et al., 2005; Huber et al., 2008; Kaufman & Segura-Ubiergo, 2001). These studies estimate linear structural models. Research in social protection shows healthy methodological diversity but with the growing availability of harmonised cross-country data regression methods are becoming dominant.

The analysis in the book will draw from these studies, but it will pay especial attention to causal inference. Causal inference has been at the

Table 1.1 Social protection and dominant forms of stratification

	1900–1940	1950–1970	1980–1990	2000–
Economic transformation	First industrialisation wave	Industrialisation	Export-led growth	'Knowledge economy'
Employment structure	Urbanisation	Growth of industrial employment	Growth of service employment	Employment polarization?
Social protection institutions	Mutual aid societies	Occupational insurance funds	Individual retirement savings plans	Social assistance – old age and conditional transfers
Dominant Stratification	Factor	Sectoral	Skill	Skill
Incorporation	Repression	First incorporation	De-incorporation	Second incorporation?

Own construction

forefront of the recent spread of impact evaluation studies of social protection interventions. The analysis in the book will seek to extend a focus on causal inference to the study of social protection institutions in the medium term. Of course, it is not possible to experiment with social protection systems, nor is it possible to control for the complexity of social change or the heterogeneity of behavioural responses. And the sample of countries is fixed at eighteen. But it is possible to pay attention to the effects of social protection institutions, identify counterfactuals and data generating processes, and account for the temporal dimension of institutions and effects. The analysis in this book will therefore make a concerted effort to identify and implement methods appropriate to capturing causal factors.

Gelman and Imbens (2013) draw a distinction between two types of enquiry. 'Causes of effects' inquiries seek to understand what factor or factors are responsible for phenomena. For example, what explains the expansion of fragmented occupational insurance funds in Latin America? Or, what explains the emergence of conditional income transfers in Mexico and Brazil? An alternative type of enquiry focuses on establishing the 'effects of causes'. Do conditional income transfers reduce labour supply among recipients? Do occupational pension benefits increase income inequality? The 'causes of effects' type of enquiry is backward looking, it attempts to find an explanation for the presence of an effect. By contrast, the 'effects of causes' enquiry is forward looking, it follows from some intervention or manipulation. Gelman and Imbens suggest that 'effects of causes' research, if properly designed and implemented, is capable of yielding (probabilistic) causal explanations, but 'causes of effects' research can only at best identify non-causal factors and suggest a list of potentially valid causal factors. Its role is to clear the ground for the formulation of 'effects of causes' type enquiries.

This is helpful in forming expectations regarding the contribution of alternative methodologies. In the Latin American context, research into the effects of social assistance interventions have been successful in delivering reliable assessments of their impact on recipients. Their approach is in the process of being replicated in other areas of social protection. Research into the factors behind the emergence and evolution of social protection in the region has been less successful in generating definite findings but has been effective in discounting the strength of some hypotheses and in the process contesting the predictions of some theories.

Paying attention to causal inference involves, as an essential first step, a concern to spell out the theoretical framework underpinning causal relations between variables. Glynn and Quinn (2013) underline the point that "a theoretical understanding of the substantive problem, particularly regarding the nature of any temporal dependencies, is an important part of a successful estimation strategy" (p. 3). It also involves a concern to spell out causal associations. There is growing interest in the use of graphical methods to identify causal relations between variables. The structural causal model of Pearl (2009) will help to establish the quality of these relationships as a first step to establishing whether identification is feasible (Elwert, 2013; Morgan & Winship, 2015). The application of graphical methods will also help to guide research towards appropriate empirical counterparts and estimation techniques.

1.4 The Approach in This Book

1.4.1 The Need for Theory

Data on the outcomes of social protection institutions in Latin America has improved exponentially in the last two decades. Information on country programmes, their reach, and financing has never been as comprehensive and reliable as the present time. The expansion of conditional income transfers has encouraged the application of quasi-experimental techniques to identify reliably their effects. This is now in the process of being extended to other type of programmes. Harmonisation of household survey data as well as attitudinal data has greatly expanded the range of research questions that can be addressed. Data gaps remain, especially in terms of reconciling survey and administrative data for occupational insurance and social assistance, but these are no impediment to detailed research on social protection in the region. Our knowledge of the design and outcomes of social protection institutions has improved significantly.

The main challenge remains to develop a theory of social protection institutions capable of explaining why Latin America has stratified social protection institutions with generous provision for skilled workers in large firms and limited or non-existent provision for the rest. How best to explain the persistence of selective and ineffective institutions? What factors can explain the compensatory, pro-old, and compensatory bias embedded in social protection institutions? How best to explain the strength of barriers to successful reform? Providing reliable answers to these questions is urgent but requires constructing a working theory of social protection institutions in the region.

1.4.2 A Late Industrialisers Perspective

Research into the development of welfare institutions in late industrialisers[13] has been heavily influenced by theories developed to study European welfare states. It is undeniable that there is much to be learned from the study of the politics of welfare states. It presents us with an advanced and sophisticated set of theoretical perspectives, empirical observations, and methodological tools (Castles et al., 2012). But it is important to avoid researching welfare institutional developments in late industrialisers through the prism of welfare states. Latin American countries show significant differences in their economic and social structures with early industrialisers, easily demonstrated by comparison of the size of their economies, level of development, and tax revenues and spending (Gough & Therborn, 2010). But this is not the primary reason for seeking to construct a distinct theory of social protection institutions in Latin America. European welfare states constitute a notable achievement, securing a set of social rights capable of protecting their citizens from the adverse effects of capitalism on workers and their dependents. In the view of some researchers, European welfare states made possible the accommodation of capitalism and democracy (Beramendi et al., 2015). However, taking a global perspective it is hard not to see welfare states as institutional developments restricted in space and time. To the extent that

[13] Terminology on this is treacherous. 'Developing' countries is dated. Low- and middle-income countries does not fit Latin America, as it now contains middle- and high-income countries. 'Late industrialisers' is a more appropriate term given the focus of the book. Early industrialisers will be reserved for European and other high-income advanced economies with welfare states.

welfare states are a special case of institutional development, theories developed to study them are unlikely to work as general theories of social protection institutions. Whilst making use of the knowledge base developed for the study of welfare states, it is important that theories of social protection institutions in Latin America, and elsewhere among late industrialisers, are constructed with a strong measure of independence.

Recent developments in the study of welfare states have emphasised the presence of distinct models of welfare state institutions, as the welfare regime literature confirms (Esping-Andersen, 1990; Farragina & Seeleib-Kaiser, 2011). Research into the evolution of welfare states over time does not provide strong support for convergence in European welfare states (Powell & Barrientos, 2004). Perhaps more relevant to the argument in this book, comparative research on welfare provision in European and Latin American countries does not provide support for a global convergence in welfare institutions.[14] The proposition that Latin American countries welfare institutions are on a development path to become welfare states in the European mould lacks sufficient supporting evidence.[15]

The challenge is to develop a theory of social protection institutions in the Latin American region that best captures the evolution, design, and outcomes of the institutions in place in these countries.

1.4.3 A Dynamic and Comparative Perspective Is Essential…

An important step forward to developing a theory of existing social protection institutions in the region is to develop an understanding of their origins, evolution, change and permanence. A dynamic perspective on these institutions is an essential building block for theoretical development.

From their origins in workers' organizations in the first industrialisation wave at the onset of the twentieth century to the rapid expansion of

[14] OECD studies on welfare institutions often underline the distance between European welfare states and Chile and Mexico, see e.g. https://data.oecd.org/socialexp/pension-spending.htm#indicator-chart.

[15] Parallels can be drawn with the course of development studies as a discipline. For a long time, it assumed a single path for late industrialisers, exemplified by Rostow's stages of growth. South Korea and China, among other countries, have highlighted the flaws in this approach.

conditional income transfers at the start of the twenty-first century, social protection institutions in the region show considerable change, but also resilience. In fact, the three main sets of institutions in place today emerged as a policy response to social change. State supported occupational insurance emerged alongside the first incorporation of worker organisations into mass politics in the second wave of industrialisation. They were stronger in countries which adopted explicit import-substitution-industrialisation (ISI) policies. Individual retirement savings plans replaced were introduced at the turn of the twenty-first century as part of the economic liberalisation imposed by export-led strategies. Occupational insurance funds undermined by labour market liberalisation and deindustrialisation. Whereas occupational insurance funds came alongside worker incorporation, individual retirement savings plans sought to reverse this process. The extent to which individual retirement savings plans replaced, competed with, or complemented, social insurance funds reflected the strength of incorporation reversals. Social assistance expansion in the twenty-first century originated in a second wave of incorporation. This time around, informal, and low paid workers were the main focus of incorporation, associated with the conflictive demands of the commodity boom, tertiarisation, and the knowledge economy. Accounting for these three sets of institutions is essential to developing a working theory of the structure of social protection in Latin American countries today.

Developing a theory of social protection in Latin America requires that we study current institutions, their evolution, and change.

1.4.4 Comparative Social Protection

The book takes a comparative approach as Latin America is a large region with significant variation in the size and composition of social protection across the countries within it. The comparative approach is multidisciplinary, with strong contribution from political economy, social policy, politics, and public finance.

The focus on Latin America as a region using a comparative perspective is justified by the distinctive features of their social protection institutions, their dynamics and resilience. Latin American countries provide an interesting set, sharing sufficient common ground to support comparative research while at the same time exhibiting sub-regional clusters in terms of economic development, state capacity, politics, and demography. Southern cone countries and Mexico industrialised earlier and more deeply, with the implication that occupational pension funds and individual retirement savings plans are more developed there. Central American countries, integrated early on with Northern markets via agricultural exports and foreign multinational investment (Sánchez-Ancochea & Martínez Franzoni, 2015; Segovia, 2022). Their industrialisation was weaker and came much later that in the larger economies of the region. Their agro-exporting model has proved resilient. Andean countries have experienced periods of intense economic growth, driven by global demand for the products of their extractive industry. A comparative perspective is essential if the aim is to construct a regional perspective that can accommodate country differences. The social protection institutions in place in the region show a sufficient degree of similarity to support the development of a common theoretical proposition. At the same time their differences help to identify the causal factors behind their evolution and outcomes.

1.4.5 Shortcuts: Pensions and Social Assistance

Social protection in Latin America includes a variety of programmes, policies, and institutions. They provide pensions, maternity benefits, unemployment support, compensation for workplace accidents and chronic illness, conditional income transfers, to name a few. Reference will be made to these programmes in the book, where relevant, but the primary focus will be on occupational pensions, individual retirement savings plans, and social assistance transfers. They are associated with critical realignments and societal change in employment and political participation. They are the principal gateways for access to social protection by the population. They account for the bulk of spending on social protection. Analytically, they are the most significant models of social protection in the region.

Applying Occam's razor, a focus on these three sets of programmes will be sufficient to reach into the core of social protection in the region, including its variation across countries. Occupational pensions and individual retirement accounts can be accurately described as instruments for horizontal redistribution. They transfer resources for the same people across their life course. Their transfers are based on group membership in the former and on personal saving in the latter. Social assistance transfers, on the other hand, are an instrument for vertical redistribution. They transfer resources from the better off to disadvantaged groups facing poverty and vulnerability. Pensions and social assistance represent the two types of redistribution at the core of social protection.

1.5 The Structure of the Book

1.5.1 Framework

Chapter 2 discusses methods appropriate to the study of social protection in Latin America. It reviews and assesses the main methodological approaches employed by researchers in the past and, building on these, it aims to identify methods appropriate to developing a theoretical perspective capable of explaining the evolution and current configuration of social protection institutions in the region. Recent trends in social research methods reveal a renewed emphasis on causal inference. The application of quasi-experimental methods in the study of the outcomes of social protection interventions, initially in the context of conditional income transfers, has focused attention on the causal effects of social protection interventions. The chapter assesses the challenges associated with the application of causal inference models in the context of research on institutions relying on observational data. It argues the potential outcomes approach offers a systematic framework for incorporating attention to counterfactuals. It makes a case for the use of graphical casual models to help discriminate causal versus non-causal association between variables, thus refining researchers' hypotheses and linking the model to potential empirical counterparts.

Chapter 3 presents the structure of the argument in the book. It introduces, develops, and applies a framework capable of explaining the emergence, structure, and dynamics of social protection institutions understood in Latin America. The central argument is that social protection institutions are an important mechanism of stratification in the capitalist economies of Latin America. The emergence of social protection institutions is explained by industrialisation. Industrialisation creates a distinct class of dependent wage earners and in doing so it sets the conditions for the emergence of social protection institutions. Once in place, the shape and dynamics of social protection institutions is best explained by their stratification effects. There are three dimensions of stratification effects that are especially relevant to understanding social protection institutions: their effects on employment, their protection effects, and their effects on the political incorporation of wage earners. The confluence of diachronic (critical realignments and the emergence of social protection institutions), synchronic (the combination of core institutions in the present), and analytical perspectives facilitates a theoretical understanding of social protection institutions in the region.

Chapter 4 is concerned with the design, implementation, and outcomes of current social protection institutions in the region. It examines in turn the three core social protection institutions: occupational pensions, individual retirement savings plans, and social assistance. Occupational pensions in Latin America are restricted to selected groups of workers, mainly skilled workers in large firms. They are also highly fragmented and dependent on public subsidies, although the level of subsidies is increasingly contested. Recent trends in labour force participation in occupational pensions largely suggest stagnation during this century. Individual retirement savings plans are grounded in individual workers saving capacity. They show three distinct institutional settings. In Colombia and Peru, individual retirement savings plans compete with occupational insurance. In Costa Rica and Uruguay, they complement occupational insurance for advantaged workers. In the rest of the countries that have adopted them, a transition process will make them the sole mandated retirement income institution. Individual retirement savings plans have not proved wildly successful in the region, and it is fair to say their institutional structures are in transition. Social assistance greatly expanded in the new century. Most countries in the region have implemented large scale old age transfers and conditional income transfer programmes. By 2015, social assistance transfers reached around one third of the population in the region.

Chapter 5 examines the stratification effects of social protection institutions on employment. The conventional approach, supported by current theories of welfare institutional development, is to assume that the structure of employment shapes social protection institutions. This makes sense when researching the origins of welfare institutions. However, once social protection institutions are in place, they exercise considerable influence on employment. The direction of causality is now from social protection to employment. The discussion in the chapter explores the stratification effects of social protection institutions on the structure of employment. The chapter discusses social protection contribution to three changes in employment in the region: tertiarisation, job polarisation and relocation, and participation in global production networks. Approaching the association between social protection and employment as a causal link brings new insights on social protection institutions in the region.

Chapter 6 studies the protection effects of social protection institutions. It involves examining the main outcomes of the core social protection institutions and of tax and transfer systems. The most significant outcome of social protection provision in Latin America is its stratification. Occupational pension schemes and individual retirement plans reach better off sections of the population while social assistance supports low-income groups dependent on informal employment. A detailed analysis of the incidence of pension benefits, from occupational pensions and individual retirement savings plans, confirmed they reach less than half the population aged 65 and over. Tracking income support for the population aged 65 and over reveals a 'hockey stick' shape, with most older people lacking income support or receiving at best a minimum level, and with a small proportion of pensioners receiving very generous pension benefits. Assessing the protection effects of social assistance has been greatly facilitated by the spread of quasi-experimental evaluation studies. Conditional income transfer programmes have measurable effects in improving the consumption of participant households. They reduce poverty in the short term and facilitate investment in schooling and health with implications for the productive capacity of participants in the longer term. Evaluation studies largely confirm the short term positive effects of conditional income transfers. Studies evaluating the protective effects of old age transfers find reductions in poverty and vulnerability among recipients and their households. Tax-transfer systems in the countries in the region have limited effects of poverty and inequality.

Chapter 7 offers an examination of the incorporation effects of social protection in Latin America. The analysis focuses on two intertwined elements in the analysis of the incorporation effects of social protection institutions and change: (i) the features of the 'critical realignments' that is the incorporation effects of the emergent institutions; and (ii) the theories that can be brought to bear to explain change. The main findings from the chapter can be summarised as follows. First, developments in social protection in the region are primarily explained by processes of incorporation and disincorporation of wage earners. Second, in Latin America the incorporation and disincorporation effects of social protection institutions confirm that intra-class (wage earners) fragmentation and aggregation is far more important than inter-class coalitions for the politics of welfare institutions. Third, identifying and studying critical realignments is essential to explaining changes in social protection institutions and the resulting processes of incorporation and disincorporation. Fourth, theoretical frameworks developed to explain the emergence of welfare states enhance our conceptual and methodological toolbox, but there are few gains in extrapolating them to the Latin American context. It makes sense to seek to develop theoretical frameworks from an understanding of the Latin American context. Fifth, the literature on the politics of social protection appears to have an in-built bias towards granting a primary role to the incentives of rulers/politicians. Focusing on the incorporation effects of social protection institutions shifts attention to wage earners, the primary actors of social protection. Research on the likelihood of broader wage earner coalitions is the gateway to more inclusive and egalitarian social protection in Latin America.

Chapter 8 examines differences and similarities in social protection institutions across countries in the region with the aim of identifying country groupings or clusters. From a comparative perspective, studying institutional differences and similarities is an important step towards theory development. The methodological approach implemented was borrowed from the literature in social policy regimes seeking to identify country clusters in the region. This literature groups and ranks countries in the region based on selected social protection indicators. A review of research on social policy regimes raised some conceptual and methodological issues. They help define an approach to grouping countries based on the causal outcomes of social protection institutions—employment, protection, and incorporation - and repeated for the periods associated with institutional development. The results from this analysis reported in the chapter largely confirm the findings in the social policy regime literature. There are three main clusters of countries: Southern cone countries plus Costa Rica, Mexico, and Panama; Andean countries including Paraguay; and Central American countries. This result is in line with the findings from the social policy regime literature and more generally the country groupings identified by early social protection research like those in Mesa-Lago (1978). Repeating the cluster analysis for different periods provides additional insights. The temporal analysis suggests a large measure of continuity in the country groupings over time, but it also shows disruption in the membership of the clusters during the neoliberal period. Cluster memberships loosen up during this period, especially for countries like Chile and Mexico. Paying attention to measures of the distribution of transfers introduces fluidity in the membership sets of Andean and Central American countries.

Chapter 9 brings together the main strands of the argumentation in the book. It will perform two main functions. It will draw out some pointers from the discussion in the book for the construction of a theory of social protection institutions in Latin America and will speculate on implications for policy.

References

Aizer, A., Eli, S., & Lleras-Muney, A. (2020). *The incentive effects of cash transfers to the poor* (Working Paper 27523; NBER Working Paper). National Bureau of Economic Research.

Alesina, A., Glaeser, E., & Sacerdote, B. (2001). *Why doesn't the US have a European-style welfare state?* (Discussion Paper 1933). Harvard Institute of Economic Research.

Antía, F. (2018). Regímenes de política social en América Latina: Una revisión crítica de la literatura. *Desafíos, 30*(2), 193–235. https://doi.org/10.12804/revistas.urosario.edu.co/desafios/a.4802

Araújo, V. (2021). Do anti-poverty policies sway voters? Evidence from a meta-analysis of Conditional Cash Transfers. *Research and Politics*, 1–9. https://journals.sagepub.com/doi/10.1177/2053168021991715

Astorga, P., & Herraz-Loncán, A. (2020). Latin America. Stalled catching up. In S. Broadberry & K. Fukao (Eds.), *The modern world. Volume II: 1870 to the present* (pp. 251–275). Cambridge University Press.

Attanasio, O., Pellerano, L., & Reyes, S. P. (2009). Building trust? Conditional cash transfer programmes and social capital. *Fiscal Studies, 30*(2), 139–177.

Avelino, G., Brown, D. S., & Hunter, W. (2005). The effects of capital mobility, trade openness, and democracy on social spending in Latin America, 1980–1999. *American Journal of Political Science, 49*(3), 625–641.

Barrientos, A. (2007). Modernising social assistance to promote social inclusion. In ILO (Ed.), *Social protection and social exclusion: Converging efforts from a global perspective*. ILO-EU-Government of Portugal.

Barrientos, A. (2013). *Social assistance in developing countries*. Cambridge University Press.

Barth, M. C., & Greenberg, D. H. (1971). Incentive effects of some pure and mixed transfer systems. *Journal of Human Resources, 6*(2), 149–170.

Bénétrix, A. S., O'Rourke, K. H., & Williamson, J. G. (2012). *The spread of manufacturing to the periphery 19870-2007: Eight stylized facts* (Working Paper 617; Department of Economics Oxford University). University of Oxford.

Beramendi, P., Hausermann, S., Kitschelt, H., & Kriesi, H. (2015). *The politics of advanced capitalism*. Cambridge University Press.

Bértola, L., & Ocampo, J. A. (2012). *The economic development of Latin America since independence*. Oxford University Press.

Castles, F. G., Leibfried, S., Lewis, J., Obinger, H., & Pierson, C. (2012). *The Oxford handbook of the welfare state*. Oxford University Press.

Cecchini, S., & Madariaga, A. (2011). *Conditional cash transfer programmes. The recent experience in Latin America and the Caribbean* (Report LC/G.2497-P). ECLAC. https://papers.ssrn.com/sol3/papers.cfm?abstract_id=1962666

Chorev, N., & Ball, A. C. (2022). The knowledge-based economy and the global south. *Annual Review of Sociology, 48*, 171–191. https://doi.org/10.1146/annurev-soc-080321-071214

Collier, R. B. (2021). Prologue: Reflections on two episodes of popular inclusion. Structuring and restructuring arenas of participation. In D. Kapiszewski, S. Levitsky, & D. J. Yashar (Eds.), *The inclusionary turn in Latin American Democracies* (pp. xxv–xlviii). Cambridge University Press.

Collier, R. B., & Collier, D. (1991). *Shaping the political arena.* Princeton University Press. https://muse.jhu.edu/book/45473

Cruz-Martínez, G. (2014). Welfare state development in Latin America and the Caribbean (1970s–2000s): Multidimensional welfare index, its methodology and results. *Social Indicators Research, 119*, 1295–1317. https://doi.org/10.1007/s11205-013-0549-7

Elwert, F. (2013). Graphical causal models. In *Handbook of causal analysis for social research*. Springer. https://doi.org/10.1007/978-94-007-6094-3_13

Esping-Andersen, G. (1990). *The three worlds of welfare capitalism.* Polity Press.

Esping-Andersen, G., & Myles, J. (2012). Economic inequality and the welfare state. In W. Salverda, B. Nolan, & T. Smeeding (Eds.), *The Oxford handbook of economic inequality* (pp. 639–664). Oxford University Press. https://doi.org/10.1093/oxfordhb/9780199606061.013.0025

Farragina, E., & Seeleib-Kaiser, M. (2011). Welfare regime debate: Past, presents and futures? *Policy and Politics, 39*(4), 583–611. https://doi.org/10.1332/030557311X603592

Filgueira, F. (2005). *Welfare and democracy in Latin America: The development, crises and aftermath of Universal, dual and exclusionary social states.* UNRISD.

Garay, C. (2016). *Social policy expansion in Latin America.* Cambridge University Press.

Garay, C. (2021). Including outsiders in Latin America. In D. Kapiszewski, S. Levitsky, & D. J. Yashar (Eds.), *The inclusionary turn in Latin American Democracies* (pp. 59–92). Cambridge University Press.

Garcia-Fuente, X. (2021). *The paradox of redistribution in time. Social spending in 53 countries, 1967-2018.* (Working Paper 815; LIS Working Papers). Luxembourg Income Study.

Gasparini, L. C., Brambilla, I., Falcone, C., & César, A. (2021). *Routinization and employment: Evidence for Latin America* (Working Paper 276; Documentos de Trabajo Del CEDLAS). CEDLAS, Universidad Nacional de La Plata. https://www.cedlas.econo.unlp.edu.ar/wp/no-276/

Gelman, A., & Imbens, G. (2013). *Why ask why? Forward causal inference and reverse causal questions* (Working Paper 19614; NBER). National Bureau of Economic Research.

Glynn, A. N., & Quinn, K. M. (2013). *Structural Causal Models and the Specification of Time-Series-Cross-Section Models* [Mimeo].

Gough, I., & Therborn, G. (2010). The global future of welfare states. In F. G. Castles, S. Leibfried, & J. Lewis (Eds.), *Oxford handbook of comparative welfare states* (pp. 703–720). Oxford University Press.

Haggard, S., & Kaufman, R. R. (2008). *Development, democracy and welfare states*. Princeton University Press.

Helmke, G., & Levitsky, S. (2004). Informal institutions and comparative politics: A research agenda. *Perspectives on Politics, 2*(3), 725–740.

Hsieh, C.-T., & Olken, B. A. (2014). The missing "Missing Middle". *Journal of Economic Perspectives, 28*(3), 89–108.

Huber, E., Mustillo, T., & Stephens, J. D. (2008). Politics and social spending in Latin America. *Journal of Politics, 70*(2), 420–436. http://www.jstor.com/stable/10.1017/s0022381608080407

Huber, E., & Stephens, J. D. (2012). *Democracy and the left in Latin America. Social policy and inequality in Latin America*. University of Chicago Press.

Illanes, M. A. (2003). *Chile des-centrado. Formación socio-cultural republicana y transición capitalista 1810-1910*. LOM Editions. http://www.memoriachilena.gob.cl/602/w3-article-82455.html

Ippolito, R. A. (1997). *Pension plans and employee performance. Evidence, analysis and policy*. University of Chicago Press.

Iversen, T., & Soskice, D. (2015). Democratic limits to redistribution. Inclusionary versus exclusionary coalitions in the knowledge economy. *World Politics, 67*(2), 185–225.

Kapiszewski, D., Levitsky, S., & Yashar, D. J. (Eds.). (2021). Inequality, democracy, and the inclusionary turn in Latin America. In *The inclusionary turn in Latin American Democracies*. Cambridge University Press.

Kaufman, R. R., & Segura-Ubiergo, A. (2001). Globalization, domestic politics, and social spending in Latin America: A time-series cross-section analysis, 1973-97. *World Politics, 53*(4), 553–587. https://www.jstor.org/stable/25054165

Lazear, E. P. (2018). Compensation and incentives in the workplace. *Journal of Economic Perspectives, 32*(3), 195–214.

Lindert, P. H. (2004). *Growing public: Social spending and economic growth since the eighteenth century* (Vol. 1). Cambridge University Press.

López-Calva, L. F., & Ortiz-Juarez, E. (2014). A vulnerability approach to the definition of the middle class. *Journal of Economic Inequality, 12*(1), 23–47.

Martínez Franzoni, J. (2008). Welfare regimes in Latin America: Capturing constellations of markets, families, and policies. *Latin American Politics and Society, 50*(2), 67–100.

Mesa-Lago, C. (1978). *Social security in Latin America: Pressure groups, stratification, and inequality*. University of Pittsburgh Press.
Mesa-Lago, C. (2007). *Reassembling social security. A survey of pensions and healthcare reforms in Latin America*. Oxford University Press.
Milanovic, B. (2019). *Capitalism alone. The future of the system that rules the world*. Belknap Press.
Moffitt, R. A. (2002). Welfare programs and labour supply. In A. J. Auerbach & M. Feldstein (Eds.), *Handbook of public economics* (Vol. 4, pp. 2394–2430). Elsevier Science B.V.
Molina Millán, T., Barham, T., Macours, K., Maluccio, J. A., & Stampini, M. (2019). Long-term impacts of conditional cash transfers: Review of the evidence. *World Bank Research Observer, 34*(1), 119–159. https://doi.org/10.1093/wbro/lky005
Morgan, S.-L., & Winship, C. (2015). *Counterfactuals and causal inference. Methods and principles of social research* (2nd ed.). Cambridge University Press.
Pearl, J. (2009). Causal inference in statistics. *Statistics Surveys, 3*, 96–146. https://doi.org/10.1214/09-SS057
Powell, M., & Barrientos, A. (2004). Welfare regimes and the welfare mix. *European Journal of Political Research, 43*(1), 83–105.
Pribble, J. (2011). Worlds apart: Social policy regimes in Latin America. *Studies in Comparative International Development, 46*(1), 191–216.
Ranaldi, M., & Milanovic, B. (2020). *Capitalist systems and income inequality* (Stone Center on Socio-Economic Inequality) [Working Paper]. City University of New York. https://stonecenter.gc.cuny.edu/research/capitalist-systems-and-income-inequality/
Ravallion, M., & Chen, S. (2015). Benefit incidence with incentive effects, measurement errors and latent heterogeneity: A case study for China. *Journal of Public Economics, 128*, 124–132.
Rehm, P. (2011). Social policy by popular demand. *World Politics, 63*(2), 271–299.
Roberts, K. M. (2021). The inclusionary turn and its political limitations. In D. Kapiszewski, S. Levitsky, & D. J. Yashar (Eds.), *The inclusionary turn in Latin American democracies*. Cambridge University Press.
Saavedra, J. E., & Garcia, S. (2017). *Educational impacts and cost-effectiveness of conditional cash transfer programs in developing countries: A meta-analysis* (Working Paper 23594; NBER). National Bureau for Economic Research.
Sánchez-Ancochea, D., & Martínez Franzoni, J. (2015). *La incorporación social en Centroamérica: Trayectorias, obstáculos y oportunidades* (Working Paper 1200). CEPAL- Mexico.

Sátyro, N., del Pino, E., & Midaglia, C. (2021). *Latin America social policy developments in the Twenty-first Century*. Palgrave Macmillan.

Segovia, A. (2022). *Las relaciones entre modelos y tipos de capitalismo: La experiencia de centroamérica* (Working Paper 198; Estudios y Perspectivas). CEPAL-Mexico.

Segura-Ubiergo, A. (2007). *The political economy of the Welfare State in Latin America*. Cambridge University Press.

Silva, E., & Rossi, F. M. (2017). *Reshaping the political arena in Latin America. From resisting Neoliberalism to the Second Incorporation*. .

UNU-WIDER. (2022). *World Income Inequality Database WIID*. UNU World Institute for Development Economic Research. https://www.wider.unu.edu/project/world-income-inequality-database-wiid

van Kersbergen, K., & Vis, B. (2014). *Comparative welfare state Politics: Development, opportunities, and reform*. Cambridge University Press.

Villatoro, P., & Cecchini, S. (2018). *¿Cuál es el alcance de las transferencias no-contributivas en América Latina?* (Estudios Estadísticos 96; Serie Estudios Estadísticos). CEPAL, División de Desarrollo Social.

Wibbels, E., & Ahlquist, J. S. (2011). Development, trade and social insurance. *International Studies Quarterly, 55*, 125–149.

Williamson, J. G. (2011). *Industrial catching up in the poor periphery 1870-1975* [Mimeo]. Harvard University.

2

Methods

This chapter discusses methods appropriate to the study of social protection in Latin America. It reviews and assesses the main methodological approaches employed by researchers in the past and, building on these, it identifies methods appropriate to developing a theoretical perspective capable of explaining the evolution and current configuration of social protection institutions in the region. The task is to select methods of data collection and analysis that will connect theoretical propositions to empirical counterparts.

By and large, the literature on social protection in Latin America has relied on case studies, cross-country institutional comparisons, linear structural equations estimated on aggregate annual data, and quasi-experimental evaluation of social protection interventions. After the turn of the century, critical improvements in data availability have supported comparative analysis. The spread, regularity, and accessibility of individual and household data[1] since the mid 1990s has facilitated the application of a wider range of analytical tools for the comparative study of

[1] CEDLAS constructs a harmonised database of household surveys for Latin America and the Caribbean (CEDLAS & World Bank, 2022) https://www.cedlas.econo.unlp.edu.ar/wp/en/estadisticas/sedlac/estadisticas/ . The Luxemburg Income Study initiative has expanded the number of countries in the region archiving data https://www.lisdatacenter.org/.

A. Barrientos, *Social Protection in Latin America*, Global Dynamics of Social Policy ,
https://doi.org/10.1007/978-3-031-49795-7_2

social protection. Dedicated beneficiary surveys in some countries in the region provide good quality detailed data on social protection.[2] More recently, impact evaluation survey data collected to assess the effects of social assistance programmes have been available to researchers. They offer an excellent resource for research on social protection outcomes.[3] Region-wide attitudinal survey data provide an essential resource to study public preferences on social protection.[4] There are also notable improvements in the availability of administrative data.[5]

Recent trends in social research methods reveal a renewed emphasis on causal inference. This is the outcome of push and pull factors. On the one hand, a growing awareness of the deficiencies associated with correlation bias in quantitative analysis. On the other, the growing application of experimental approaches to data collection and analysis (Angrist & Pischke, 2008; Banerjee & Duflo, 2008; Gelman & Imbens, 2013). The application of quasi-experimental methods in the study of the outcomes of social protection interventions, initially in the context of conditional income transfers, has focused attention on the causal effects of social protection interventions.

The issue to be discussed in this chapter is the extent to which these methodological developments can guide research on social protection institutions. There are significant challenges to causal inference in social protection research. Arguably, the study of social protection institutions could be seen as fundamentally different to the study of whether conditional income transfers have specific effects on their recipients. There are obvious limits to the application of experimental techniques in the study of social protection institutions and policies. Institutions evolve in time making it hard to keep conditions unchanged. Controls groups

---

[2] See Chile's Encuesta de Protección Social https://www.previsionsocial.gob.cl/sps/biblioteca/encuesta-de-proteccion-social/ ; and Uruguay's https://www.bps.gub.uy/15328/encuesta-longitudinal-de-proteccion-social.html.

[3] Mexico has led the way, see https://www.coneval.org.mx/Evaluacion/IEPSM/Paginas/default.aspx.

[4] See the Americas Barometer (LAPOP) https://www.vanderbilt.edu/lapop/ and Latinobarometro https://www.latinobarometro.org/latContents.jsp.

[5] On individual retirement savings plans see the database at AIOS at https://www.aiosfp.org/estadisticas/boletin-estadistico-aios.html. On social assistance see CEPAL's Base de Datos de Programas no Contributivos at https://dds.cepal.org/bpsnc/. On social spending see; and on revenue see https://www.oecd.org/tax/revenue-statistics-in-latin-america-and-the-caribbean-8b555412-en.htm.

can be hard to identify in the context of social policy. Implementation issues can be significant in the context of decentralised programmes affected by territorial diversity (Niedzwiecki, 2018).

Nevertheless, causal inference studies are increasingly being implemented in the study of social policy (Morgan & Winship, 2015). Taking causal inference seriously promises to deliver significant gains. The implementation of graphical causal models forces researchers to examine critically the relationships between the variables of interest on the basis of their theoretical frameworks (Elwert, 2013). Sifting causal from non-causal factors associated with social protection systematically, as opposed plugging multiple control variables in regression exercises, is a welcomed discipline. The potential outcomes approach can be usefully applied in the context of observational data, providing the preconditions for its applicability are considered carefully (Imbens, 2019). And alternatives to times-series-cross section studies that avoid post-treatment bias and omitted variables can support credible and reliable causal inference (Blackwell & Glynn, 2018). Identifying the challenges of implementing causal inference methods in social protection research could contribute to our understanding of these institutions in the region.

The materials in this chapter are arranged as follows. Section 2.1 will provide a brief review of the methods employed in the current literature on social protection in Latin America. Section 2.2 will make a case for adopting methods focused on causal inference. Section 2.3 discusses the implications of distinguishing between 'effects of cause' and 'causes of effects' for our approach to methods. Sections 2.4 and 2.5 offer a brief introduction to two causal inference tools: the potential outcomes approach and directed acyclic graphs. Section 2.6 identifies causality deficits in current social protection research. Section 2.7 summarises methodological challenges associated with placing greater emphasis on causal models. A final section concludes.

2.1 Methods in the Comparative Literature

The comparative literature on social protection in the region, especially in the last quarter of the last century, relied mainly on country and cross-country case studies. Case studies described institutional patterns and their evolution over time, focusing on the institutional set up in specific countries or focusing on specific institutions and instruments. In the new century, case studies focusing on multiple countries and regional comparisons have expanded.[6] Regional reports from ECLAC, ILO, IADB, UNDP and from the World Bank regularly offer comprehensive regional perspectives on social protection.[7] This comparative literature provides a substantive knowledge base on social protection policies and practices in the region. The analytical interest is often the identification of trends, cross-country and sub-regional differences in institutional performance, responses to the issue of the day, and comparisons with other regions or countries.

The identification of country clusters has generated a lively literature grouping countries according to the key features of their institutions. The relevant studies will be covered in some detail in a later chapter. Here the interest is to identify the methods employed. Studies on country clusters follow up on the welfare regime literature on welfare states pioneered by the work of Esping-Andersen (1990). This approach distinguishes welfare systems according to the institution that dominates their welfare provision: markets, the state, and families. This comparative approach has generated a great deal of research interest because it claims to unveil fundamental differences in the structure of capitalism among high income countries.[8] The main analytical tools employed in this literature cluster countries by extracting an index of differences or similarities from multivariate data (Barrientos, 2015). Cluster analysis is a commonly used approach (Abu Sharkh & Gough, 2010; Gough, 2001; Hirschberg et al., 1991; Powell & Barrientos, 2004). Martínez Franzoni (2008) has applied this approach to social policy in Latin America. Alternative data reduction techniques have been implemented in the region. Cruz-Martínez (2014, 2017b) employs principal components analysis to reduce several

[6] Recent contributions to the comparative literature have added a longitudinal dimension (Cruz-Martínez, 2019; Midaglia et al., 2018; Sátyro et al., 2021).

[7] See inter alia (Bosch et al., 2013; CAF, 2020; CEPAL, 2007, 2023; Fiszbein & Schady, 2009; ILO, 2022; OECD/IDB/The World Bank, 2014). Regular publications such as Social Panorama, Fiscal Panorama, Panorama Laboral provide excellent coverage of data and trends on social protection.

[8] The substantive contribution of this approach will be discussed in more detail in Chap. 8.

indicators supporting the construction of indexes which are then combined into a multidimensional welfare index. Countries are then ranked by their scores on this welfare index. Two points from this literature need to be underlined at this juncture. First, a crucial underlying assumption is that welfare institutions are multidimensional, hence the need to implement data reduction. Second, country groupings are helpful, analytically, in distinguishing multiple configurations of welfare institutions in the region, but they also have a normative content is as much as they reveal good and bad outcomes.

Qualitative Comparative Analysis (QCA) has proved especially useful in the study of institutions, their configuration, and change over time (Kangas, 1994; Kvist, 2007; Vis, 2012). It has been applied to the study of welfare institutions in Latin America (Cruz-Martínez, 2017a, 2019; Segura-Ubiergo, 2007). Simulation studies are also effective in providing a comparative perspective on social protection (Altamirano Montoya et al., 2018).

Time-series-cross-section and panel data are employed extensively in economic and political studies which include social protection institutions. Studies have considered whether globalisation has undermined social expenditure (Avelino et al., 2005; Huber et al., 2008) or whether democracy or conflict are associated with social programmes and expenditure (Yörük, 2022). Studies have relied on time-series-cross-section data to investigate the factors associated with the origins and evolution of welfare institutions (Haggard & Kaufman, 2008; Huber et al., 2008; Kaufman & Segura-Ubiergo, 2001; Segura-Ubiergo, 2007). Time-series-cross-section and panel data analysis are grounded on structural linear equation models unveiling correlations among variables of interest. The statistical models estimated are scrutinised as regards the significance of the estimated coefficients and the strength of the model's ability to reduce unexplained variance.

Event studies are helpful in identifying the factors constraining or facilitating the emergence of specific social protection institutions. They focus on unveiling correlates of foundational events (Knutsen & Rasmussen, 2018; Rasmussen & Knutsen, 2017; Schmitt, 2015; Schmitt et al., 2015).

More recently, the availability of evaluation and observational data has encouraged quasi-experimental techniques to study the impact of social protection interventions. In Latin America the spread of conditional income transfers helped bed in the collection of evaluation data and techniques for their evaluation. Mexico's *Progresa* was the pioneer (Skoufias, 2005). Exploiting a scheduled implementation of the programme, difference in difference estimates of its impact on poverty helped to protect it from contracting government budgets (Levy, 2006). Impact evaluations of old age transfers estimate the effects of the programmes by focusing on the differences in social indicators around the age of eligibility, a regression discontinuity design (Galiani et al., 2014). Regression discontinuity design can be implemented where programme regulations or their change over time generate exogenous breaks in benefit entitlements (Barrientos & Villa, 2015). Comparative studies extract information from the estimated impact of specific programme. Meta studies of the impact of conditional income transfers on education (Saavedra & Garcia, 2017); child mortality (Cavalcanti, 2023); labour supply (Alzúa et al., 2010); or elections (Araújo, 2021) provide a comparative perspective on social assistance. The rapid spread of evaluation data and quasi-experimental analytical techniques have greatly refined our understanding of the impact of social protection interventions in the region.

2.2 Shifting Attention to Causality

The growing use of experimental and quasi-experimental in social protection, especially in the study of the effects of social assistance programmes is part of a methodological shift focused on causal inference. In the context of social assistance programmes this focus on causality has greatly benefited from the design of impact evaluations and the availability of quasi-experimental data. This will be discussed in detail in the Protection chapter. This approach is predicated on the presence of an ad hoc intervention, social assistance transfers for example, capable of leading to a change in the behaviour of recipients. Dividing potential participants into two equivalent groups and implementing the intervention to the treatment group makes it possible to measure the difference in outcomes across the treatment and control groups after the intervention. This measure is a representation of the causal effect of the intervention.

There are multiple ways in which social protection institutions, like occupational pension funds or individual savings plans, are likely to have more complex effects than conditional income transfers. It is harder, and often unfeasible, for governments to experiment with large scale pension schemes, if anything because of the time horizons required. To a significant extent, researchers can only rely on observational data to try to understand social protection institutions. Generalising from local experiments is perilous as the causal effects identified by impact evaluation studies trade off external validity for external validity. These and other issues have persuaded researchers examining social protection institutions to sidestep causal inference in favour of associational models, qualitative and quantitative.

The aim of the materials discussed here is to argue there is path towards a causal examination of social protection institutions in Latin America. The main argument is that causal models are essential to unveil the factors explaining existing social protection in the region. The causal framework should not be limited to the study of the effects of local interventions but can also be deployed to study the configuration of social protection institutions in the region. To do this successfully, we need to integrate a set of methodological tools into our research together with an understanding of their limitations or, what is the same, an understanding of the conditions in which they can help advance understanding.

2.3 'Effects of Causes' and 'Causes of Effects' Explanations

Gelman and Imbens (2013) make a distinction between two types of causal explanations in the social sciences. First, a forward explanation that answers to the question: 'what are the effects of causes'? This is at the core of the experimental methods revolution. A second set of explanations consist of backward explanations answering the question: 'what are the causes of effects? They start from a set of effects and seek to understand what factors caused them. Impact evaluation studies of conditional income transfers belong to the first set of explanations, the 'effects of causes', while studies aiming to explain the origins of occupational insurance funds in Latin America in terms of associated features of society, politics, or the economy belong to the second set of explanations, the 'causes of effects'. Yamamoto (2012) argues that 'causes of effects' explanations "are about *attribution*, instead of effects, because their primary concern is the extent to which the actual occurrence of events can be attributed to a suspected cause" (2012, p. 1). This is closer to the term in common use. This distinction is relevant to the methodological approach in this book.

The 'experimental revolution' involved shifting the focus from 'causes of effects' to 'effects of causes. In Gelman and Imbens' view, estimating causal relations can only be done with forward causal questions. Studies attempting to explain causes of phenomena usually begin by identifying a set of potential causal factors and then test for the presence or absence of these factors in the antecedents of the phenomena. The presence of the effect often precludes consideration of possible counterfactual. Even when attention is paid to counterfactuals, reverse causation studies find multiple explanatory factors capable of confounding the potential link between causes and the effect. Research findings are on stronger ground if they can dismiss, falsify, the influence of some factors on the presence of the phenomena.

The current dominance of 'effects of causes' methodologies, especially experimental methods, has cast doubt on the contribution that 'causes of effects' studies can make (Goertz & Mahoney, 2012) and on whether this approach can be accommodated within statistical or econometric estimation models (Gelman & Imbens, 2013). Some researchers go further and argue that only an external intervention or manipulation can support causal inference. Experimental data is needed to support causal inference, observational data lacking an intervention in the data generating process will not be capable of supporting causal inference.

It can be argued this view is too restrictive, that 'causes of effects' explanations have a role to play in advancing causal knowledge. Experimental methods are unfeasible in many social protection or social policy contexts that motivate social protection researchers in Latin America. However, a 'causes of effects' approach could be helpful in the task of identifying non-causal factors, the factors that are not causally linked to social protection institutions; in refining existing models capable of capturing the relationships involved, and perhaps in helping formulate hypotheses to be explored using 'effects of causes' research methods. Identification of causal and non-causal factors is a first step (Morgan & Winship, 2015, Chapter 3). It makes explicit the assumptions that are required to claim causal status. Searching for causes of effects or inverse causal inference could lead to improvements in the maintained model or suggest its replacement with a better one. Gelman and Imbens suggest that 'causes of effects' questions fit into statistics and econometrics not as inferential questions to be answered with estimates or confidence intervals, but as the identification of statistical anomalies that motivate improved models" (Gelman & Imbens, 2013, p. 4).

In fact, the identification of relevant factors capable of explaining the emergence of social protection institutions has been the primary objective in the quantitative literature. In some contributions, this relates to conditions required for social protection institutions, for example the level of economic development, or democracy, or openness, or urbanisation. Studies interrogating times series cross-section data have focused on the identifying the main correlates of social expenditure. The underlying statistical model is a linear structural equation model including a range of variables to 'control' for potential confounders and estimated using regression analysis. Studies using times-series-cross-section data (Segura-Ubiergo, 2007) and panel data (Haggard & Kaufman, 2008) provide some examples.

'Causes of effects' or reverse causation studies have contributed to refining the identification of the factors explaining the emergence and evolution of social protection institutions in the region. They have helped to clear the ground for 'effects of causes' research leading to reliable causal inference. But perhaps the most significant methodological challenge is to extend the application of 'effects of causes' to the study of social protection institutions in the region. It requires shifting the focus of research from conditions to effects. The following sections introduce some of the relevant tools.

2.4 The Potential Outcomes Framework

The potential outcomes framework provides a foundation for causal inference (Imbens, 2019). Assume that education is a unit treatment, so that an individual is a college graduate or only manages to complete basic education. It is a well-established fact that college educated workers command higher salaries than workers with only basic education. In an experimental setting, an individual selected at random will have two potential outcomes denoted y_1 if offered college education or y_0 is offered only basic education. In theory the difference between the two outcomes, y_1–y_0, would be the college premium. In practice, only one outcome can be observed for an individual although in theory there are two potential outcomes. For the individual who completes college education, the salary of the individual without college education is the counterfactual, and vice versa. Researchers examining a sample of individuals, some 'treated' with college education and others in the 'control' group can measure the average college premium, the payoff to the treatment.

There are some complications the researcher must address (Angrist & Pischke, 2008). In the real world, individuals in the sample might not start from the same position. Some will have benefited from wealthy parents, or from a privileged social position, or their mothers' attention in early life. Variables that influence both the treatment and the outcome are referred to as confounders. Some might have genetic advantages while others might be affected by learning difficulties. Random assignment of individuals to the treatment, the experimental approach, could overcome these complications and lend credibility to the findings from the research. The design of the experimental research requires some rules guiding the random assignments. If random assignment is not feasible, identifying groups in the sample that share the same characteristics is essential. Grouping individuals according to the income level of their parents or the education level reached by their mothers might strip away some of the confounders such that the college premium can be measured across comparable groups. This strategy is referred to as 'quasi-experiment' in that researchers do not have full control over the assignment but are able to find ex-post that conditions are equivalent to a random assignment. Evaluating average potential outcomes requires appropriate assumptions.

The potential outcome framework can be stated more formally for an individual i as

$$y_i = y_i 1 - y_i 0$$

Where y_i is the outcome for individual i; $y_i 1$ denotes the outcome if treated and $y_i 0$ the outcome if not treated.[9] Aggregating across the sample, it is possible to evaluate the sample average treatment effect (SATE).

$$Y_{\text{sate}} = \frac{1}{n}\sum_{i=1}^{n}\left(y_i 1 - y_i 0\right)$$

Several assumptions are required to ensure validity for the SATE (Hernán, 2020). The ignorability assumption refers to the requirement that the random assignment is independent of the potential outcomes. This assumption can be formalised as $t \perp y^0, y^1$. The stable unit treatment assumption requires that the potential outcome for unit i depends only in the treatment. This implies the requirement that there are no hidden treatments and no spillovers among units.

The potential outcomes framework facilitates thinking through causality in the context of social protection institutions. It emphasises the role of counterfactuals, that is the road not taken.

2.5 Directed Acyclical Graphs

Directed acyclical graphs (DAGs) provide a tool for assessing causal models that could potentially deliver causal inference (Elwert, 2013; Morgan & Winship, 2015; Pearl, 2010). DAGs are visual representations of hypothesised qualitative causal relationships. In constructing directed acyclical graphs, researchers encode their perceptions about how the world works aided by a set of formal logical rules (Pearl, 2010). Elwert emphasises two primary uses for DAGs "First, DAGs can be used to

[9] Assuming, for simplicity that there is a single treatment.

prove or disprove the identification of causal effects, that is, the possibility of computing causal effects from observable data… Since identification is always conditional on the validity of the assumed causal model, it is fortunate that the second use of DAGs is to present those assumptions explicitly and reveal their testable implications, if any" (Elwert, 2013, p. 246).

Elwert describes DAGs as nonparametric structural equation models (NPSEM), including a range of (parametric) linear structural equation model as special cases. The fact that DAGs are non-parametric implies that the relationships identified do not require the specification of the distribution of the variables involved, nor the functional form or the size of the causal effects. In this sense nonparametric structural equation models (NPSEM) identify causal relationships at a more basic level than identification in (parametric) linear structural equation model. DAGs can tell us whether causality can be ascertained in theory, assuming the relevant observable data and appropriate statistical models are available.[10]

DAGs encode assumption about qualitative causal relationship by arrows pointing to the outcomes. Arrows are directed edges linking nodes or random variables. Missing arrows indicate the absence of a causal effect.[11] Causal paths represent all paths in which the arrows point away from the treatment and towards the outcome. Non-causal paths are all other paths. Variables directly caused by another variable are referred to as their children, whilst the causing variables are referred to as their parents. Descendants are all variables directly and indirectly related to a

[10] "Structural equation modelling (SEM) has been the main vehicle for effect analysis in economics and the behavioural and social sciences …. However, the bulk of SEM methodology was developed for linear analysis and, until recently, no comparable methodology has been devised to extend its capabilities to models involving dichotomous variables or nonlinear dependencies. A central requirement for any such extension is to detach the notion of "effect" from its algebraic representation as a coefficient in an equation, and redefine "effect" as a general capacity to transmit changes among variables."(Pearl, 2009, p. 107). For the correspondence between DAGs and structural equation models see Elwert (2013) and Morgan and Winship (2015).

[11] "It is important to note that, in path diagrams, causal assumptions are encoded not in the links but, rather, in the missing links. An arrow merely indicates the possibility of causal connection, the strength of which remains to be determined (from data); a missing arrow represents a claim of zero influence."(Pearl, 2009, p. 105).

parent. A collider is a variable with two arrows pointing into it. A DAG is a directed acyclic path because it does not contain a path that returns to the original variable, a cyclic path.[12] This requirement rules out simultaneous causality, as in 'trade unions and social spending cause each other'.

In Fig. 2.1(a) the causal path X→ B → Y represents that Y is the outcome of X. 2.1(b) represents the same causal path X → B → Y, but now with a non-causal path from X to D or D ← X. 2.1(c) show B as a collider in that both X and Y influence B or X → B ← Y. 2.1(d) shows that B is a common cause of X and Y or X ← B → Y.

DAGs encode researchers' beliefs about how the world works and. Paying attention to a small number of rules, they can help translate researchers' beliefs into models of associations that can be potentially observable in the data. DAGs rules can also help exclude non-causal paths. DAG rules for identification offer interesting insights into assessing these causal models. For example, in Fig. 2.1(a) variable X has a marginal effect on the outcome Y. The presence of B does not prevent the association between X and Y. In fact, estimation of a statistical model that 'controls' for B would fail to compute the effect of X on Y.[13] In Fig 2.1(b) computing the causal relation of X on Y should ignore the non-causal path from X to D as it does not affect the primary causal relationship.

In Fig. 2.1(c) there is no causal path between X and Y, the two variables are not dependent on each other. However, an estimation of the association between X and Y that controls for B, a common outcome, could produce a spurious association between the two. This is commonly described as 'endogenous selection bias'. In Fig 2.1(d), X and Y are not dependent on each other but share a common cause. In this case B is a 'confounder' because it influences both X and Y, and 'controlling' for B would lead to the identification of the association between X and Y (none in this case).

Figure 2.2(a) borrowed from Morgan and Winship (2015), represents the effect of E earnings on Y income, A is a common cause of earnings and income, say unobserved ability, and C is a confounding variable also

[12] "Causal analysis in graphical models begins with the realization that all causal effects are identifiable whenever the model is Markovian, that is, the graph is acyclic (i.e., containing no directed cycles) and all the error terms are jointly independent."(Pearl, 2009, p. 110).

[13] Elwert (2013) describes this as 'overcontrol bias'.

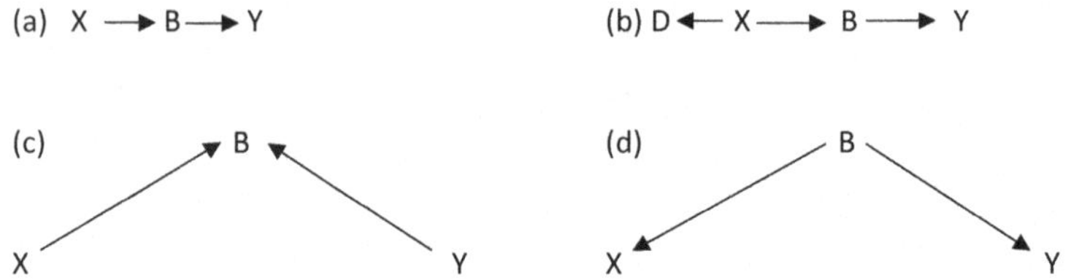

Fig. 2.1 DAGs showing causal and non-causal paths

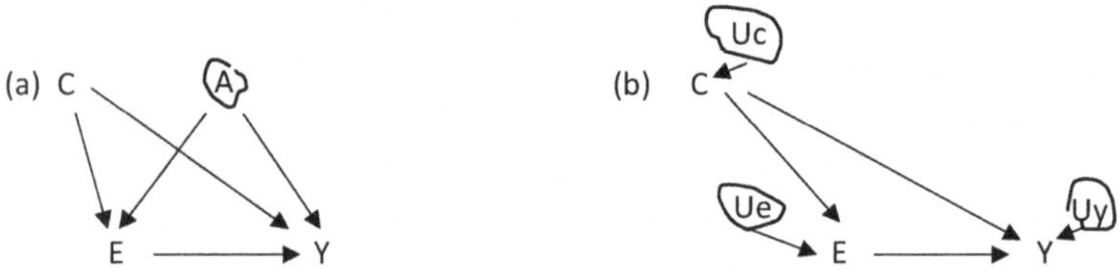

Fig. 2.2 Confounders

affecting earnings and income. Note that 'controlling' for the confounding variable will bias any estimation of the direct effect. Because A is unobserved, controlling for C would not support an unbiased estimate of the effect of education on earnings. Figure 2.2(b) points to another issue in DAGs, unobserved error terms associated with variables can be included, as in Uc, Ue and Uy in the Figure. To the extent that they could be described as independent of each other and as 'idiosyncratic' causes of each variable, they are usually left out of the DAG. This practice would not apply if the unobserved error terms were judged to influence more than one variable.

As can be seen, applying some basic rules to the encoding of researchers' beliefs concerning the phenomena under investigation adds precision to the description of causal and non-causal relations between variables, and suggests appropriate strategies for the analysis of observable counterparts.

2.6 Causality Deficits in Social Protection Research

As noted in the Introduction, an incipient application of causal inference in social protection research can be traced back to Mesa-Lago's (1978) *Social Security in Latin America: Pressure Groups, Stratification, and Inequality*. There he sketches three models of social security development, using arrows to underline causal linkages between pressure groups PG, the state S, Social Security SS, and political parties PP. The first model describes an acyclical path from occupational pressure groups the state from the state to social security institutions, PG → S → SS. This model requires democratic pluralism he associated with conditions in Chile. The second model describes a causal path from the state to social security institutions, with a further link from the state to pressure groups denoting their co-optation, this can be represented as PG ← S → SS. Here the state is a common cause of both pressure groups and social security. Co-optation of pressure groups and the establishment of publicly supported social security institutions are sourced to authoritarian state elites. The third implicit model is more complex, it has an edge from the state to social security, and edge from pressure groups to the state, and an edge from pressure groups to political parties and political parties to the state. This can be interpreted as political parties acting as a common cause of both pressure groups and the state, or PG ← PP → S → SS plus PG→ S. Mesa-Lago offered an early insight into mapping the causal links between the different actors. This methodological approach was not developed further in the literature.

The availability of harmonised cross-country data on aggregate social spending has enabled researchers to construct panels of repeated observations for countries in the region. Quantitative research[14] on social protection in Latin America has made use of panel and time-series-cross section data to investigate determinants of social protection dynamics. Time-series-cross-section data open a new range of potential research questions

[14] The discussion in this section focuses on quantitative studies largely because of my limited expertise in qualitative research. For a discussion of causal approaches in qualitative research see (Goertz & Mahoney, 2012).

associated with changes in social protection provision over time. At the same time, these data present some challenges for researchers as regards appropriate statistical estimation (Beck & Katz, 1995, 1996, 2011; Plumper et al., 2005; Wilson & Butler, 2007). It is likely that pooling repeated observations for countries in the region will show serial correlation in that spending in one year will be correlated with spending in previous years. It is also the case that the different units or countries will show temporal and spatial correlation, as with the impact of crises or conflict. Differences in social protection across countries may be permanent or at least persistent if due to differences in natural resources, population, history, or legal or constitutional frameworks. The point is that pooled observations cannot be assumed to be independent random draws from nature. It is essential to take account of these potential biases in the estimation model.[15]

The workhorse is some form of error correction estimating model that takes care of serial correlation and panel heteroskedasticity (Beck & Katz, 2011). Starting from a static regression model as in

$$\text{Static model}: Y_t = \alpha + \beta_0 X_t + u_i$$

Where Y_t is the outcome of interest, X_t are the determinant factors and ui is an iid error term.

An error correction models (ECM) will include lagged variables (first order autoregressive, and independent variables in levels and rate of change

$$\text{Error correction model}: Y_t - Y_{t-1} = \alpha + \gamma_1 Y_{t-1} + +\beta_0 X_{t-1} + \beta_1 \left(X_t - X_{t-1}\right) + u_t$$

ECM will have several advantages in estimating TSCS data. Assuming the autoregressive correlation is AR(1) the ECM models the dynamics in the data generating process. Estimated by OLS with panel corrected standard errors, it addresses both serial correlation and panel heteroskedasticity.

[15] This, in addition to having a workable model of how the world works, a causal or theoretical model, and challenges, like measurement error, that are associated with all empirical work.

An important assumption in ECMs is that the data are drawn from a stationary process, that is observations are mean reverting, and that the best long-run forecast of a stationary process is that mean. We can think of the mean is "the 'equilibrium' of a stationary process" (Beck & Katz, 2011, p. 333). ECM are therefore appropriate to the study of the way in which 'shocks' impact on the variables of interest, so that the coefficients associated with the independent variable describe the rate of adjustment to the equilibrium.

Among the studies on social protection in Latin America using ECM, Kaufman and Segura-Ubiergo (2001) and Avelino et al. (2005) investigate the influence of economic openness on social spending in the region. Following the literature on OECD countries, they test alternative explanations of social spending responses to globalisation. Increased competition brought about by globalisation could force governments to reduce the costs of welfare provision to improve efficiency and competitiveness, or alternatively to raise their social spending to compensate citizens for any adverse effects of globalisation. Kaufman and Segura-Ubiergo (2001), relying on data from 1973–1997, find that populist governments squeeze all social spending, while democratic governments increase spending in health and education and reduce spending on social security. Avelino et al. (2005) on the other hand, using data from 1980–1999 harmonised using purchasing power parity as opposed to exchange rates, find that openness tends to enhance rather than diminish social spending. They also find that the effects of globalisation differ across the components of social spending. As they put it, "… Latin America's heightened exposure to international competition does not affect all social programs equally. In fact, our results suggest that politicians in open economies both compensate certain groups (spend on social security) and undertake policies that raise the level of efficiency in an economy (spend on education). In addition, democracies enhance the prospects for investing in human capital while preserving social security payments." (Avelino et al., 2005, p. 634).

A study of the effects of protests and democracy on social spending shows another relevant application of the ECM (Zarate Tenorio, 2014). In this study, interacting a democracy indicator variable with variables capturing alternative types of protest generates interesting findings. Zarate does not "…find evidence that democracy has an independent effect on social security spending, neither in the short nor in the long run." (Zarate Tenorio, 2014, p. 1961). In fact, "…the effect of democracy on social security spending is conditioned by organized labor protest. Their organizational capacity inherited from earlier periods puts them in a better position relative to other groups to effectively mobilize to defend their entitlements. However, mass protest has also had important consequences for human capital spending. While democratic leaders increase human capital spending as a consequence of electoral incentives, mass protest inhibit cutbacks in these areas in democratic regimes "(Zarate Tenorio, 2014, p. 1965).

Huber et al. (2008) also examine the effect of openness and domestic politics on social spending in the region for the period 1970 to 2000. They are interested in the determinants of long-term patterns of social spending. They aim to explain the level of social spending rather than the rate of change or adjustment towards an equilibrium. They argue that democracy and partisanship does not produce change instantly, but over time. It is long-term periods of unbroken democracy or left partisan coalitions in power, rather than instantaneous change, that are held to influence the level of social spending. Accordingly, their model does not include a lagged dependent variable and the independent variables are estimated in levels. They also avoid including fixed country effects.[16] The find that democracy matters for social spending in the longer term for both social security and education and health spending. Authoritarian regimes, on the other hand, maintain health and education spending at low levels but raise social security and welfare spending. This finding, shared by the other studies discussed above, is predicated on the acute regressivity of occupational insurance provision in the region.

Altman and Castiglioni (2020) study the influence of political and growth factors on the egalitarian character of social policy expansion in Latin America. They construct a panel of countries for the period 1990 to 2013. Their estimation method includes lagged independent variables, country fixed effects and 5-year dummies. They find that political

[16] Their methodological decisions are influence by Achen (Achen, 2000) on the issue of the issue of including a lagged dependent variable and by Plumper et al. (Plumper et al., 2005) on the issue of country fixed effects.

competitiveness and civil society strength, rather than left-right partisanship, influenced the egalitarian character of social policy expansion in the region (Altman & Castiglioni, 2020).

Studies of social protection spending in the region using panel or time-series-cross-section (TSCS) data have adopted ECMs or panel corrected standard errors (PCSE) of levels to account for the dynamics of spending and its determinants and in the process account for serial correlation and panel heteroskedasticity. The models are appropriate to address the effects of 'shocks' to stationary data. However, as demonstrated by Huber et al. (2008) ECM models are less appropriate to the study of the longer-term determinants of social protection since the relevant data reveals the presence of a trend, as opposed to stationary data. The adoption of alternative methods reflects the research questions they address.

As anticipated by the discussion on 'cause of effects' research, the findings from the literature examining the influence of globalization and democracy on social spending in Latin America are helpful but meagre (Flechtner & Sánchez-Ancochea, 2022). Overall, they confirm the influence of political regimes on social spending but fail to throw much light on the actual mechanism through which this influence is exercised. There is some consensus around the view that partisanship is not as important as it appears to be in the welfare state literature, a hypothesis that echoes the cleavage literature (Bornschier, 2009; Dix, 1989; Roberts, 2002). The studies find agreement on the need to disaggregate social spending into its component parts: social protection and basic service. This is based on the view that the each of the components have a different underlying political logic. The studies are inconclusive as regards the influence of democracy, measured as a continuum, or the role of interest groups, in explaining spending on social security. They offer contested findings on the influence of authoritarian regimes on the persistence of social security spending and on the influence of democracy on the expansion of service spending.

To an important extent, the frailties of studies based on time-series-cross-section and panel data are well known (Kittel, 2006; Plumper et al., 2005; Wilson & Butler, 2007) and perhaps it is unfair to blame the tools. The assumptions underlying ECMs might be the real issue. At its core is the issue whether the social protection data generating process in Latin

America is characterised by stationarity or alternatively it is characterised by a trend. This has implications for whether estimated coefficients are constant or variable over time. It is important to keep in mind that the TSCS literature reviewed above focuses on the neoliberal phase in the region and the findings might apply to this period only.

Structural equation models in quantitative studies of social protection generally focus on correlation, not causation. This is made explicit in Kaufman and Segura-Ubiergo (2001) estimation of the association of democracy and globalization with social spending in a cross-section panel of Latin American countries. They are careful to interpret the estimated coefficients in their model as associations or correlations, precluding causality claims. In the spirit of 'causes of effects' or attribution studies, their study helps shape an 'effects of causes' research strategy. Discussing the finding that democratic governments are more likely to raise education and health spending while authoritarian governments are more likely to protect spending in pensions, they note that if "our analysis cannot definitely uncover the causal mechanisms that underlie the statistical findings, however, it does provide a frame of reference that might orient future research."(Kaufman & Segura-Ubiergo, 2001, p. 582).

Structural equation models can underscore thinking about social protection implicitly. Levy and Cruces (2021) develop a model in which a long list of variables is taken to influence social protection and each other. They do not move forward to estimate such a model although it is implicit from their approach that they have a linear structural equation model in mind. As all the relevant variables are assumed to influence each other simultaneously, this approach precludes any consideration of causal associations.

Dynamic models emphasising feedback effects are often employed in institutional analyses of social protection. They hypothesise simultaneous influences among the variables of interest. They are essentially ruled out by a DAG causal model. In DAG causal models the aim is to "'redefine' effects as a general capacity to transmit changes among variables."(Pearl, 2009, p. 107). Approaching feedback mechanisms and simultaneous associations between variables from a causal perspective would require separating out different causal relationships in time and treating them as separate phases lending themselves to separate causal models.

2.7 Methodological Challenges

The review of methods in social protection research in Latin America points to several challenges for this book. They are associated with expanding the implementation of causal models. The potential outcomes and directed acyclical graphs discussed above could productively complement the range of current methodological approaches to the study of social protection in Latin America.

Graphical methods can encourage a deeper consideration of the quality of association between variables and discriminate between causal and non-causal association. This approach points to the need for close attention to theory. This is shared across methodological approaches. Noting areas of consensus between structural equation modelling and structural causal modelling Glynn and Quinn (2013) note that "a theoretical understanding of the substantive problem, particularly regarding the nature of any temporal dependencies, is an important part of a successful estimation strategy" (p. 3).[17] They recommend recourse to graphical methods associated with the structural causal model of Pearl (Pearl, 2009) to establish the quality of these relationships.

Awareness of the limitations of linear structural models in capturing the influence of time-varying covariates has encouraged work on estimation models embedding potential outcomes and treatment histories (Blackwell & Glynn, 2018). In the ECM model presented above, the effects of lagged covariates are included in several ways, the effect of X_{t-1} on Y_t, the effect of X_{t-2} and X_{t1} on Y_t through the inclusion of the lagged dependent variable Y_{t-1}. This complex set of interactions are hard to model and lead to estimation biases, especially where time-varying covariates are present. Note that in the static model, covariates are assumed to be constant, only their current value is considered. In the single shot scenario, covariates can be included as part of a strategy to control for baseline conditions or for preintervention variables. In a dynamic context, some covariates are time varying. Take the example of past social protection spending that strengthen trade union or supportive political

[17] This point was raised by Plumper et al. (2005) as the primary concern for researchers using time-series-cross-section data.

parties that could themselves influence current social protection spending. In this case TSCS models will include trade union or partisan strength as a covariate. These variables qualify as posttreatment. TSCS or panel regression can avoid posttreatment bias by not including them as control variables, but this exacerbates any omitted variable bias. TSCS models with time-varying covariates find themselves in a dilemma. Including time-varying covariates leads to omitted variable bias but including them results in posttreatment bias. Blackwell and Glyn (2018) explore marginal structural models with treatment histories as a potential solution.

2.8 Conclusions

This chapter has provided a review of methodological approaches in social protection research. The availability of harmonised cross-country data on social protection in the region has encouraged the application of a wider range of methods, qualitative and quantitative. Step improvements in data availability and methodological innovation will make it possible for researchers to address an expanding range of research questions on social protection.

The discussion in the chapter focused on applications of parametric structural equation models estimated with times-series-cross-section and panel data in the context of Latin American social protection institutions. They have contributed to our understanding of the influence of globalisation, democracy, and conflict on social spending, including spending on social protection. At the same time, these studies demonstrate some weaknesses associated with the lack of fit between their assumptions regarding the data generating process, and the characteristics of the relevant data for Latin America. The model assumptions are too restrictive. Their findings privilege correlation over causation.

The chapter has made a case for paying greater attention to causal models in social protection research. It discussed three main areas where this strategy can be advanced.

First, it made a distinction between 'causes of effects' and 'effects of causes' type of research enquiry. In 'causes of effects' enquiries the aim is to attribute phenomena to specific causes. It is important define the potential contribution of this type of research to our understanding of social protection. Attribution studies can help sift through possible causal factors primarily by identifying non-causal factors and can shape follow up 'effects of causes' research. The latter aims to establish the effects of changes in causal factors, for example the consumption effects of conditional income transfers. 'Causes of effects' type enquiry accounts for the bulk of research on social protection institutions in Latin America. More recently, experimental, and quasi-experimental methods have been implemented in the study of the effects of social protection interventions. They signal a shift towards 'effects of causes' research methods. There are challenges to the application of 'effects of causes' methods in the context of research on institutions relying on observational data. Second, the potential outcomes approach offers a systematic framework for incorporating attention to counterfactuals. Third, graphical casual models offer a range of tools for assessing the association between variables in a systematic fashion. Directed acyclic graphs offer a representing of researchers' beliefs of researchers regarding the way the world works. The application of a set of basic rules (Pearl, 2010) help discriminate causal versus non-causal association between variables, refining researchers' hypotheses and linking the model to potential empirical counterparts.

References

Abu Sharkh, M., & Gough, I. (2010). Global welfare regimes: A cluster analysis. *Global Social Policy, 10*(1), 27–58.

Achen, C. (2000). *Why lagged dependent variables can suppress the explanatory power of other independent variables* [Mimeo]. University of Michigan.

Altamirano Montoya, A., Berstein, S., Bosch, M., & García Huitrón, M. (2018). *Presente y futuro de las pensiones en América Latina y el Caribe*. Inter-American Development Bank.

Altman, D., & Castiglioni, R. (2020). Determinants of equitable social policy in Latin America (1990–2013). *Journal of Social Policy, 49*(4), 763–784. https://doi.org/10.1017/S0047279419000734

Alzúa, M. L., Cruces, G., & Ripani, L. (2010). *Welfare programs and labour supply in developing countries. Experimental evidence for Latin America* (Documento de Trabajo 95). CEDLAS-UNLP.

Angrist, J. D., & Pischke, J.-S. (2008). *Mostly harmless econometrics: An empiricist's companion*. Princeton University Press.
Araújo, V. (2021). Do anti-poverty policies sway voters? Evidence from a meta-analysis of Conditional Cash Transfers. *Research and Politics*, 1–9. https://journals.sagepub.com/doi/10.1177/2053168021991715
Avelino, G., Brown, D. S., & Hunter, W. (2005). The effects of capital mobility, trade openness, and democracy on social spending in Latin America, 1980–1999. *American Journal of Political Science, 49*(3), 625–641.
Banerjee, A. V., & Duflo, E. (2008). *The experimental approach to development economics* (NBER Working Paper 14467). National Bureau of Economic Research. http://www.nber.org/papers/w14467
Barrientos, A. (2015). "A veritable mountain of data and years of endless statistical manipulation": Methods in the Three Worlds and after. *Social Policy and Society, 14*(2), 259–270.
Barrientos, A., & Villa, J. M. (2015). Antipoverty transfers and labour force participation effects. *Journal of Development Studies, 51*(9), 1224–1240.
Beck, N., & Katz, J. N. (1995). What to do (and not to do) with time series cross-section data. *American Political Science Review, 89*, 634–647.
Beck, N., & Katz, J. N. (1996). Nuisance vs. substance: Specifying and estimating time-series-cross-section models. *Political Analysis, 6*, 1–36.
Beck, N., & Katz, J. N. (2011). Modeling dynamics in time-series-cross-section political economy data. *Annual Review of Political Science, 14*(1), 331–352.
Blackwell, M., & Glynn, A. N. (2018). How to make causal inferences with time-series cross-sectional data under selection on observables. *American Political Science Review, 112*(4), 1067–1082.
Bornschier, S. (2009). Cleavage politics in old and new democracies. *Living Reviews in Democracy, 2009*, 1–13.
Bosch, M., Melguizo, A., & Pages, C. (2013). *Mejores pensiones, mejores trabajos*. Inter-American Development Bank.
CAF. (2020). *Los sistemas de pensiones y salud en América Latina. Los desafíos del envejecimiento, el cambio tecnológico y la informalidad*. Corporación Andina de Fomento.
Cavalcanti, D. M. (2023). Evaluation and forecasting analysis of the association of conditional cash transfer with child mortality in Latin America, 2000-2030. *JAMA Network/Open, 6*(7), 1–11. https://doi.org/10.1001/jamanetworkopen.2023.23489
CEDLAS, & World Bank. (2022). *Socio-economic database for Latin America and the Caribbean*. CEDLAS.

CEPAL. (2007). *Panorama Social 2006*. CEPAL.
CEPAL. (2023). *Panorama Fiscal de América Latina y el Caribe 2023* [Panorama Fiscal]. Comisión Económica para Amèrica Latina y el Caribe.
Cruz-Martínez, G. (2014). Welfare State development in Latin America and the Caribbean (1970s–2000s): Multidimensional Welfare Index, its methodology and results. *Social Indicators Research, 119*, 1295–1317. https://doi.org/10.1007/s11205-013-0549-7
Cruz-Martínez, G. (2017a). Is there a common path that could have conditioned the degree of welfare state development in Latin America and the Caribbean? *Bulletin of Latin American Research, 36*(4), 459–476.
Cruz-Martínez, G. (2017b). Welfare state development, individual deprivations and income inequality: A cross-country analysis in Latin America and the Caribbean. *Social Indicators Research, 134*, 955–979. https://doi.org/10.1007/s11205-016-1465-4
Cruz-Martínez, G. (Ed.). (2019). *Welfare and social protection in Contemporary Latin America*. Routledge.
Dix, R. H. (1989). Cleavage structures and party systems in Latin America. *Comparative Politics, 22*(1), 23–37.
Elwert, F. (2013). Graphical causal models. In *Handbook of causal analysis for social research*. Springer. https://doi.org/10.1007/978-94-007-6094-3_13
Esping-Andersen, G. (1990). *The three worlds of welfare capitalism*. Polity Press.
Fiszbein, A., & Schady, N. (2009). *Conditional cash transfers: A world bank policy research report*. The World Bank.
Flechtner, S., & Sánchez-Ancochea, D. (2022). Why is the accumulation of knowledge so hard? Exploring econometric research on the determinants of public social spending in Latin America. *Latin American Research Review, 57*, 258–277. https://doi.org/10.1017/lar.2022.21
Galiani, S., Gertler, P., & Bando, R. (2014). *Non-contributory pensions* (NBER Working Paper w19775). NBER.
Gelman, A., & Imbens, G. (2013). *Why ask why? Forward causal inference and reverse causal questions* (Working Paper 19614; NBER). National Bureau of Economic Research.
Glynn, A. N., & Quinn, K. M. (2013). *Structural causal models and the specification of time-series-cross-section models* [Mimeo].
Goertz, G., & Mahoney, J. (2012). *A tale of two cultures. Qualitative and quantitative research in the social sciences*. Princeton University Press.
Gough, I. (2001). Social assistance regimes: A cluster analysis. *Journal of European Social Policy, 11*(2), 165–170.

Haggard, S., & Kaufman, R. R. (2008). *Development, democracy, and welfare states. Latin America, Asia and Eastern Europe*. Princeton University Press.

Hernán, M. A. (2020). *Causal inference: What if*. CRC Press.

Hirschberg, J. G., Maasoumi, E., & Slottje, D. J. (1991). Cluster analysis for measuring welfare and quality of life across countries. *Journal of Econometrics, 50*, 131–150.

Huber, E., Mustillo, T., & Stephens, J. D. (2008). Politics and social spending in Latin America. *Journal of Politics, 70*(2), 420–436. http://www.jstor.com/stable/10.1017/s0022381608080407.

ILO. (2022). *Panorama de la protección social en América Latina y el Caribe*. International Labour Office.

Imbens, G. W. (2019). *Potential outcomes and directed acyclic graph approaches to causality: Relevance for empirical practice in Economics* (Mimeo arXiv:1907.07271v1). Stanford University.

Kangas, O. (1994). The politics of social security: On regressions, qualitative comparisons, and cluster analysis. In T. Janoski & A. M. Hicks (Eds.), *The comparative political economy of the welfare state* (pp. 346–364). CUP.

Kaufman, R. R., & Segura-Ubiergo, A. (2001). Globalization, domestic politics, and social spending in Latin America: A time-series cross-section analysis, 1973–97. *World Politics, 53*(4), 553–587. https://www.jstor.org/stable/25054165

Kittel, B. (2006). A crazy methodology? On the limits of macro-quantitative social science research. *International Sociology, 21*(5), 647–677.

Knutsen, C. H., & Rasmussen, M. (2018). The autocratic welfare state: Old-age pensions, credible commitments and regime survival. *Comparative Political Studies, 51*(2), 659–695.

Kvist, J. (2007). Fuzzy set ideal type analysis. *Journal of Business Research, 60*, 474–481. https://doi.org/10.1016/j.jbusres.2007.01.005

Levy, S. (2006). *Progress against Poverty. Sustaining Mexico's Progresa-Oportunidades program*. Brookings Institution Press.

Levy, S., & Cruces, G. (2021). *Time for a new course: An essay on social protection and growth in Latin America* (Working Paper 24; UNDP LAC Working Paper). UNDP.

Martínez Franzoni, J. (2008). Welfare regimes in Latin America: Capturing constellations of markets, families, and policies. *Latin American Politics and Society, 50*(2), 67–100.

Midaglia, C., Ordoñez, G., & Valencia Lomelí, E. (Eds.). (2018). *Políticas sociales en América Latina en los inicios del siglo XXI*. CLACSO. http://www.jstor.com/stable/j.ctvn96gmn.1

Morgan, S.-L., & Winship, C. (2015). *Counterfactuals and causal inference. Methods and principles of social research* (2nd.). Cambridge University Press.
Niedzwiecki, S. (2018). *Uneven social policies. The politics of subnational variation in Latin America*. Cambridge University Press.
OECD/IDB/The World Bank. (2014). *Pensions at a glance: Latin America and the Caribbean*. OECD Publishings.
Pearl, J. (2009). Causal inference in statistics. *Statistics Surveys, 3*, 96–146. https://doi.org/10.1214/09-SS057
Pearl, J. (2010). An introduction to causal inference. *The International Journal of Biostatistics, 6*(2), 1–59.
Plumper, T., Troeger, V., & Manow, P. (2005). Panel data analysis in comparative politics: Linking method to theory. *European Journal of Political Research, 44*(2), 327–354.
Powell, M., & Barrientos, A. (2004). Welfare regimes and the welfare mix. *European Journal of Political Research, 43*(1), 83–105.
Rasmussen, M., & Knutsen, C. H. (2017). *Party institutionalization and welfare state development* (Working Paper 2017.55). V-Dem Institute University of Gothenburg.
Roberts, K. M. (2002). Social inequalities without class cleavages in Latin America's Neoliberal Era. *Studies in Comparative International Development, 36*(4), 3–33.
Saavedra, J. E., & Garcia, S. (2017). *Educational impacts and cost-effectiveness of conditional cash transfer programs in developing countries: A meta-analysis* (Working Paper 23594; NBER). National Bureau for Economic Research.
Sátyro, N., del Pino, E., & Midaglia, C. (2021). *Latin America social policy developments in the Twenty-first Century*. Palgrave Macmillan.
Schmitt, C. (2015). Social security development and the colonial legacy. *World Development, 70*, 332–342.
Schmitt, C., Lierse, H., Obinger, H., & Seelkopf, L. (2015). The global emergence of social protection: Explaining social security legislation. *Politics and Society, 43*(4), 503–524.
Segura-Ubiergo, A. (2007). *The political economy of the welfare state in Latin America*. Cambridge University Press.
Skoufias, E. (2005). *Progresa and its impacts on the welfare of rural households in Mexico*. International Food Policy Research Institute.
Vis, B. (2012). The comparative advantage of fsQCA and regression analysis for moderately large-N analysis. *Sociological Methods and Research, 41*(1), 168–198.

Wilson, S. E., & Butler, D. M. (2007). A lot more to do: The sensitivity of time-series-cross-section analysis to simple alternative specifications. *Political Analysis, 15*(2), 101–123.

Yamamoto, T. (2012). Understanding the Past: Statistical analysis of causal attribution. *American Journal of Political Science, 56*, 237–256. https://doi.org/10.1111/j.1540-5907.2011.00539.x

Yörük, E. (2022). *The politics of the welfare state in Turkey. How social movements and elite competition*. University of Michigan Press.

Zarate Tenorio, B. (2014). Social spending responses to organized labor and mass protests in Latin America, 1970-2007. *Comparative Political Studies, 47*(14), 1945–1972.

3

Framework

This chapter presents the structure of the argument in the book. It introduces, develops, and applies a framework capable of explaining the emergence, structure, and dynamics of social protection institutions understood in Latin America.

In a nutshell, the book argues that social protection institutions are an important mechanism of stratification in the capitalist economies of Latin America. The object of social protection institutions is a class of wage earners, the population group they influence and stratify. The emergence of social protection institutions is explained by industrialisation.

Industrialisation creates a distinct class of dependent wage earners and in doing so it sets the conditions for the emergence of social protection institutions. Once in place, the shape and dynamics of social protection institutions is best explained by their contribution to the forms of social stratification they generate. Explaining these institutions requires that we develop an understanding of their stratification effects. There are three dimensions of stratification effects that are especially relevant to understanding social protection institutions: their effects on employment, their protection effects, and their effects on the political incorporation of wage earners. These three dimensions will be explored in greater detail in

A. Barrientos, *Social Protection in Latin America*, Global Dynamics of Social Policy ,
https://doi.org/10.1007/978-3-031-49795-7_3

subsequent chapters of the book. Study of these three effects in the context of Latin America helps identify empirical counterparts offering the possibility of testing the validity of this theoretical framework.

In the context of the development of social institutions in Latin America there is a fortunate coincidence of diachronic and synchronic perspectives. Currently, the most important institutions in the region are occupational pensions, individual retirement savings plans and social assistance. They provide a primary focus for the analysis in the book. Each of them emerged in the context of separate critical realignments, defining a periodisation of the evolution of social protection institutions in the region. Occupational pensions emerged in the context of state-led-development policies seeking to support industrialisation. Individual retirement savings plans emerged as a component of economic liberalisation seeking to dismantle the selective protection of import-substitution-industrialisation and to vacate the role of labour organisations in social protection. The expansion of social assistance has emerged hand in hand with the strong economic growth associated with the commodity boom and participation in global production networks. The main social protection institutions in place today reflect critical realignments in the region, a confluence of diachronic and synchronic perspectives.

Overlaid with the confluence of diachronic and synchronic perspectives, there is an analytical perspective associated with dominant forms of stratification. Social protection institutions emerged with processes of industrialisation and a wage earner class. The then dominant form of stratification is factor stratification, social stratification based on ownership of the factors of production. In countries experiencing early industrialisation in 1890–1930 a nascent urban industrial wage earner class began to develop mutual aid associations, the precursors of social protection institutions. Post-WWII state-led development policy favoured specific sectors, the dominant form of stratification becoming sectoral. Finally, export-led development models replacing import-substitution-industrialisation made skill stratification the dominant form. The emergence and evolution for social protection institutions are consistent with changes in the dominant form of stratification.

The confluence of diachronic, synchronic, and analytical perspectives is fortunate because it facilitates advance towards a more theoretical understanding of social protection institutions in the region. The search for a more general approach necessarily smooths over significant variation in social protection structure and dynamics across countries and sub-regions. Central American countries embraced import-substitution-industrialisation much later than the more industrialised countries of South America and in a more limited fashion. Andean countries show an industrialisation trajectory in between these two groups of countries. Tracing the emergence of occupational insurance funds in Latin America, Mesa-Lago (1978) identifies pioneer countries, intermediate countries and latecomers, for example. It is also the case that individual retirement savings plans did not spread to all countries in the region. Social assistance, on the other hand, has spread to all countries in the region. Country and sub-regional diversity are important and will be discussed in more detail later in the book, but setting out an overall framework to study social protection institutions is the main challenge for this chapter.

The materials in this chapter are arranged as follows: Section 3.1 discusses the framework in a more detail. Section 3.2 will trace key shifts in the trajectory of social protection institutions in Latin America. This is not intended as a historical account. There are excellent scholarly contributions available based on rigorous research on which the discussion in this chapter is based.[1] The aim is to develop a framework matching these three institutional developments to critical realignments in the expectation that it will help us to develop an understanding of the contribution of social protection institutions to social and economic cooperation. Section 3.3 develops a perspective on stratification, linking dominant form of stratification and social protection institutions, in line with the periodisation discussed in the previous section. Section 3.4 focuses on the effects of social protection institutions on employment, protection, and incorporation. A final section concludes.

[1] They include inter alia the extensive work of Mesa-Lago (1978, 2007), Mesa-Lago and Bertranou (1998); contributions by Malloy (1979) and Lindert (2004, 2021), the recent compilation by Monsalve Cuéllar (2017); and (Borzutzky, 2002).

→ employment stratification effects

Industrialisation → social protection → protection stratification effects

→ incorporation effects

Factor stratification | Sectoral stratification | Skill stratification

Fig. 3.1 A causal framework

3.1 Framework

The structure of the argument in the book focuses on the causal links existing between its components. The analytical framework can be described succinctly. Industrialisation is the main causal factor in the emergence of social protection institutions through the creation of an urban wage earner class wholly reliant in their capacity to sell their labour. Once social protection institutions are in situ, they effect further stratification effects within the wage earner class. Here we are especially interested in employment effects, protection effects, and political incorporation effects. Figure 3.1 summarises the main causal linkages and dominant forms of stratification.

This framework represents a confluence of synchronic, diachronic, and analytical perspectives on social protection institutions in the region. They will be discussed in turn below.

3.1.1 Synchronic: Core Institutions

Current social protection in the region is dominated by three main types of institutions managing core programmes: occupational pensions; individual retirement savings plans; and social assistance including conditional income transfers and social pensions.[2] Together, these programmes account for most of the population directly engaged in social protection as contributors or beneficiaries. They also account for the bulk of public and private expenditure on social protection. Focusing on these institutions will help to organise the materials covered in this chapter and much of the book. Complementary social protection programmes are in place in some countries of the region: employment protection, unemployment insurance, and occupational health insurance are the most significant. In the analysis in this book, they will be discussed where relevant, but the focus will be on the three main programmes.

Occam's razor offers a strong justification for adopting this approach. Complementary social protection programmes are not present in all countries or even in most of them. The population groups they serve are those already covered by the three main social protection institutions. Participation in complementary programmes is often dependent on access to the main programmes. Unemployment insurance schemes, for example, are add-on programmes to occupational pension or individual retirement savings plans. Moreover, complementary programmes often serve a sub-sample of the population groups covered by the three main programmes. Severance subsidies in the event of employment termination, for example, are restricted to participants in pension schemes with long and continuous record of contributions (Holzmann & Vodopivec, 2012). Complementary social protection programmes reinforce the stratification generated by the core programmes.

To an important extent, complementary programmes exhibit the same dynamics as the core programmes they complement. Reforms to complementary programmes are implemented in line with reforms to the main

[2] A consistent and precise terminology of social protection institutions is lacking. Institutions imply permanent and stable administrative organisations, implementing a set of rules. A broader meaning of institutions describes them as the rules of the game followed by agents in society. Both meanings would apply to occupational pension schemes for example. Programmes also imply stable administrative structures, but perhaps with shorter horizons and with specific objectives. Policies describe a set of objectives and instruments guiding organisations. I trust readers will discern the nuances of these terms contextually.

programmes and share the orientation and objectives of the reforms to the main programmes. For example, unemployment savings plans have been introduced in parallel to individual retirement savings plans (Ferrer & Riddell, 2011; Sehnbruch et al., 2020).[3] In practice, focusing on the three main institutions does not imply an important gap in our understanding of the trajectory of social protection in the region.

At the same time, there are significant gains available when focusing in these three institutions. They will be made clear in the discussion on diachronic and analytical perspectives below.

3.1.2 Diachronic: Critical Realignments

The emergence of each of these institutions was associated with structural changes in the political economy of countries in the region. In their research on social policy, Haggard and Kaufman (2008) found it useful to focus on the political dimension of structural change, described as a 'critical realignment'. 'Critical realignments' reflect "…discontinuities in patterns of political domination…" consistent with "…the emergence of new ruling coalitions and political incorporation or exclusion of working-class and peasant organizations." (p. 7). This approach proved effective in developing theoretical insights on the development of social policy across all regions of the world. With some minor modification, the discussion that follows will draw on this approach to study the trajectory of social protection in Latin America. Identifying 'critical realignments' will throw light on key shifts in social protection institutions.

In the Latin American context, it is relatively straightforward to identify three instances of a 'critical realignment' associated with changes in social protection. They are: (i) industrialisation in the post WWII period and the emergence of publicly supported occupational insurance funds; (ii) trade and labour market liberalisation in the final third of the twentieth century and pension reform including individual retirement savings

[3] Health insurance programmes are larger than unemployment insurance and have expanded in the recent past, but in the main they cover the same population as the three programmes above (Atun et al., 2015; Cotlear et al., 2015).

plans; and (iii) the commodities boom and globalization wave in the early decades of this century and social assistance expansion.

Critical realignments coincide with the emergence and expansion of the three main social protection institutions identified above. Occupational insurance funds became established at scale following mid-20th century industrialisation. Their expansion accelerated in countries with state-led import substitution industrialisation policies following growing state recognition and support. Individual retirement savings plans emerged as an important component of neoliberal responses to the exhaustion of import-substitution-industrialisation policies. They were an explicit component of the liberalisation of the economies of the region, intended to facilitate export-led-growth strategies. Finally, the expansion of social assistance in the twenty-first century has been associated with rapid economic growth generated by the commodity boom following China's accession to global markets. The expansion of social assistance was further encouraged by left coalitions gaining power in the region.

Critical realignments linked structural changes in the nature of the political economy of the Latin American economies with significant changes in social protection institutions. The main periods in Latin America's social protection are summarised in Table 1.1.[4]

Each of these core institutions is associated with a distinct form of incorporation or exclusion of wage earners, the distinguishing feature of a critical realignment in Haggard and Kaufman. The growth to scale of occupational insurance funds is associated with the incorporation of labour organization and left political parties into mass politics (Collier & Collier, 1991). The first incorporation of workers was highly selective, hence the Bismarckian flavour to Latin American occupational insurance funds. Mesa-Lago (1978) aptly describes the expansion of occupational insurance funds as the 'massification of privilege', a direct counterpart to the massification of politics. Individual retirement savings plans came hand in hand with a retrenchment of welfare provision. They were

[4] Space restrictions prevent me from considering more carefully whether the emergence of embryonic labour organizations and mutual aid associations with the first wave of industrialisation around the turn of the 19th century constitutes a fourth (initial) 'critical realignment' (Illanes, 2003; Monsalve Cuéllar, 2017).

intended to contribute to efforts to liberalise the workings of the labour market and to reduce government deficits. Individual retirement savings plans were successfully institutionalised in countries with strong neoliberal coalitions in power (Mesa-Lago, 2020; Mesa-Lago & Müller, 2002). Efforts to introduce individual savings instruments as part of structural social protection reforms were explicitly aimed at excluding labour organisation and left political parties from social protection provision. The expansion of social assistance has been explicitly associated with a further wave of incorporation, this time incorporation of groups associated with low income and informal employment, often described as 'popular sectors' to distinguish them from the industrial working class involved in the first incorporation (Garay, 2016; Kapiszewski et al., 2021; Silva & Rossi, 2017).

3.1.3 Analytic: Dominant Stratification

A central argument in the book is that social protection institutions should be understood primarily as stratification mechanisms in capitalist economies. Applying this perspective, critical realignments and their associated core social protection institutions can be shown to support distinct dominant forms of stratification. Considering the evolution of social protection in Latin America, it will be useful to distinguish three main forms of stratification that have been dominant in particular periods. They are factor stratification, sector stratification, and skill stratification. They are discussed in turn below.

Factor stratification refers to the separation of the owners of factors of production into distinct classes.[5] In the region, the emergence of a wage earner class resulted from the dispossession of land labourers and artisans, from the end of slavery, and from domestic and international migration.

[5] Wibbels and Ahlquist (2011) develop a factor model of social insurance, distinguishing between labour abundant and labour scarce countries and the implications for occupational insurance institutions. In countries with scarce labour and capital, political coalitions supported closed economies and extracted surpluses from landowners to finance development. These conditions maximise the power of workers in securing occupational insurance. Countries with abundant labour, on the other hand, empower coalitions pursuing trade openness leading to adverse conditions for workers and denial of their social protection demands.

Institutionalised social protection plays a very limited role in the processes associated with factor stratification.[6] An independent wage earner class is a precondition for the emergence of public or publicly supported occupational insurance funds (Atkinson, 1991; Iversen & Rehm, 2022). Institutionalised forms of social protection emerge only after the processes leading to the formation of a class of independent wage earners have taken their course.

There is considerable variation in the timing of these processes across countries and sub-regions but dominant factor stratification in the more industrialising countries in the region has been associated with the period spanning the 1890s to the 1930s (Williamson, 2011). Patterns of urbanisation and internal migration can pinpoint this period more precisely for specific countries or sub-regions. Mutual aid societies managed by worker organisations are the main protection instrument. They aimed to mitigate the income effects of mortality and morbidity among their members and to provide training in particular trades (Illanes, 2003; Monsalve Cuéllar, 2017). Illanes (2003) describes the development of mutual aid societies in Chile, their scope and growing political engagement. Legislation and force were the main instruments helping shape a wage earner class. In Central American countries, as agro-exports dominated their economies, the power of landowners ensured the that factor stratification was sustained by legislation and force far longer than in the southern cone countries with implications for the strength of social protection institutions (Segovia, 2022).

Social protection institutions emerged in the industrialising countries of the region as sector stratification replaced factor stratification as the dominant form. Following the first wave of industrialisation at the turn of the twenty-first century and the subsequent decline in trade due to the two world wars, import-substitution-industrialisation encouraged sectoral differentiation through the selective protection of sectors in the economy. In some countries this process was reinforced by proactive government policies, described as state-led-development (Bértola & Ocampo,

[6] Monsalve Cuéllar (2017) provide information on mutual aid provision in pre-Columbian and early Hispanic periods for all countries in Latin America. Non-institutionalised social protection predates the Spanish conquest.

2012). They emerged first in the industrialising countries and later in a more limited form in agro-exporting countries of Central America (Segovia, 2022). State-led-development required broad coalitions in support of industrialisation policies and in opposition to land interests. The extension of the franchise and the incorporation of labour organisation and political parties signalled their entry into mass politics. The emergence of Bismarckian occupational insurance funds is directly associated with state-led import-substitutions industrialisation. It extended the selective support for economic sectors through legal and political recognition of occupational insurance funds or *cajas de previsión*.

Where sectoral stratification combined with Fordist organisation of production in large enterprises, workers with diverse skills sets could access expanding occupational insurance funds. This dynamic reached furthest in the more developed countries in the Southern cone, where most wage earners would eventually access social protection. However, even in countries with large scale manufacturing and primary resource exploitation, occupational insurance funds often differentiated provision for specific groups of workers. Some governments sought to consolidate and streamline the governance of occupational funds, but their efforts often failed to integrate workers into the same scheme.[7]

The exhaustion of the import-substitution-industrialisation model, marked by financial and economic crises, led to the liberalisation of the economies of the region and to the spread of authoritarian regimes. Economic policy was now directed to dismantling selective sector protection and enforcing greater competition within more open economies. Skill stratification emerged as the dominant form of stratification.

Stratified occupational insurance funds became the subject of reform and retrenchment in the last quarter of the century. The implementation of individual retirement savings plans is the most salient aspect of this process. Pension reforms brought in individual retirement savings plans to replace, compete with, or complement occupational insurance funds. As will be discussed in detail below, individual savings instruments, whether for pension provision or unemployment insurance, encouraged

[7] As was the case under the Nordic notion of universalism (Brady & Bostic, 2010; Martínez-Franzoni & Sánchez-Ancochea, 2017).

the reallocation of collective worker protection to the individual workers themselves and their savings capacity. They minimised the role of labour organisations in the management of social protection and aimed to facilitate labour mobility.

In countries where individual retirement savings plans fully substituted occupational insurance funds—Chile, Bolivia, Dominican Rep., El Salvador—or where they are expected to become the dominant instrument in a transition from occupational insurance funds to individual retirement savings plans—Mexico, Panama, Peru—their introduction dismantled sectoral distinctions in social protection provision. They offer workers a single mode of participation with common rules on entitlements. Differentiation in entitlements depend solely on savings capacity and a minimum contribution history. The correlation existing between skills, earnings, and savings capacity for workers in the labour market ensure that entitlement differentials reflect the distribution of skill levels. In Uruguay and Costa Rica where individual retirement saving plans are complementary to defined benefit schemes, participation in these is limited to higher earning workers.

Individual retirement savings plans accommodate stratification by skill, as elements collective provision and redistribution present in occupational insurance funds are eliminated. Some elements of design redistribution are retained in some countries, to the benefit of low and high skilled workers. The inclusion of minimum pension guarantees, whether financed by better off plan members or from public subsidies, favours workers with lower skills and short term labour market engagement who might be able to access minimum guaranteed pensions. They also favour workers with high skill levels with long term labour market engagement (Altamirano Montoya et al., 2018). To the extent that individual retirement savings plans are open to own account workers, they ensure that social protection for these workers is also stratified by skill.

Participation in social protection pension schemes is primarily correlated with firm size. This would suggest that the association of pension schemes and skills stratification applies at the firm level. Workers with low education and/or low income are more likely to participate if they are working in a large firm than in a smaller firm (CAF, 2020; Eslava et al.,

2021). This would also suggest that, as far as the incentives for participation in occupational pensions and individual retirement savings accounts are concerned, firm requirements trump worker characteristics.[8]

Explanations as to why participation in pension schemes is higher in large firms abound. The costs of firm compliance with social protection regulations have been discussed in the context of middle-income countries. Larger firms are constrained in their capacity to avoid or evade tax and labour market regulations. They are therefore more likely to comply with existing regulations. But this assumes rule compliance is exogenous. A substantial share of research on firm size and compliance takes firm size as itself endogenous to compliance (Herrera & Lora, 2005). Firms may reconstitute themselves in response to labour regulations and the intensity of compliance regulation.

The issue of monitoring might be relevant. Monitoring worker performance is more of an issue in larger firms and requires that greater attention is paid to costly monitoring and alternatives. Using pension entitlements as means of ensuring worker performance and motivation is consistent with occupational pensions plans (Ippolito, 1997). Individual retirement savings plans fail to offer an alternative to costly monitoring. Earlier career payroll savings contribute more to the final pension pot at retirement than large payroll savings in the final years of employment, due to the dominant role of interest in savings plans. The incentives in defined benefit occupational pensions work the other way around. Defined benefit pensions would be preferable to firms facing high monitoring costs.

Firms facing high retention and recruitment costs would benefit from pension plans in which workers sustain losses in pay or future entitlements by leaving a firm. This would recommend wage premiums that rise with workers engagement with a firm, or escalating pension benefits. In labour markets with considerable employment volatility, as is the case in Latin America, the incentive effects of pension entitlements rising faster

[8] Research on earnings differentials in Latin America suggest that the decline in wage inequality in the first decade and a half of this century is primarily explained by a compression of labour earnings within groups of workers distinguished by skill than across skills or worker characteristics (Messina & Silva, 2018).

than productivity would be enhanced. Individual retirement pension plans are neutral with respect to firm retention but occupational pensions with defined benefit could alter benefit schedules to strengthen retention incentives, as in the armed forces for example.

Skills stratification becomes the dominant effect of social protection in the twenty-first century. The expansion of social assistance in the new century is also consistent with dominant skill stratification, but its effects apply to low skilled workers and employment. Conditional income transfers with their focus on social investment, associated with schooling and health conditions, reflect a concern with improving general skills among low income groups dependent on informal employment (Barrientos, 2022b).[9]

Social assistance in Latin America undermines sector specific stratification because it decouples social protection provision from (sector-specific) employment. The literature on social assistance, and especially conditional income transfers, has not identified significant indirect effects on employment associated with participation. A disproportionate amount of research on social assistance has examined the labour supply incentives of conditional income transfers and old age transfers.[10] The main finding is that transfers have marginal effects on the labour supply of adults and reducing effects on the labour supply of children and older people (Barrientos & Malerba, 2020). The recent evolution of social assistance, as in the replacement of conditional income transfers by schooling subsidies in Mexico, has reinforced a focus on improvements in the productive capacity of lower income households.

The segmentation in social protection provision in the region today demonstrates that the dominant form of stratification is along skill. To generalise, occupational pensions serve routine non-manual workers in the public sector and non-routine cognitive workers in the public and private sectors (CAF, 2020). Individual retirement savings plans, in countries where they are the main or dominant pension instrument, serve the same groups, but with greater flexibility in time and across firms due to

[9] This is in contrast with social investment programmes in high income countries that are focused on high income groups (Garritzmann et al., 2022).

[10] This will be discussed in more detail in Chap. 6.

the individualised nature of savings. With variation across countries, social assistance reaches routine non-cognitive manual workers (Barrientos, 2009, 2019a).

This analytical framework will guide the argument developed in this book. It combines a diachronic perspective which links the core social protection institutions to critical realignments, a synchronic perspective which focuses on the three main social protection institutions in place today, and an analytical perspective which links dominant forms of stratification in the region to the core social protection institutions. The next section discusses in more detail the main stratification effects of the core social protection institutions.

3.2 Stratification and Theories of Welfare Institutions: A Digression

The three forms of dominant stratification have close associations with existing theories of welfare institutions. This section will make a short detour to underline this point.

Factor stratification is at the core of power resources theories of the development of welfare institutions as a response to the demands of an emerging industrial working class. Factor stratification is deployed to support what can be described as a demand-side theory of welfare institutions. It argues that industrialisation generates classes with an incentive for collective organisation and action. The power resources approach to class[11] makes a distinction between blue collar workers, white collar workers, and a group of vulnerable workers and citizens. They are described as, respective, a working class, a middle class, and the poor. Their interests overlap because of the changes the distribution of social risks brought about by industrial production. According to Korpi and Palmer, "socio-economic class generates differences in risks to which citizens are exposed during the life course. While some life-course risks are generated by

[11] "A more productive starting point is to define class as categories of individuals who share relatively similar positions, or situations, in labour markets and in employment relationships. This definition raises the empirical question of the extent to which and how such similarities in opportunities and constraints result in collective action and group identification"(Korpi, 2006, p. 174).

universal processes, most risks, such as those associated with aging, illness, work accidents, unemployment, poverty and rearing of children, are instead unequally distributed among individuals occupying different positions in socio-economic class structures" (Korpi, 2006, p. 173). Collective action arises from workers' perceived need to mitigate the adverse effects of these risks. In democracies, coalitions of workers and the middle class can successfully push through demands for social protection which lead to the establishment of comprehensive welfare states.

The 'paradox of redistribution' emphasises the political implications of stratification: the "…targeted model creates a zero sum conflict of interests between the poor and the better off workers and the middle class who must pay for the benefits of the poor without receiving any benefits…[targeting] drives a wedge between the short-term interests of the poor and those of the rest of the population "universalism" brings low income groups into the same institutional structures [supporting] the formation of cross-class coalitions" (Korpi & Palme, 1998, pp. 672; 682).

The absence of democracy or a limited overlap in the social risks faced by blue and white collar workers results in welfare institutions that are differentiated by sector, as in Bismarck's stratified social insurance (Palier, 2010). There is a genealogical line linking Bismarckian welfare institutions and occupational insurance funds in Latin America (Barrientos, 2019b) and more generally occupational insurance developments in late industrialisers (Mares & Carnes, 2009). Bismarckian social protection institutions are associated with dominant sectoral stratification.

A different approach to sectoral stratification can be found in outsider-insider models of welfare state dualism. Their argument is that dualism is a hangover from powerful insiders into the new globalised world economy. In the European context, "systems of social protection built upon ex ante protections have proven poorly adapted to a world of open economies. Such systems limit the capacity of workers to enter the formal economy, reduce their incentives to gather human capital (the returns of which are low in the informal sector), and encourage investments in low productivity sectors. As a result, labour regulations that date to protectionist processes of industrialization have contributed to the growth of informal sectors, weak labor productivity, and income inequality." (Rueda et al., 2015, p. 108).

This approach tallies with explanations of the highly segmented occupational insurance funds in Latin America. Wibbles and Alqhist argue that many "... early import substituters continue to struggle economically and see powerful anti-market movements twenty years after liberalization. Indeed, as social spending on protected sectors has been difficult to retrench and labor markets have proven particularly resistant to reform, these governments have struggled to provide social support to the truly poor and investments in human capital that would increase productivity. Labor markets in such countries are sharply divided between labor market insiders and outsiders" (Wibbels & Ahlquist, 2011, p. 144).

Varieties of capitalism theories emphasise the critical role of skills accumulation as the source of welfare institutions (Iversen & Soskice, 2001). They envisage two main economic sectors: an advanced sector that makes extensive use of skilled workers and a vulnerable sector that relies mainly on a less skilled workforce. In their view, social protection is offered by governments to the advanced sector of the economy. This is because government coalitions are necessarily, and electorally, committed to economic growth and have strong incentives to ensure that workers in this sector invest in their skills. By contrast, governing coalitions have no incentives to provide social protection to workers in the vulnerable sector.

Whether any form of social protection is available to workers in the vulnerable sector depends wholly on whether supporting political parties participate and have any influence on governing coalitions. In their model, "...redistribution towards the vulnerable sector does not involve the institutional framework that supports the advanced sector...those aspects of the welfare state relevant to advanced capitalism (its insurance but not redistributive function)" (Iversen & Soskice, 2015, p. 79). In respect of social protection, varieties of capitalism can best be described as a supply-side theory of welfare institutions.

Drawing a connection between dominant forms of stratification and theories of welfare institutions acknowledge the central role of stratification in the theoretical underpinnings of welfare institutions. However, these theories have been developed largely in the context of European welfare states, with the implication that they cannot be directly extrapolated to Latin America or elsewhere. To the extent that they have been developed in the context of special cases, using them in the context of this book necessitates a preliminary scrutiny of their relevance. The purpose of the discussion here is to reinforce the analytical import of stratification in examining social protection institutions.

3.3 Stratification Effects

This section discusses the main stratification effects of social protection. It focuses on three areas of stratification that are central to understanding social protection as a stratification mechanism. Social protection institutions generate stratification in three main areas: they help manage labour for productive activity, they protect selected workers and their families from income risks brought about by work interruptions, and they influence the political inclusion of groups of wage earners. Social protection institutions influence specific stratification outcomes in these three main areas. These effects will be introduced here and will be considered in detail in separate chapters of this book.

These three dimensions of stratification play a key role in the framework and in the accompanying analysis. Focusing in these three key stratification effects connects the framework in the chapter to the institutional and empirical outcomes associated with social protection. It helps identify empirical counterparts to the stratification effects, provide indicators capturing the quantitative dimension of these effects and their change over time, offers an empirical basis for testing hypotheses on the causal linkages existing between social protection institutions and their effects. The three dimensions of stratification also enable a metrics capable of supporting normative assessments of the extent to which social protection institutions fall short of social expectations on their work.

The advantage of approaching the latter task within this framework is that assessments are consistent with a theoretical understanding of the role of social protection in the capitalist economies of the region, instead of basing this assessment on external aspirational norms. Normative assessments of social protection institutions based on a theoretical understanding of their role will help reduce the excess normativity in current research and policy appraisal of social protection in the region.

The identification of these three dimensions in the framework developed in this book could not claim originality. In fact, these three stratification effects are well embedded in theory and policy research associated with social protection.

Take the employment stratification effects of social protection, for example. Concerns with the labour supply of social protection have encouraged a large literature assessing the effects of social assistance on the employment of recipient households (Alzúa et al., 2010; Barrientos & Malerba, 2020). In fact, old age transfers are expected to lead to a reduction in the labour supply of older recipients (Bosch et al., 2013). Similarly, access to pension benefits, from occupational insurance funds or individual retirement savings plans, facilitate and in cases require the withdrawal of recipients from employment. Child and family transfers often encourage the reduction of child labour in recipient households (de Hoop & Rosati, 2014). Social protection programmes are explicitly designed to be incentive-compatible, that is to be synergetic with work incentives and productive employment. The employment effects of social protection are an important area of research and policy.[12]

The protection effects of social protection are at the core of all research and policy assessments, encouraging large efforts in data collection and analysis as well as highly charged policy debates on the merits and demerits of policy innovation and reform (Arenas de Mesa, 2019). This involves preventing poverty and destitution, as well as reducing wage earner vulnerability to employment and life course risks. The spread of experimental evaluation methods has been motivated by the search of improved measures of the protection effects of social protection (Deaton, 2010). In fact, a substantial proportion of research and policy debates on social protection is aimed at unveiling the protection effects of social protection institutions.

The literature on the incorporation effects of social protection institutions has not reached a comparable level of consolidation and methodological innovation than the literature on employment and protection effects. Nonetheless, the power resources approach, which has

[12] Welfare states are a particular configuration of social protection institutions claimed to deliver a workable compromise on the productive and protective roles of social protection, capable of ensuring the successful combination of democracy and capitalism (Cantillon, 2011; Rueda et al., 2015).

incorporation effects at its core, has been very influential in studies on social protection in the region (Collier & Collier, 1991; Huber, 1996; Huber & Stephens, 2012). Research on the politics of pension reform (Carrrera & Angelaki, 2021; Kritzer et al., 2011; Mesa-Lago & Müller, 2002) and on the spread of social assistance (Barrientos, 2022a; Borges, 2019; Hunter & Borges Sugiyama, 2014) examine incorporation effects associated with social protection reform.

The presence of social protection institutions can best be understood by focusing on their stratification effects. There is a direct connection between the main social protection programmes, the specific forms of stratification they facilitate, and intra wage earners differentiation and coalitions.

If there is a measure of distinctiveness in the framework, it has to do with its hypothesis that the stratification effects of social protection institutions can be better studied in a causal inference framework along these three dimensions. To a lesser extent the explicit inclusion of political incorporation in the set and the attention paid to the interaction of the three effects could claim to be distinctive.

Significant change in social protection institutions over time can be explained by processes of contestation and change associated with these three dimensions of stratification. Changes in the employment structure, the relative reach and generosity of social protection components, and contestation over political incorporation explains social protection reform.

3.4 Testing the Framework

Now that the different components of the framework are in place, the next task is to identify empirical counterparts, collect the necessary data, and test the validity of the causal links suggested by the discussion.

Testing for the framework comes in two parts. The first part will focus on the relatively easier task of establishing the causal link between industrialisation and the emergence of occupational insurance funds. The second part will examine the causal links existing between social protection institutions and their stratification effects. Readers interested in exploring the stratification effects hypotheses empirically are encouraged to access data and estimation models (R and Stata) at https://github.com/armando295/spla.

3.4.1 Origins

The first part is relatively straightforward because the causal link existing between industrialisation and social protection institutions is widely accepted in the literature. The less straightforward task is to identify appropriate empirical counterparts and to select an appropriate statistical method to test their relationship.

The causal model can be described as: Industrialisation --> Occupational insurance funds. To capture industrialisation the model will rely on a measure of the ratio of manufacturing value added to agriculture value added. The relevant annualised data has been consolidated and harmonised in the Montevideo-Oxford Latin America dataset and covers all the countries in the region from the beginning of the 20th century (MOxLAD, n.d.). This ratio is a reliable measure of industrialisation. It rises with industrialisation, rising faster in the countries that industrialised more intensely.

The share of the labour force participating in occupational insurance funds offers a good measure of expansion of occupational insurance funds. It is important to keep in mind several issues regarding these data. Cross-country comparable measures of the participation share can be sourced from administrative data and from survey data. Early administrative data are not very reliable because of differences in the way they were constructed in different countries. This is especially true in the period before governments moved to consolidate the governance of occupational insurance funds. Mesa-Lago (1978) provides an early cross-country comparable data on participation and he carefully describes the weaknesses associated with these data. More recently, Arenas de Mesa (2019) constructs a series on administrative data from 2000 to 2018. He also describes with care the weaknesses associated with the data series. Survey data provides an alternative source of participation share data. These data are patchy in its coverage before countries began to collect regular household surveys in the mid-1990s. For our purposes this is significant because the expansion of occupational insurance funds in the region spans the period 1950s to 1970s. There is therefore a trade-off between focusing on earlier periods with data available for fewer countries or focusing on later periods with data available for most, if not all, countries.

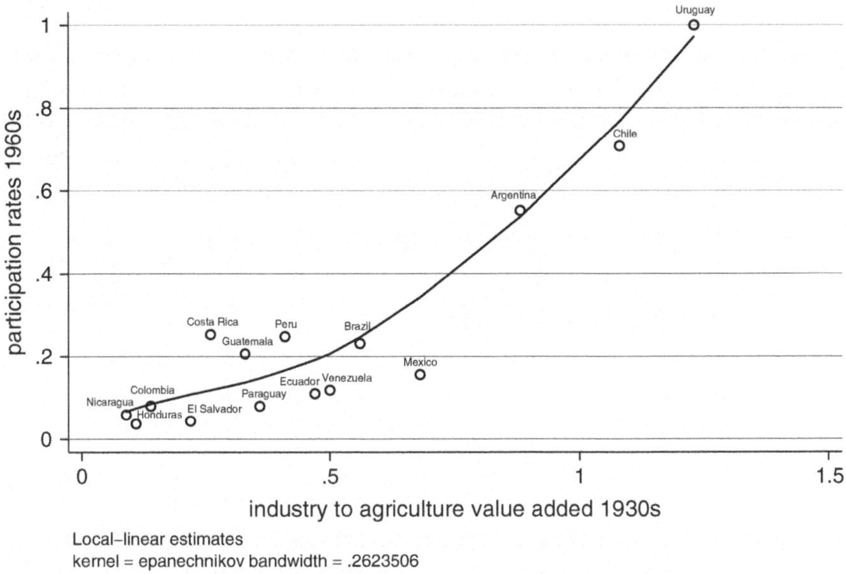

Fig. 3.2 Industrialisation and occupational insurance fund participation

To maximise the reliability and coverage of the data, the analysis below will work with decade averages.

The simplest model to estimate the causal effect of industrialisation on the expansion of occupational insurance fund participation is to regress participation shares on earlier industrialisation with country level data. This strategy has the advantage of avoiding post-treatment bias and minimising omitted variables bias (Blackwell & Glynn, 2018) (Fig. 3.2).

The Figure shows the relationship existing between industrialisation, measured by the ratio of industry to agriculture value added and occupational insurance fund participation in the 1960s.

The Figure reports on the crosstabulation of industry to agriculture value added on insurance funds participation rates in 1960. The latter comes from Mesa-Lago (1978) figures from administrative data. It is important to keep in mind the deficiencies of these data as reported by him. The issue of double counting in contexts where workers could affiliate to multiple insurance funds is apparent for Uruguay. Delayed and irregular updates of the insurance fund records overestimate participation rates. The fitted line is from a nonparametric kernel regression. The line indicates a non-linear relationship existing between early industrialisation and the expansion of occupational insurance fund in the immediate post-WWII period. Given the period captured in the data, the exercise offers some support for the causal relationship hypothesised above. Industrialisation leads to the expansion of occupational insurance funds in Latin America.[13]

3.4.2 Stratification Effects

Once social protection institutions are in place the focus shifts to testing for the stratification effects of social protection. The framework developed in this chapter identifies three important areas of stratification which are the focus of analysis: employment, protection, and incorporation. The analysis below examines the causal effects linking social protection institutions and their effects on these three areas. It also examines the relationship between these areas.

The general model is: Social protection --> [employment | protection |incorporation]. Define 's' for social protection, 'e' for employment, 'p' for protection and 'i' for incorporation. We are now able to examine alternative configurations of the three sets of effects, drawing insights from the existing literature in social protection.

The literature on social protection institutions in Latin America suggest it is less likely these effects are independent from each other. Disciplinary boundaries often result in each research investigating these effects on their own, say, labour economists studying employment effects, social policy scholars considering protection effects, and political science researchers looking at the electoral effects of social protection. It is also the case that disciplinary studies often cross these boundaries and point to the appropriateness of accounting for the relationships existing between these effects and the need to pay attention to their ordering. Alternative theorising of these orderings is at the core of alternative explanations of social protection in Latin America, and elsewhere.

---

[13] Including Vdem variables capturing (i) expert assessment of trade union engagement as a share of the population and (ii) the influence of economic power in political decision making in the model failed to add information.

Possible orderings of causal links, and the relevant literature, are discussed in turn below. Orderings are represented by moving from inside the brackets to outside them. Arrows represent the direction of causality.

i(p(e)) stands for employment first: incorporation ← protection ← employment.

This is the configuration of causal links common in studies of social protection in Latin America, and elsewhere. It is dominant in labour economics, for example in microfoundational explanations of the role of pensions in shaping employment relationships, recruitment, retention, firm-specific skill investment, and productivity (Ippolito, 1997; Lazear, 1983). This is also dominant in Varieties of capitalism approaches to social protection, see Iversen and Soskice 's asset theory (2001, 2015). From this perspective, economy wide changes in employment cascade into protection and incorporation. Arguably, this could be described as the underlying model in Segura-Ubiergo and in Haggard and Kaufman's approach to social protection and more generally in industrialisation theories of social change.

p(i(e)) is a possible variant of the employment first configuration. Here incorporation comes before protection. It fits bottom up perspectives on the incorporation of workers in Latin America (Collier & Collier, 1991). It also fits well with Mesa-Lago model of interest group pressure leading to social protection institutional development. It fits with corporatist models of incorporation in the region, especially Argentina (Isuani, 2008; Malloy, 1979). It does not fit well with top down models of incorporation, where authoritarian elites introduce social protection as a means to delaying incorporation (Filgueira, 2005; Mares & Carnes, 2009).

e(p(i)) stands for politics first: employment ← protection ← incorporation.

In this configuration, incorporation is the primary effect, leading to demands for social protection which in turn influences employment. It is closest to the power resources approach, where social protection is a consequence of democratic struggle (Korpi, 1980). It is also present in approaches to social protection institutions emphasising the primary role of democracy in enabling social demands to gather force. In a welfare state context, social protection institutions are considered as the 'linchpin of democracy and capitalism' (Beramendi et al., 2015). They are essential to ensure that the destructive forces of capitalism are moderated, the essence of European social democracy. Iversen and Soskice (2006) description of social protection provision to the less skilled sector of the economy as wholly dependent on the participation of political parties representing the interests of workers in this sector in governing coalitions is another example of this configuration.

In the Latin American context, the discussion surrounding the politics of social assistance takes for granted a model with these characteristics (Levitsky & Roberts, 2012; Silva & Rossi, 2017). The politics first approach fits a version of the emergence of social assistance as predicted on elite responses to electoral competition (Garay, 2016). It also fits accounts of the second wave of incorporation. Direct access to social policy formulation by social movements and political groupings, or the emergence of political groupings from political movements in the process of re-democratisation, results in social assistance programmes that facilitate and support employment of low-income workers.

Discussions of the retrenchment phase in Latin America depart from a negative version of the politics first variant: -e(-p(-i)). Limited incorporation undermines protection resulting in a downgrading of labour standards and employment. It also applies with force to explanations for the undeveloped social protection in Central American countries (Sánchez-Ancochea & Martínez Franzoni, 2015).

Inverting the relationship between employment and protection, as in p(e(i)), appears less promising as a model, except perhaps as a reinforcement of the cycle. It could provide an insight into the incorporation of women politically. The hypothesis is that women's political participation leading to the reduction of discrimination in employment would enforce changes in protection. Studies on the evolution of family benefits, maternity provision for example, fail to confirm this sequence (Rossel, 2013).[14]

e(i(p)) stands for policy first: employment ← incorporation ← protection.

In policy first models, a change in policy leads to changes in incorporation and eventually employment. Baldwin's (1990) description of occupational insurance is a good example of this ordering. Occupational insurance

[14] A study on the effects of women's franchise on public expenditure in Latin America fails to confirm the presence of a strong link (Aidt & Jensen, 2009).

pools groups of workers with similar social risks who then vie for state legal recognition and support leading - in a context of expanding franchise and competitive electoral processes - to incorporation and a stable employment structure. Criticism of occupational insurance funds during the retrenchment phase emphasised their role in preventing structural adjustment, prolonging unemployment, and increasing informality. Levy (2008) argues that the interaction of institutionally separate or unintegrated occupational insurance and social assistance reinforces informality in Latin America.

i(e(p)) is less likely in the Latin American context.

What about joint effects? In theory, it is also possible to propose joint effects: i(p, e) describes the joint effects of employment and protection influencing incorporation. It fits with accounts of employment first social protection effects with dominant trade unions in the first incorporation phase. e(p, i) could apply to social assistance expansion in Latin America. Its potential effects on reservation wages in turn having an influence on employment. p(e, i) combines the policy and politics first approaches. Joint effects are useful to identify the assumptions underlying theorisation on social protection.

Additive or multiplicative effects? y(p, e, i) ordering can be conceived as additive: y(p + e + i); multiplicative y(p x e x i); or combinatorial y(p, e, i) with or without weights.

3.5 Conclusion

This chapter has presented an analytical framework capable of explaining the origin and evolution of social protection institutions in Latin America. The core proposition guiding this analysis is that social protection institutions are primarily a stratification mechanism, with core stratification effects in employment, protection, and incorporation. The framework combines diachronic, synchronic, and analytical perspectives on social protection institutions.

Critical realignments are associated with key changes in social protection institutions. Industrialisation led to the formation of an urban working class wholly dependent on labour earnings, factor stratification. Import-substitution-industrialisation enforced by the trade disruption in the first half of the twentieth century later supported by state-led development policies led to the expansion of occupational insurance funds for selected groups of workers, sectoral stratification. Retrenchment under neoliberal policies was associated with large scale reform of occupational insurance funds and the implementation of individual retirement savings plans in some countries. The commodity boon in the 2000s and the pink tide of left government coalitions is associated with the expansion of social assistance.

The core social protection institutions in the region are occupational pensions, individual retirement savings plans and social assistance. A synchronic perspective on these institutions provides an entry point into the stratification effects of social protection. Research into these stratification effects yields an analytical perspective explaining their influence on social and economic interaction, the basis of a theory of these institutions in the region. The chapter discussed in turn the causal links between industrialisation and the expansion of occupational insurance funds, and alternative orderings of the stratification effects of these institutions. The next chapters will consider these effects in more detail.

References

Aidt, T. S., & Jensen, P. S. (2009). Tax structure, size of government, and the extension of the voting franchise in Western Europe, 1860-1938. *International Tax and Public Finance, 16*, 362–394.

Altamirano Montoya, A., Berstein, S., Bosch, M., & García Huitrón, M. (2018). *Presente y futuro de las pensiones en América Latina y el Caribe*. Inter-American Development Bank.

Alzúa, M. L., Cruces, G., & Ripani, L. (2010). *Welfare programs and labour supply in developing countries. Experimental evidence for Latin America* (Documento de Trabajo 95). CEDLAS-UNLP.

Arenas de Mesa, A. (2019). *Los sistemas de pensiones en la encrucijada. Desafíos para la sostenibilidad en América Latina* (159; Libros de La CEPAL). *Comisión Económica para América Latina y el Caribe.*

Atkinson, A. B. (1991). Social Insurance. *The Geneva Papers on Risk and Insurance Theory, 16*(2), 113–131.

Atun, R., Monteiro de Andrade, L. O., Almeida, G., Cotlear, D., Dmytraczenko, T., Frenz, P., Garcia, P., Gómez-Dantés, O., Knaul, F., Muntaner, C., Braga de Paula, J., Rígoli, F., Castell Florit Serrate, P., & Wagstaff, A. (2015). Health-system reform and universal health coverage in Latin America. *The Lancet, 385*(9974), 1230–1247.

Baldwin, P. (1990). *The politics of social solidarity. Class bases of the European welfare state 1875-1975*. Cambridge University Press.

Barrientos, A. (2009). Labour markets and the (hyphenated) welfare regime in Latin America. *Economy and Society, 38*(1), 87–108.

Barrientos, A. (2019a). Social protection in Latin America: One region, two systems. In G. Cruz-Martínez (Ed.), *Welfare and social protection in contemporary Latin America* (pp. 59–71). Routledge.

Barrientos, A. (2019b). *The rise and fall of Bismarckian social policy. A hundred years of social protection in Latin America* [Mimeo]. CRC 1342 Gobal Dynamics of Social Policy, University of Bremen.

Barrientos, A. (2022a). Social Assistance Expansion and Political Inclusion in Latin America. *Journal of Politics in Latin America, online.*

Barrientos, A. (2022b). Social investment and social assistance in Low- and Middle-income countries. In J. Garritzmann, S. Häusermann, & B. Palier (Eds.), *The world politics of social investment* (Vol. 1, pp. 173–193). Oxford University Press.

Barrientos, A., & Malerba, D. (2020). Social assistance and inclusive growth. *International Social Security Review, 73*(3), 33–53.

Beramendi, P., Hausermann, S., Kitschelt, H., & Kriesi, H. (2015). *The politics of advanced capitalism*. Cambridge University Press.

Bértola, L., & Ocampo, J. A. (2012). *The economic development of Latin America since independence*. Oxford University Press.

Blackwell, M., & Glynn, A. N. (2018). How to make causal inferences with time-series cross-sectional data under selection on observables. *American Political Science Review, 112*(4), 1067–1082.

Borges, F. A. (2019). Adoption and Evolution of Cash Transfer Programs in Latin America. In *Oxford Research Encyclopedia*. Oxford University Press. https://doi.org/10.1093/acrefore/9780190228637.013.1521

Borzutzky, S. (2002). *Vital connections. Politics, social security and inequality in Chile*. University of Notre Dame Press.

Bosch, M., Melguizo, A., & Pages, C. (2013). *Mejores pensiones, mejores trabajos*. Inter-American Development Bank.

Brady, D., & Bostic. (2010). Paradoxes of social policy: Welfare transfers, relative poverty, and redistribution preferences. *American Sociological Review, 80*(2), 268–298.

CAF. (2020). *Los sistemas de pensiones y salud en América Latina. Los desafíos del envejecimiento, el cambio tecnológico y la informalidad.* Corporación Andina de Fomento.

Cantillon, B. (2011). The paradox of the social investment state: Growth, employment and poverty in the Lisbon era. *Journal of European Social Policy, 21*(5), 432.

Carrrera, L., & Angelaki, M. (2021). Bringing back the state: Understanding varieties of pension re-reforms in Latin America. *Latin American Politics and Society, 63*(22–44).

Collier, R. B., & Collier, D. (1991). *Shaping the Political Arena. Princeton University Press.*. https://muse.jhu.edu/book/45473

Cotlear, D., Gómez-Dantés, O., Knaul, F., Atun, R., Barreto, I. C. H. C., Cetràngolo, O., Cueto, M., Francke, P., Frenz, P., Guerrero, R., Lozano, R., Marten, R., & Saenz, R. (2015). Overcoming social segregation in health care in Latin America. *The Lancet, 385*(9974), 1248–1259.

de Hoop, J., & Rosati, F. C. (2014). *Cash transfers and child labor* (Policy Research Working Paper 6826). The World Bank.

Deaton, A. (2010). Instruments, randomization, and learning about development. *Journal of Economic Literature, 48*, 424–455.

Eslava, M., Meléndez, M., & Urdaneta, N. (2021). *Market concentration, market fragmentation, and inequality in Latin America* (Working Paper 11; UNDP LAC Working Paper). UNDP.

Ferrer, A. M., & Riddell, W. C. (2011). *Unemployment insurance savings accounts in Latin America: Overview and assessment* (Discussion Paper 5577; IZA Discussion Paper). IZA - Institute of Labor Economics.

Filgueira, F. (2005). *Welfare and democracy in Latin America: The development, crises and aftermath of Universal, dual and exclusionary social states.* UNRISD.

Garay, C. (2016). *Social policy expansion in Latin America.* Cambridge University Press.

Garritzmann, J., Häusermann, S., & Palier, B. (2022). *The world politics of social investment: Welfare states in the knowledge economy* (Vol. 1). Oxford University Press.

Haggard, S., & Kaufman, R. R. (2008). *Development, democracy, and welfare states. Latin America, Asia and Eastern Europe.* Princeton University Press.

Herrera, A. M., & Lora, E. A. (2005). Why so small? Explaining the size of firms in Latin America. *The World Economy, 28*(7), 1005–1028.

Holzmann, R., & Vodopivec, M. (Eds.). (2012). *Reforming severance pay. An international perspective*. The World Bank.
Huber, E. (1996). Options for social policy in Latin America: Neoliberal versus social democratic models. In G. Esping-Andersen (Ed.), *Welfare states in transition. National adaptations in global economies*. Sage.
Huber, E., & Stephens, J. D. (2012). *Democracy and the left in Latin America. Social policy and inequality in Latin America*. University of Chicago Press.
Hunter, W., & Borges Sugiyama, N. (2014). Transforming subjects into citizens: Insights from Brazil's Bolsa Família. *Perspectives on Politics, 12*(4), 829–845.
Illanes, M. A. (2003). *Chile des-centrado. Formación socio-cultural republicana y transición capitalista 1810-1910*. LOM Editions. http://www.memoriachilena.gob.cl/602/w3-article-82455.html
Ippolito, R. A. (1997). *Pension Plans and Employee Performance. Evidence, Analysis and Policy*. University of Chicago Press.
Isuani, E. A. (2008). La polìtica social argentina en perspectiva. In G. Cruces, J. M. Moreno, D. Ringold, & R. Rofman (Eds.), *Los programas sociales en la Argentina hacia el Bicentenario* (pp. 169–198). The World Bank.
Iversen, T., & Rehm, P. (2022). *Big data and the welfare state. How the information revolution threatens social solidarity*. Cambridge University Press.
Iversen, T., & Soskice, D. (2001). An asset theory of social policy preferences. *American Political Science Review, 95*(4), 875–893.
Iversen, T., & Soskice, D. (2006). Electoral institutions and the politics of coalitions: Why some democracies redistribute more than others? *American Political Science Review, 100*(2), 165–181.
Iversen, T., & Soskice, D. (2015). Politics for markets. *Journal of European Social Policy, 25*(1), 76–93.
Kapiszewski, D., Levitsky, S., & Yashar, D. J. (Eds.). (2021). *The Inclusionary turn in Latin American democracies*. Cambridge University Press.
Korpi, W. (1980). Social policy and the distributional conflict in the capitalist democracies: A preliminary comparative framework. *West European Politics, 3*, 296–316.
Korpi, W. (2006). Power resources and employer-centered approaches in explanations of welfare state and varieties of capitalism: Protagonists, consenters, and antagonists. *World Politics, 58*(2), 167–206.
Korpi, W., & Palme, J. (1998). The paradox of redistribution and strategies for equality: Welfare state institutions, inequality and poverty in the Western Countries. *American Sociological Review, 63*(5), 661–687.
Kritzer, B. E., Kay, S. J., & Sinha, T. (2011). Next generation of individual account pension reforms in Latin America. *Social Security Bulletin, 71*(1), 35–76.

Lazear, E. P. (1983). *Incentive effects of pensions*. NBER.
Levitsky, S., & Roberts, K. M. (2012). *The resurgence of the Latin American Left*. The John Hopkins University Press.
Levy, S. (2008). *Good intentions, bad outcomes. Social policy, informality and economic growth in Mexico*. The Brookings Institution.
Lindert, P. H. (2004). *Growing public: Social spending and economic growth since the eighteenth century* (Vol. 1). Cambridge University Press.
Lindert, P. H. (2021). *Making social spending work*. Cambridge University Press.
Malloy, J. M. (1979). *The politics of social security in Brazil*. University of Pittsburgh Press.
Mares, I., & Carnes, M. (2009). Social policy in developing countries. *Annual Review of Political Science, 12*, 93–113.
Martínez-Franzoni, J., & Sánchez-Ancochea, D. (2017). *The quest for universal social policies in the South*. Cambridge University Press.
Mesa-Lago, C. (1978). *Social security in Latin America: Pressure groups, stratification, and inequality*. University of Pittsburgh Press.
Mesa-Lago, C. (2007). *Reassembling social security. A survey of pensions and healthcare reforms in Latin America*. Oxford University Press.
Mesa-Lago, C. (2020). *Evaluación de cuatro décadas de privatización de pensiones en América Latina (1980-2020): Promesas y realidades* [Report]. Fundación Friedrich Ebert en México.
Mesa-Lago, C., & Bertranou, F. (1998). *Manual de Economía de la Seguridad Social*. Centro Latinoamericano de Economía Humana.
Mesa-Lago, C., & Müller, K. (2002). The politics of pension reform in Latin America. *Journal of Latin American Studies, 34*(3), 687–715.
Messina, J., & Silva, J. (2018). *Wage inequality in Latin America. Understanding the past to prepare for the future*. The World Bank.
Monsalve Cuéllar, M. E. (Ed.). (2017). *Historia de la Seguridad Social en América Latina*. Universidad de Medellín.
MOxLAD. (n.d.). *Montevideo-Oxford Latin American Economic History Data Base* [Database]. Montevideo-Oxford Latin American Economic History Data Base. http://moxlad.cienciassociales.edu.uy/en#
Palier, B. (Ed.). (2010). *A long goodbye to Bismarck? The politics of Welfare Reform in Continental Europe*. Amsterdam University Press.
Rossel, C. (2013). *Politicas para las familias en America Latina: Panorama de políticas de reduccion de pobreza y reconciliacion entre trabajo-familia* [Mimeo]. Universidad Catolica del Uruguay.

Rueda, D., Wibbels, E., & Altamirano, M. (2015). The origins of dualism. In P. Beramendi, S. Hausermann, H. Kitschelt, & H. Kriesi (Eds.), *The politics of advanced capitalism* (pp. 89–111). Cambridge University Press.

Sánchez-Ancochea, D., & Martínez Franzoni, J. (2015). *La incorporación social en Centroamérica: Trayectorias, obstáculos y oportunidades* (Working Paper 1200). CEPAL-Mexico.

Segovia, A. (2022). *Las relaciones entre modelos y tipos de capitalismo: La experiencia de centroamérica* (Working Paper 198; Estudios y Perspectivas). CEPAL-Mexico.

Sehnbruch, K., Carranza, R., & Contreras, D. (2020). *Unemployment insurance in Chile: Lessons from a high inequality developing country* (Working Paper 54; III Working Paper Series). London School of Economics.

Silva, E., & Rossi, F. M. (2017). *Reshaping the political arena in Latin America. From resisting Neoliberalism to the Second Incorporation.* University of Pittsburgh Press.

Wibbels, E., & Ahlquist, J. S. (2011). Development, trade and social insurance. *International Studies Quarterly, 55*, 125–149.

Williamson, J. G. (2011). *Industrial catching up in the poor periphery 1870-1975* [Mimeo]. Harvard University.

4

Institutions

This chapter is concerned with the design, implementation, and outcomes of current social protection institutions in the region. As discussed in the Introduction, the book will focus on three core social protection institutions: occupational pensions, individual retirement savings plans, and social assistance. These three institutions are the core of social protection provision in the region, secondary or complementary social protection programmes are often offshoots of them and serve a sub-group of their participants. The three main institutions reflect diachronic dimensions, their origins and evolution, as well as synchronic dimensions in their deployment across countries. They also provide a fertile and effective entry point for the comparative analysis of social protection in the region and theory development.

The chapter is organised as follows: Section 4.1 reviews indicators and data, probing the strengths and weaknesses of survey and administrative data. Section 4.2 studies pension schemes covering in turn occupational pensions and individual retirement savings plans. Section 4.3 examines social assistance, including conditional income transfers and old age transfers. Section 4.4 offers a brief review of secondary provision covering unemployment insurance, family and children, and active labour market policies. A final section concludes.

A. Barrientos, *Social Protection in Latin America*, Global Dynamics of Social Policy,
https://doi.org/10.1007/978-3-031-49795-7_4

4.1 Data and Indicators

It will be helpful to start with a brief discussion on social protection data sources and indicators. There are currently two main sources of data on social protection institutions: household surveys and administrative registers, each have strengths and limitations.

Administrative data on social protection schemes are collected by the relevant agencies with the objective of selecting participants and of monitoring implementation, entitlements, and costs. Administrative data on participation are affected by gaps and errors associated with lags in record updating (Rofman & Oliveri, 2012). Where a multiplicity of agencies are involved, gaps and data harmonisation can be an important issue (Arenas de Mesa, 2019). Consistent historical administrative data is scarce due to repeated institutional change affecting the relevant agencies. Cross-country administrative data requires a common approach to data collection and presentation by the countries involved.

Regular collection of household surveys by the countries in the region began in the 1990s and has become an important source of information for social protection researchers. Household surveys provide regular, consistent, and up to date information on participation in social protection programmes. However, they have several limitations. First, they are subject to limitations in their sampling, associated with groups harder to reach such as the very rich or the very poor, and with people living in insecure communities or remote rural areas. Sampling limitations can have a measurable impact on estimates. Second, in common with all household surveys they are subject to errors and omissions in reporting. Third, restrictions in the time available for respondent interviews imposes restrictions on the selection of social protection programmes included in the collection of information.

Comparison of administrative and survey data on social protection programme participation suggest their limitations can bias their information in different directions. Villatoro and Cecchini (2018) compared administrative and survey data capture of social assistance participants. They found that survey data underestimated participation in conditional income transfers (old age and disability transfers) by 13% (21.9%) on average. They attributed the disparities principally to household survey sampling deficiencies.

In the literature, participation in social protection schemes is usually measured through indicators of coverage. The latter are used as an indicator of the reach of social protection schemes, that is the population they benefit. The term coverage has its provenance in insurance approaches to social protection. A standard insurance scheme draws a premium from all members to compensate the fraction of them affected by the insured contingencies. Coverage, measured as a proportion of the labour force or population, indicates the proportion of that group that stands to be compensated by the scheme. The ILO's measure of 'legal' coverage comes close to capturing this narrative (ILO, 2021). In social assistance programmes, reach is a more appropriate measure of participation than coverage.[1]

In the Latin American context, 'legal' coverage is very limited as an indicator of the reach of social protection programmes. In part this is because in practice not all workers with a legal entitlement might be protected. In unemployment insurance schemes, for example, there are additional requisites workers might be expected to meet to access entitlements: to have continuous employment prior to the separation, a minimum set of contributions with a specified period. Behavioural responses might prevent access to entitlements. Even if explicitly included in the programme, workers are likely to stay away if they expect to find it difficult to meet these requirements. Occupational pensions often exclude workers who are not in a regular and permanent employment relationship. Own account workers, unwaged workers, workers in short-term or intermittent employment, domestic, and rural workers find it hard to access unemployment protection. In practice, 'actual' coverage of insurance programmes is likely to diverge substantially from 'legal' coverage. Examining Chile's individual savings unemployment insurance, Sehnbruch et al. (2020) find that only 11.8% or workers with a permanent contract were actually entitled to make a claim and only 2.9% of workers with fixed term contracts were entitled to do so. Ceilings on the period time covered by unemployment insurance, say 3–6 months, represents a further restriction on 'coverage'. It is more accurate to describe

[1] Social assistance could be described as insurance in conditions where it applies to the population in its entirety, taxes as premiums and transfers as compensation (Varian, 1980). For all practical purposes, it makes more sense to describe the scope of social assistance transfers by the term reach.

'legal' coverage as 'conditional' coverage because it is conditional on meeting a battery of programme requisites. In pension schemes, vesting periods describe the length of time participants need to make contributions before accessing pension benefits. Assessing coverage on an annual basis does not tell us whether workers will reach the age of retirement with 20–30 years of contribution required to access entitlements.

A measure of the share of workers participating in pension programmes is described as 'active' coverage, whereas a measure of the share of persons over the retirement age who are in receipt of a pension benefit is described as 'passive' coverage. These measures are calculated or estimated on an annual basis, often at the end of the year. As will be discussed in more detail below, these measures require contextualisation in the context of Latin America. Due to large volatility in employment and vesting periods, 'active' coverage could significantly over-estimate the proportion of workers who will be able to access pension benefits at retirement. This will be discussed in some detail below. 'Active' pension scheme coverage does not provide a reliable measure of old age income security, for example. On the other hand, 'passive' coverage does provide a reasonable measure of old age income security, assuming minimum pension benefits are adequate. The generosity of social protection programmes is usually measured by the share of earnings they are likely to replace, or replacement rates.

Improvements in the availability of cross-country administrative and survey data on social protection participation in recent times has facilitated comparative research. Issues of data comparability across survey and administrative data and lack of precision in some of the indicators in common use recommend care should be exercised in their interpretation.

4.2 Pension Schemes

This Section provides a description and analysis of pension schemes, including occupational pension schemes and individual retirement savings plans.[2] Old age income security has been the dominant concern of social protection policy in Latin America since the emergence of

[2] They are also referred to in the literature as formal or contributory pension schemes.

occupational pension funds. Pensions are the largest component of social protection expenditure, enjoy a high degree of institutionalisation, and monopolise the attention of policy makers (national and international) and researchers. They signal a strong age bias in the development and current structure of social protection provision in Latin America.

Table 4.1 summarises the institutional set up of pension schemes in the region. The distinction between schemes based on defined benefits and those based on defined contributions serves as the main organising concept. Defined benefit schemes establish a formula to calculate

Table 4.1 Pension schemes in Latin America

		(1)	(2)	(3)	(4)
Country	Pension Design	All Contributors (DC in brackets) as % EAP (2017)	Vesting (years)	Guaranteed minimum	Segmentation
Argentina	DB	56.2	30	B	Highly segmented
Bolivia	DC	16.9	15	B	Unified
Brazil	DB	58	15	M	Highly segmented
Chile	DC	63.4 (64.2)		M/T	Relatively unified
Colombia	DB/DC	30.5 (21.5)	26	/M	Highly segmented
Costa Rica	DB + DC	63.6 (70.5)	25/-	T	Relatively unified
Ecuador	DB	37	30	T	Segmented
El Salvador	DC	24.5 (24)	25		Highly segmented
Guatemala	DB	18.1	20		Relatively unified
Honduras	DB	19.1	15		Highly segmented
Mexico	DC	36.3 (34.9)	25	B/M	Highly segmented

(*continued*)

Table 4.1 (continued)

		(1)	(2)	(3)	(4)
Country	Pension Design	All Contributors (DC in brackets) as % EAP (2017)	Vesting (years)	Guaranteed minimum	Segmentation
Nicaragua	DB	31.3	15		Relatively unified
Panama	DC	64.1 (10.1)	20		Unified
Paraguay	DB	23.7	25	M	Highly segmented
Peru	DB/DC	26.9 (17.3)	20		Segmented
Dominican Rep.	DC	41.3 (35.5)	30	M	Segmented
Uruguay	DB + DC	81.1 (45.8)	30	T	Highly segmented
Venezuela	DB		15		Highly segmented

Notes: Pension Design reports destination, with some countries , Mexico and Panama for example, currently transitioning. DB is Defined Benefit; DC is Defined Contribution; "/" indicates parallel schemes; "+" indicates integrated schemes. (1) EAP is Economically active population; numbers in brackets are Defined Contribution pension scheme contributors. Source for All Contributors is Arenas de Mesa (2019). Source for defined benefit contributors is AIOS (2019). They are collected independently and therefore some figures might not match. (2) Vesting Period is the minimum contribution record required to access entitlements. Source is Altamirano Montoya et al. (2018). (3) Indicates whether pension schemes have a guaranteed minimum; B indicates a basic minimum pension benefit for all; M indicates a minimum benefit if accumulated entitlements are insufficient; T indicates a minimum benefit is paid if accumulated entitlements are insufficient and contributor has low socio-economic status. Source is OECD (2014). (4) Source is Mesa-Lago (2007)

retirement benefits, normally based on years of service and final salary parameters. Defined benefit schemes in the region are unfunded, or pay-as-you-go, with current pension contributions and public subsidies financing current benefits. They are managed by public or semi-public agencies and are stratified for different occupations. Defined contribution pension schemes, on the other hand, set the contribution rate as a share of labour earnings. Savings are collected in individual retirement accounts managed by private or public pension funds. At retirement, workers use their accumulated balances to make pension arrangements. The options include purchasing an annuity from an insurance provider guaranteeing a fixed monthly income during retirement or agreeing a schedule of withdrawals from the pension funds.

As can be seen from the Table, countries in the region show a variety of arrangements. Nine countries have defined benefit schemes only—Argentina, Brazil, Cuba, Ecuador, Guatemala, Honduras, Nicaragua, Paraguay, and Venezuela. Five countries have defined contribution schemes only or are transitioning to it—Bolivia, Chile, El Salvador, Dominican Republic, and Mexico and Panama.[3] Five countries have both defined benefit and defined contribution pension schemes deployed in different combinations. Colombia and Peru have competing defined benefit and defined contribution schemes, meaning that workers can be in one or the other but not both. Costa Rica and Uruguay have defined benefit schemes as a first pillar with defined contribution schemes as a second pillar. Some countries that initially embraced individual retirement accounts have subsequently reformed them, a process referred to as 're-reform' (Mesa-Lago, 2020). In 2008 Argentina transitioned back from individual retirement plans to a defined benefit scheme. In 2010 Bolivia opted to transition to a public defined contribution scheme, not yet fully implemented.

The Table shows the share of the active labour force contributing to pension schemes, with the numbers in brackets indicating the share in defined contribution schemes for those countries that have them. Uruguay stands out with just over 80% of the active labour force contributing to pension schemes. In Chile, Costa Rica, and Panama, around two thirds of the active labour force contribute to a pension scheme, with Argentina and Brazil just behind them. In the rest of the countries, between a fifth and a quarter of the active labour force are engaged in pension schemes. Overall, participation in pension schemes is higher in the more economically developed countries of the region. For the region taken as a whole, less than one in two workers contribute to an occupational scheme or individual retirement account.

[3] Countries with only defined contribution schemes may have defined benefit schemes for privileged groups of workers. Chile has a defined benefit pension scheme for members of the Police and Armed Forces. When individual retirement plans were introduced in 1981, the military government preserved the occupational pension schemes for them. Chile's and Mexico's old defined benefit pension scheme are closed to new entrants but remain in place.

The numbers in brackets show the share of the active labour force saving in individual retirement plans, where the two types of pension schemes coexist. Aside from Chile and Costa Rica, individual retirement plans reach a small proportion of the active labour force. In Peru and Panama, the share of the active labour force contributing to individual retirement plans is very small.

Figure 4.1 draws on administrative data to provide a picture of pension programmes participation rates for Latin American countries for the period 2000–2018. There is a group of countries showing sustained higher rates of participation of the labour force. They are Argentina, Brazil, Chile, Costa Rica, Panama, and Uruguay. They have participation rates around the 60% mark for a significant portion of the period. Unsurprisingly, aside from Costa Rica these countries experienced deeper industrialisation and early implementation of occupational insurance funds. Another group of countries have participation rates at around

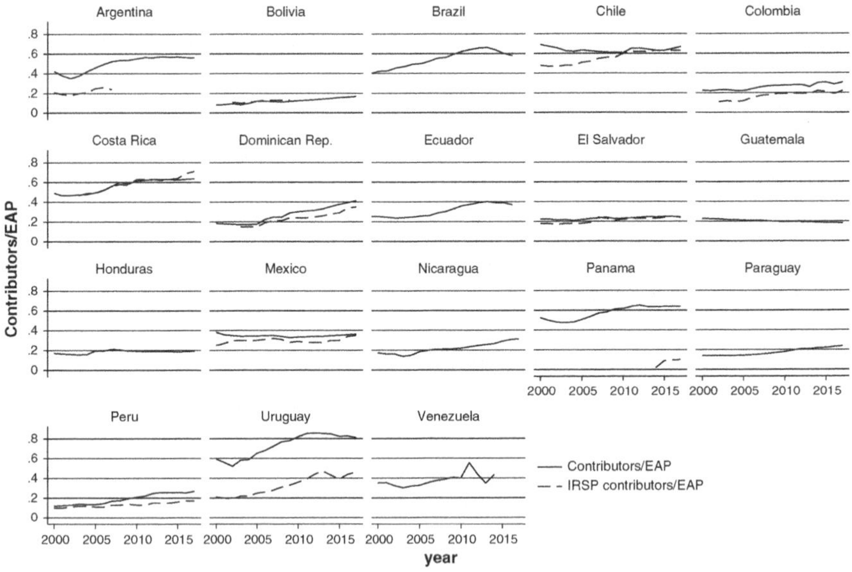

Fig. 4.1 Pension scheme contributors as fraction of the economically active population. Data sources: All Contributors from Arenas de Mesa (2019); Individual retirement savings plan contributors (Asociación Internacional de Organismos de Supervisión de Fondos de Pensiones, 2022)

40% for significant portions of the period. They include Ecuador, Mexico, and Venezuela. A third group of countries have very low participation rates, around the 20% mark. They are Central American and Andean region countries.

The Figure shows contributors to pension schemes, and participants in individual retirement savings plans, as a fraction of the economically active population.

Overall, participation rates paint a frozen picture of pension programme coverage in the region. Uruguay and Brazil are perhaps the exception. Their participation rates rising during the first decade of the new century but registering a decline in the second decade. Chile shows a sustained decline over the period. There are few changes in group membership for the period, with only a weak rising trend for some countries in the middle of the period that stabilises around 2015.

The Figure shows changes in participation rates in individual retirement savings plans as a separate trend. This series can be expected to rise over time, as the newly introduced individual retirement savings plans attract new entrants to the labour market and, depending on the rules, workers switching to the new programmes. However, the Figure does not show a sustained rising trend in individual retirement savings plans participation. In countries where individual retirement savings plans are intended to substitute existing defined benefit programmes, Bolivia, Chile, Dominican Republic, El Salvador, Mexico and Panama there is no observable net increase in participation. In Costa Rica, and Uruguay, where individual retirement savings plans are complementary to existing defined benefit programmes, participation rates have increased as expected. In countries like Colombia and Peru, where defined contribution pension programmes are in direct competition with defined benefit programmes, there is very little change over time.

Figure 4.2. draws on household survey data to measure participation. Participation rates are captured by the share of workers who report having pension rights. The participation rates are based on household survey data harmonised by CEDLAS (2012). The survey data enable measuring participation rates for all workers and separately for salaried workers. Participation is expected to be higher for salaried workers as non-salaried workers face restricted access to pension schemes.

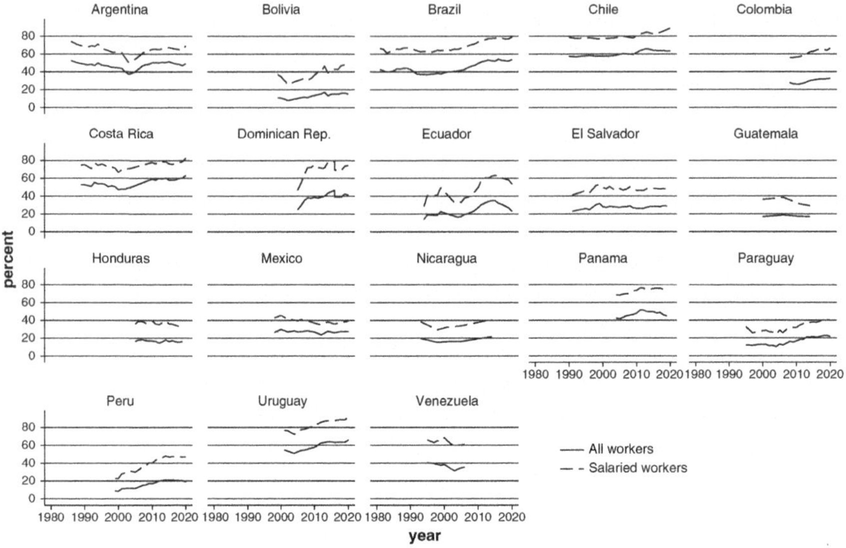

Fig. 4.2 Share of workers with pension rights. Data source: CEDLAS (CEDLAS & World Bank, 2012)

The Figure shows the estimated share of workers who report having pension rights in household surveys. It shows pension scheme participation rates as estimated in survey data.

The participation rates estimated from survey data confirm the general trends observed with administrative data. Country groupings also remain the same. Participation rates are higher when only salaried workers are considered, underlining the exclusion of workers in informal employment from pension schemes. Widening or shrinking gaps between the two series provide information on changes in the share of workers in informal employment in the countries of the region or changes in access to pension schemes.[4] In the interest of comparability, it makes sense to focus on participation rates for the labour force. The longer span of the survey data helps to contextualise some of the trends observed from administrative data shown in Fig. 4.1. In Argentina, for example, coverage appears to have a 'U' shape, with participation higher at the begin-

[4] Informality is often measured by whether workers are contribution to pension schemes.

ning of the period than at the end. The relaxation of access to entitlements following the 2001 financial crisis might be responsible for the upward trend in participation in the latter period.

Pension participation is higher for males, workers with higher educational qualifications and higher labour earnings, and workers in larger firms (CAF, 2020; Eslava et al., 2021; OECD/IDB/The World Bank, 2014). This applies to all pension programmes in the region (Rofman & Oliveri, 2012). These correlates of pension participation are common to countries in the region and are relatively constant in time. In sum, participation in pension schemes in Latin America shows significant stability over time, even in countries that have implemented far-reaching pension reforms.

The rest of the section discusses features and issues that are specific to each pension programme design and then examines issues they have in common.

4.2.1 Occupational Pensions

4.2.1.1 Bismarck vs. Beveridge

In the more industrialised countries in the region, occupational pension schemes originated in worker led self-protection institutions. State-led developmental policies, and the first wave of worker incorporation associated with it, explain to government attempts to influence, and control over the independent insurance funds. This involved changes in the financing of occupational pension funds to a pay-as you-go-basis and efforts to consolidate and streamline the governance of the schemes. According to Mesa-Lago (1989), the occupational pension funds emerging in intermediate countries—Andean, Costa Rica and Panama—from the 1940s were controlled by governments from the outset. They attempted to follow more closely Beveridgean guidelines, advocated by the ILO, than the Bismarckian logic in the pioneer countries. However, surveying occupational pension funds today it is hard not to come to the conclusion that Bismarck won the contest (Bertranou et al., 2018).

Government led reforms, motivated by financial considerations, sought to streamline the governance of occupational pension funds, but their fragmentation has proved resilient. What is sometimes presented in the literature as 'social insurance systems' are nothing of the sort. 'Systems' are in fact common governance structures enabling large differentials in access and entitlements for different groups of workers, military and police, civil service, teachers, etc. Large exclusions, implicit and explicit, remain in the face of repeated attempts at improving inclusivity in the 2000s (see Arenas, 2019). Even where common governance structures apply to the unified pension programmes, some workers have access to special voluntary complementary programmes. Mesa-Lago concludes that "the process of unification of multiple contributory pension programs and schemes in the region has been difficult, prolonged and uneven" (Mesa-Lago, 2007, p. 83). Mesa-Lago places Argentina, Colombia, El Salvador, Mexico, Uruguay, Brazil, Honduras, Paraguay, and Venezuela in the group of countries with highly segmented pension programme provision (See Table 4.1). This is at the core of large inequalities in pension benefits despite common governance administrative structures.

4.2.1.2 Membership Entitlements

To the extent that occupational insurance funds are insurance instruments, they emphasise ex ante resource pooling to address idiosyncratic risk and ex post redistribution from the fortunate to the less fortunate. They reflect strong incentives to form common groups with similar risk profiles. As such they reinforce status differentials in the labour market. Their underlying logic of entitlements based on group membership follows directly from their stratified risk pooling (Baldwin, 1990). It explains the resilience of pension programme segmentation in the face of sustained governmental attempts at consolidation and streamlining.

In practice occupational insurance funds are an instrument of employment stratification. Occupational insurance funds reinforce intra-class differentials within wage earners. This is just another way of making the same point, but with the advantage that it throws light on the employment effects of social protection. Their stratification effects work in two ways. First by excluding groups of workers with less advantageous risk profiles: agricultural workers, domestic workers, urban informal workers, workers in small firms, women, and new entrants (Garay, 2021). Latin American governments have over time made repeated efforts to reduce legal and regulation barriers to the participation of these workers in pension programmes, with mixed success.

Second, pension scheme design features often act as a deterrent to the participation of outsiders despite common governance. For example, long vesting periods, the density of contributions required to access pension benefits, preclude workers in intermittent formal employment accessing their entitlements. Long vesting periods redistribute pension funds from workers with shorter than vesting period contributions at retirement to workers with permanent and secure employment who will find it easier to meet the vesting requisite.[5] This applies especially to women who are likely to have large contribution gaps.

There has been a recurrent argument in policy debates as to why Latin American countries failed to extend the reach of social protection schemes along the lines of European welfare states. Leaving aside for the moment the issue whether all, or indeed most, European countries really achieved this standard (Marx & Nelson, 2012), it is not a productive way to approach this issue. It is the same as asking why Latin American countries failed to construct welfare states. Acute differentiation of wage earners since the 1980s has removed the possibility that homogeneous risks pools among wage earners could have created the conditions for the emergence of inclusive social protection institutions.

4.2.1.3 A Less Advantaged Worker Perspective

It is informative to consider participation in pension schemes from the perspective of less advantaged workers. By less advantaged, I mean workers who are less likely to benefit from stable, continuous, and reasonably

[5] This will be discussed in more detail below.

well-paid employment. For advantaged workers' pension schemes participation decisions take the conventional form of paying contributions to secure a pension benefit related to their final earnings in accordance with the scheme entitlement formula (say 1/80th of final salary per year of service). For less advantaged workers, on the other hand, it makes sense to look at pension schemes participation decisions as a bet - an option in financial market terms—on securing a guaranteed minimum pension benefit. This is an important distinction because for the less advantaged worker pension participation decision is a binary choice, securing a guaranteed minimum pension or not. It is not surprising that for workers in Latin America who fall in the disadvantaged group, the regulations on the minimum pension are all that matters. In fact, as we will find in the next chapter, in Latin American countries most pension recipients access the minimum pension guarantee.

Altamirano et al. (2018) study replacement rates from participation in pension schemes in Latin America and the Caribbean. They simulate replacement rates as predicted to apply to workers with average employment and pay in each of the countries.[6] They find that defined benefit pension schemes in Latin America and the Caribbean have a replacement rate of 68.7% on average while defined contribution schemes have a replacement rate of 38.9% on average. They calculate the net subsidy to pension recipients as the difference between (i) the benefit they are likely to receive according to pension scheme entitlement regulations; and (ii) the pension generated by savings equivalent to the contribution rate accumulated at a fixed rate of interest. The net subsidy to pension recipients, in percentage points of the replacement rate, turns out to be 28.3 pp for defined benefit programmes and 12.4 pp for defined contribution programmes. Given the design parameters of the simulation, the net subsidy necessarily comes from two sources: provisions for guaranteed minimum pension leading to pensioners getting a higher benefit than that merited by their contributions; and redistribution from participants who at retirement fail to meet the requisites for securing a benefit in defined benefit programmes. In defined contribution pension schemes only the

[6] The simulation parameters include workers retiring in 2015, married, starting work aged 20 and retiring at minimum retirement age, with median formal salary rising by 2% a year.

first source of a net subsidy applies, that is minimum pension guarantees. In defined benefit pension programmes, most of the net subsidy is in fact a net tax on workers who fail to meet access conditions. The findings from this study underline the adverse redistribution inbuilt into defined benefit programmes faced by less advantaged workers.[7]

In sum, occupational insurance funds are designed to redistribute resources away from workers with low density of contributions and towards workers with high density of contributions. In the Latin American context, this involves a redistribution of pension benefits from the mass of disadvantaged workers to a minority of advantaged workers.

There are sustained pressures on occupational insurance funds in the region. Secular demographic change and changes in family structures threaten the male breadwinner model under which Bismarckian pension schemes were designed. Rising contribution rates, the ending of service pensions, and an extension of the retirement age, could contribute to counteract the effects of ageing populations, but they generate significant resistance. Changes in employment are also a significant threat. A decline in stable longer-term employment relationships brought in by harsher business competition in increasingly open economies will undermine the conditions in which occupational insurance funds thrive. Governments are everywhere under pressure to lower subsidies to pensions programmes that benefit advantaged workers (Arenas de Mesa, 2020), especially as consumption and corporate taxes provide the bulk of fiscal revenues in Latin America.

4.2.2 Individual Retirement Savings Plans

Individual retirement savings plans have been available from financial institutions for high net worth customers in Latin America and elsewhere for some time. The policy change we are interested in here is the adoption of mandated individual retirement savings plans. Beginning with Chile in 1981, ten governments in the region legislated to compel workers to save a proportion of their earnings in dedicated accounts with newly

---

[7] The study also concludes: "In the majority of the countries, non-contributive pensions manage to fully compensate for the 'taxes' on workers with low density of contributions generated by pension programmes" (Altamirano Montoya et al., 2018, p. 48 my translation).

established ad hoc pension fund managers (Barrientos, 1998a). The purpose of these mandates was to create a pension fund market. Pension fund managers collect the savings from workers and invest them in a range of government regulated assets. On reaching retirement age, workers can access the balances in their accounts and make appropriate retirement income arrangements.

Advocates of pension reform claimed a wide range of potential advantages: improving the working of the labour market and productivity, reducing old age poverty and vulnerability, lifting governments' fiscal deficits, and strengthening financial markets (Edwards, 1996; Orszag & Stiglitz, 1999; World Bank, 1994). An assessment of then existing occupational insurance funds in the region emphasised the strong incentives for rent-seeking offered by the stratification in provision. Powerful labour organisations successfully lobbied governments for pension privileges and funding, in the process setting barriers to the mobility of workers to their most productive employment. A gap opened between contributions and entitlements with deleterious effects in incentives for human capital accumulation and effort. Individual retirement savings plans, it was argued, would restore the direct connection between contributions and entitlements with favourable outcomes for human capital accumulation, labour market competition, and productivity. Current or projected occupational insurance funds' deficits underlined the need for growing fiscal support (Mesa-Lago, 2020). Mandating individual retirement savings plans would lift the threat of impending deficits and restore government fiscal balances. Shallow financial asset markets in the region were held responsible for low investment rates, short-termism, firm concentration and uncompetitiveness. They contributed to recurrent financial crises and low productivity and competitiveness. The emerging pension fund market was expected to deepen financial markets by redirecting workers' retirement savings through the financial sector, while pension fund managers could provide the kind of institutional investors that would push through reforms and practices to strengthen the allocative role of financial markets (Barrientos, 1999). Individual retirement savings plans would have far-reaching effects on the performance of the region's economies. The outcomes of pension reform failed to fulfil the transformational claims made on its behalf (Gill et al., 2004). Forty years after the Chilean reform, it continues to be contested.

Table 4.2 outlines the key features of individual retirement savings plans in Latin America. The first column reminds readers of the relationship existing between occupational insurance funds and individual retirement savings plans in countries' pension design, whether occupational insurance funds are transitioning to individual retirement plans, individual retirement savings plans are in competition with occupational insurance funds or are integrated with them. The next four columns focus on the parameters of pension entitlements for the countries involved. In individual retirement savings plans, there is more scope for participants to make retirement decisions. The absence of redistributive features means that the consequences emanating from these decisions will not affect other participants. Column 2 notes the legal retirement age in the country, as a reference point, however in most countries it is possible for participants to access their individual funds balances earlier. There are, of course, implications for the government as the protector of last resort, hence some countries set a minimum vesting period before participants can claim any minimum pension guarantees.

In the same prudential vein, there are restrictions on the form of entitlements. Under a life annuity, participants are required to use their accumulated balances to contract a life annuity with an insurance company. This has the effect of protecting the government from individual's retirement funds running out. Unfortunately, insurance financial sectors are relatively thinly developed in Latin American countries with the implication that annuity rates are rather expensive. Two issues are important. First, the fact that financial markets trade very few long-term instruments makes it difficult for insurance companies to manage long-term liabilities. Second, the choice of mortality tables used in the calculation of annuities can be distorted by the selective nature of individual retirement savings plans participants.[8] Population-wide mortality tables would significantly underestimate life expectancy after retirement for more advantaged workers. Alternatively, individual retirement savings plans can replace the purchase of an annuity with arrangements for scheduled withdrawals, effectively an annual pension which generosity is dependent on

[8] This applies to gender differences in mortality and labour market engagement (Arza, 2017; Barrientos, 1998b).

Table 4.2 Main features of Individual retirement savings plans in Latin America

	1	2	3	4	5	6	7	8
Country	Design	Legal retirement age	Vesting (years)	Benefit design	Guarantees (Target as % mean earnings)	Funds as % GDP Dec. 2019	# Managers (% top 2)	Real fund returns (3 years to Dec 2021)
Bolivia	Transition	55(50)	10(15) min	Life annuity	Top-up 56–70)		1	
Chile	Transition	65(60)	none	Life annuity or programmed withdrawal	Top-up (36)	80.8	7(54.1)	5.4
Colombia	Parallel	62(57)	25	Programmed withdrawal	Top-up (60)	24.5	4(80.8)	9
Costa Rica	Integrated	65	none	Annual pension	Minimum pension (28)	18.6	6(60.3)	9.7
Dominican Rep.	Transition	60	25	Price indexed life annuity or programme withdrawal	Minimum pension (40)	12.2	7(58.6)	6.1
Mexico	Transition	65	25 -min	Annual pension	Top-up (23)	16.3	10(35.7)	7.8
Panama	Transition	62(57)	20	Programme withdrawal	Minimum pension (25)	1.2	3(98.9)	3.7
Peru	Parallel	65	20 -min.	Programme withdrawal	Minimum pension (30)	22.8	4(66.6)	6.4
El Salvador	Transition	60(55)	25 - min.	Programme withdrawal	Minimum pension (45)	43.8	2	3.3
Uruguay	Integrated	60	30	Annual pension	Top-up (20-44)	29.1	4(73.4)	7.7

Notes: (2) (3) (4) (5) mainly from IMF 2018; (6) (7) (8) from AIOS (2022). Transition implies individual retirement savings plans will eventually replace occupational pensions. Parallel implies individual retirement savings plans will remain in competititon with occupational pensions. Integrated individual retirement savings plans complement occupational pensions the fund balances at retirement. In Uruguay and Costa Rica individual retirement pension plans provide an annual pension supplement to the defined benefit pillar.

From the perspective of less advantaged workers, likely a plurality of mandated participants, minimum pension guarantees are paramount. Individual retirement savings plans have two main modalities of guaranteed minimum provision. Some offer a top up where fund balances could only finance an annuity below a pre-defined threshold (Valdés-Prieto, 2009). This threshold is shown in brackets in the Table as a proportion of mean labour earnings. It varies in generosity across countries, but the mode is around a quarter of mean salary (IMF, 2018). In other countries, participating in individual retirement savings plans guarantees a minimum pension level which replaces the annuity otherwise generated by the fund. These guarantees are financed from additional solidarity contributions or, in their absence, from public funds.

A deeper question surrounding individual retirement savings plans is whether they are 'pensions'. A defining feature of pension schemes is that they protect the population from longevity risk, the risk that they may outlive their resources. This is a necessary and arguably sufficient condition for retirement arrangements to be described as pensions. By themselves, individual retirement savings plans are at best a conditional pension, that is conditional on participants accumulating sufficient funds - taking account of annuity rates - and conditional on meeting relevant vesting periods. Individual retirement savings plans could only qualify as pension schemes where governments can act as guarantors of contracted annuity income streams or where governments provide minimum pension guarantees.

As discussed above, individual retirement savings plans advocates made a great deal of their potentially favourable effects on financial markets. The Table shows that over time IRAs have accumulated large funds as a proportion of GDP. The Table shows accumulated funds at the end of 2019 prior to the COVID19 pandemic. The latter resulted in large withdrawals that may or may not be recovered in the future (Kay & Borzutzky, 2022). Chile's accumulated fund is the largest, reflecting early reform and a sizeable share of the labour force as participants. Debates on the composition of fund asset portfolios are recurrent in all the countries involved, for example as regards investment in foreign assets. Government regulations must strike a balance between the need to maximise rates of return for participants, ensure that funds deepen domestic financial markets, and ensure they help finance public debt. Real rates of return of individual retirement savings plans are variable, but as the Table shows recent rates of return are healthy. Pension fund markets are highly concentrated. Popular levels of dissatisfaction are apparent in the interaction between pension fund managers and participants.

The fact that individual retirement savings plans now control a large share of financial assets has not led to a transformational change in the nature of financial markets or indeed the orientation of the economy (Gill et al., 2004). It has not led to a change in the distribution of assets in the economy. Discussing the distribution of income form labour and income from capital in different countries, Ranaldi and Milanovic (2020) draw a distinction between 'class' economies, where the vast majority of labour income is captured by workers and most income from capital is captured by capitalists, and 'diversified' economies where the income from capital and labour is more widely distributed across workers and capitalists. Empirically, they place Latin American countries as 'class' economies. However, classifying pension wealth as a private asset can nuance this assessment. As "…the share of older people is on the rise in many advanced countries and the use of private pensions becomes more popular, one can envisage a somewhat novel form of "classless" society where relatively equal shares of capital and labor across distribution are achieved through savings over active life and capital returns once in retirement." (Ranaldi & Milanovic, 2020, p. 22). individual retirement savings plans fund in Chile are equivalent to 80% of annual GDP, but they have not provided wage earners with any influence over economic policy, or over the preferred structure of the economy, or over the distribution of assets. individual retirement savings plans participants have less influence on social policy than the managers of pension funds. If anything, individual retirement savings plans have delivered huge political and financial power to fund managers who have deployed it to preclude structural pension reform in Chile (Castiglioni, 2005; Dorlach, 2020; Fairfield & Garay, 2017).

Pension reforms implementing individual retirement savings plans in Latin America have not been entirely successful, certainly not in terms of the claims made by advocates. Attempts at reforming the reforms confirm this to be the case (Arza, 2017; Carrera & Angelaki, 2021). They map a direction of travel towards growing government involvement in supporting and regulating private pension plans. Argentina went back to a pay-as-you-go defined benefit pension programme in 2008. Bolivia legislated to retain individual retirement savings plans but under a single public fund manager, although the reforms have not been fully implemented to date. In successive reforms, Chile has strengthened the budget-financed first pillar basic pension and offered publicly funded graduated incentives for individual savings plans for lower income groups. The 2007 financial crisis and the COVID19 pandemic have underlined individual retirement savings plans exposure to financial volatility.

Individual retirement savings plans have a role in the institutional architecture securing income security in old age, mainly as voluntary instruments open to workers with the capacity and desire to save for retirement. Promoting retirement savings is a sensible policy in the context of population ageing. Uruguay and Costa Rica offer examples of pension reforms making individual retirement savings plans mandatory for advantaged workers as a means to supplement defined benefit pension schemes that are mandatory for all (de Melo et al., 2019).

4.2.3 Pressure Points for Pension Provision

Measures of pension scheme participation in the labour force are informative of compliance with of labour market regulation, but they are less reliable as a measure of prospective old age income security. Employment volatility and the temporary nature of the employment relationship characteristic of countries in the region means that only a fraction of those currently participating in pension schemes will eventually manage to secure adequate entitlements. Research indicates that due to spells of unemployment and under-employment, job transitions, gaps in compliance and fraud, pension contribution density in the region is around 50% (Altamirano Montoya et al., 2018). Applying this figure linearly into the future suggests only one half of the workers currently participating in pension schemes will secure an adequate pension at retirement.

Pension participation decisions for disadvantaged workers is equivalent to an option value, the value of retaining options for the future. Design pension scheme features, especially those relating to the bottom line like vesting periods and minimum pension guarantees, become highly salient. In occupational pension schemes, minimum pension benefits are often easier to access and more generous than in individual retirement savings plans. In individual retirement plans vesting periods tend to be high, around twenty years of contributions. The implication is that for a significant proportion of those currently in the labour force participation in a pension scheme is best described as an option on the minimum pension benefit guarantee. The expansion of old age transfers, to be examined below, is also relevant to the bottom line. Perhaps the takeaway point is that, in the context of Latin America, reforms affecting the bottom line are hugely important.

Pension reform, and 're-reform', have generated a debate around the privateness-publicness of pension schemes (Mesa-Lago, 2020). Some researchers predicts a return of the state in pension provision (Carnes & Mares, 2015). The distinction between defined benefit and defined contribution pension schemes can overlap with the privateness-publicness spectrum (Mesa-Lago, 2020). But this can be exaggerated. As noted above, the 'first incorporation' in the 1950s and 1960s resulted in growing government involvement in occupational pension schemes.[9] Latin American governments have had since a significant stake in the design, implementation, and financing of occupational pension schemes, especially as no other institution could effectively manage and sustain a pay-as-you-go financing model. Governments also have a large stake in the design, implementation, and financing of individual retirement plans. Governments mandate contributions; set the financial, tax, and regulatory frameworks; and ensure minimum pension guarantees. Individual retirement plans are not feasible without government involvement. Government also provide or regulate minimum pension guarantees without which individual retirement plans would most likely fail in the context of volatile employment. The privateness-publicness of pension schemes in Latin America is not its defining dimension. Governments are firmly positioned in the pension business (Blinder, 1988).

[9] No country in the region has achieved Nordic universalism in their pension provision. The latter requires that all participants are un the same scheme under the same rules. Bismarckian stratification has proved hard to undo.

4.3 Social Assistance

Large scale social assistance provision emerged in the region following the decline of the neoliberal economic model and the return to democracy in the 1990s. It is associated with a 'second incorporation'. Two social protection instruments dominate the growth of social assistance in the region: old age and disability transfers and conditional income transfers to families.

Figure 4.3. shows the expansion of social assistance in the new century. It tracks the reach of social assistance and old age transfers over time. Reach measures as the share of direct and indirect beneficiaries of social assistance programmes. Direct beneficiaries are transfer recipients while indirect beneficiaries include other household members. Conditional income transfers explicitly support households. Old age transfers are paid

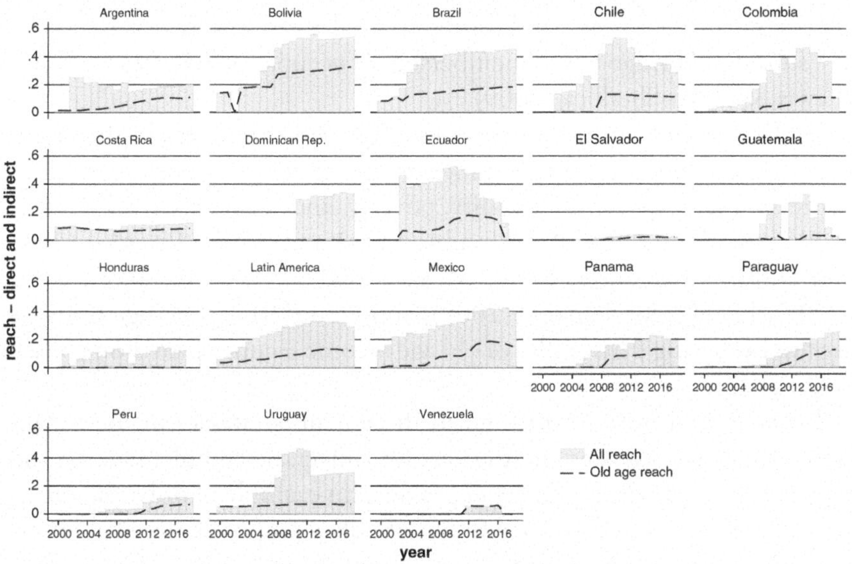

Fig. 4.3 Reach of social assistance. Notes: Reach is a measure of direct and indirect beneficiaries (co-residents). Data from CEPAL (2020) and Barrientos (2018). Estimate of the reach of Old age transfers constructed by applying average household size from UNDESA (2017) to direct recipient data

to qualifying older people but are shared within households. Reach is a more accurate measure of the population groups who benefit from social assistance transfers.

Table 4.3 provides an overview of current social assistance institutions by country, with information on expenditure levels, and age of entitlement and adequacy for old age transfers.

A discussion of key features of old age and conditional income transfers follows.

4.3.1 Old Age Transfers

Old age and disability transfers[10] were introduced early in the pioneer social protection countries. They were initially designed to complement or facilitate occupational insurance funds. Uruguay is credited with the first budget financed transfer programme for poor older. Brazil's FUNRURAL, introduced in the early 1970s to cater for informal workers in agriculture, mining and fishing in rural areas, was intended to serve as a subsidised bridge to full membership of occupational insurance funds (Lewis & Lloyd-Sherlock, 2009).

In the new century, most countries in the region have established budget financed old age transfer programmes as self-standing institutions addressing old age and disability poverty and vulnerability:[11] Bolivia (1996), Argentina (2003), Colombia (2003 and 2013), Ecuador (2003 and 2009), Guatemala (2005), Mexico (2007, 2012 and 2013), Chile (2008), El Salvador, Panama (2009), and Peru (2011). Old age transfers are fast becoming a first pillar of old age income security provision (Bosch et al., 2013).

Rofman et al. (2013) distinguish three main strategies in the expansion of old age transfers in the region: universal, complementary and targeted. Bolivia's *Renta Dignidad* provides an example of universal provision. It emerged in the mid 1990s out of policy proposals aimed at lowering public opposition to the privatisation of the energy sector, promising to redistribute dividends from partial public shareholding in the

[10] In the literature they are also described as social pensions or non-contributory pensions.

[11] The incidence of disability rises steeply in later age. It makes sense to combine old age and disability transfer programmes.

Table 4.3 Social assistance in Latin America—Programmes and budgets

Country	Old age transfers Programme year (start/last reform) (1)	Age (2)	Exp. % GDP 2015 (3)	Transfer %GDP pc 2016 (4)
Argentina	Pensión Universal para el Adulto Mayor 2018 Pensión no contributiva por vejez 1997 70+	65	0.79	30.9
Bolivia	Renta Dignidad 2008	60	1.25	19.3
Brazil	Beneficio de Prestacao Continuada 1994	65	0.12	0.33
Chile	Pension Basica Solidaria de Vejez 2008	65	0.39	11.8
Colombia	PPSAM 2003	57/52	0.15	8.1
Costa Rica	Regimen No Contributivo	65	0.45	20.2
Dominican Rep.				
Ecuador	Pension para Adultos Mayores 2009	65	0.4	10.1
El Salvador	Pension Basica Universal 2009	70	0.09	20.7
Guatemala	Aporte economico del Adulto Mayor 2005	65	0.9	14.9
Honduras				
Mexico	65 y mas 2012	65	0.21	4.5
Nicaragua				
Panama	100 a los 70 2009	70	0.34	11
Paraguay	Pension alimentaria 2010	65	0.39	17.6
Peru	Pension 65 2011	65	0.13	7.8
Uruguay	Pensiones no contributivas	70	0.53	21.5
Venezuela	Gran Mision Amor Mayor	60/55	0.12	38.7

Country	Conditional income transfers Current programmes (start year) (5)	Exp. % GDP 2015 (6)	Exp.% social protection 2015 (7)
Argentina	Asignación Universal por Hijo 2009	0.59	5.5
Bolivia	Bono Juancito Pinto 2006 Bono Madre Niño-Niña Juana Azurduy 2009	0.2	4.5
Brazil	Programa Bolsa Família 2003 Programa Bolsa Verde 2011 Programa de Erradicação do Trabalho Infantil 1996	0.5	5.2
Chile	Chile Solidario 2002 Ingreso Ético Familiar 2012	0.15	2.4
Colombia	Más Familias en Acción 2001 Red Unidos 2007	0.27	24.2
Costa Rica	Avancemos. 2006	0.17	6.1
Dominican Rep.	Progresando con Solidaridad. 2012	0.43	23.6

(*continued*)

Table 4.3 (continued)

Country	Conditional income transfers Current programmes (start year) (5)	Exp. % GDP 2015 (6)	Exp.% social protection 2015 (7)
Ecuador	Bono de Desarrollo Humano 2003	0.66	73.7
	Desnutrición Cero 2011		
El Salvador	Programa de Apoyo a Comunidades Solidarias 2005	0.24	23.4
Guatemala	Mi Bono Seguro. 2012	0.06	5
Honduras	Bono Vida Mejor 2010	0.2	30.7
Mexico	Prospera 2014 (discontinued in 2019)	0.23	7
Nicaragua			
Panama	Red de Oportunidades. 2006	0.1	8.2
	Bonos Familiares para la Compra de Alimentos 2005		
Paraguay	Tekopora 2005	0.22	4.5
	Abrazo 2005		
Peru	Juntos. 2005	0.43	7.7
Uruguay	Asignaciones Familiares – Plan de Equidad. 2008	0.39	5.7
	Tarjeta Uruguay Social. 2006		
Venezuela			

Notes: (1) (4) data sources from (OECD/IDB/The World Bank, 2014) updated from (Arenas de Mesa, 2019; Barrientos, 2018); (4)–(7) data sourced from (Barrientos, 2018; Cecchini & Atuesta, 2017)

privatised energy corporations. After several permutations, it became a budget financed transfer paid to all citizens over 60 years of age. In countries with large scale pension schemes - e.g., Argentina, Uruguay, Brazil, Chile -, old age transfers have a complementary role. They reach the older population without access to pension scheme benefits. Consideration of work and saving incentives usually restrict the generosity of complementary old age transfers. In countries with limited pension scheme provision – e.g., Colombia, Ecuador, El Salvador, Peru -, old age and disability transfers have a poverty reduction role and are targeted to vulnerable group. Access to transfers is dependent on socio-economic status re-assessed at specified intervals. The complementary and targeted strategies can be embedded in different programmes. In Brazil, *Previdência Social Rural*, a follow up to FUNRURAL, represents the complementary strategy while *Beneficio de Prestação Continuada* represents the poverty reduction strategy (Barrientos, 2013). Today people with disabilities account for a plurality of Beneficio de Prestação Continuada.[12]

The rapid expansion of old age and disability transfers, especially among women, in the region has greatly improved old age income security in the region (Barrientos, 2021).

4.3.2 Conditional Income Transfers

Conditional income transfers are the most significant innovation in social protection systems in the region. Brazil's *Bolsa Escola* and Mexico's *PROGRESA* (Programme for the Advancement of Health and Education) are the pioneer programmes (Levy, 2006; Rocha, 2013). Introduced in mid-1990s they became large scale social assistance programmes providing regular and reliable transfers to families in poverty or at risk of falling into poverty. Transfers are conditional on children's schooling and on household's primary health care utilisation. All three core features of conditional income transfers, they are budget financed family subsidies, with a social investment orientation, are significant innovations in the context of Latin America (Barrientos, 2019). Conditional income transfers also reflect a fourth, crucial, innovation: Latin American governments' newfound commitment to poverty reduction.

Between 1997 and 2006 conditional income transfers spread to all countries in the region. As expected, conditional income transfer programmes show diversity in design, scope and implementation (Cecchini & Madariaga, 2011a; Fiszbein & Schady, 2009; Ibarrarán et al., 2017). They are rules-based in the sense that entry and exit from the programme, and entitlements, follow the application of pre-established rules. Entry conditions are based on household demographics, the presence of children of school age for example, and socio-economic conditions. The latter is assessed via income or proxy means tests. Participant households' compliance with programme conditions ensure the continuation of the transfers. Administration of programme conditions necessitates coordination between the programme agency and education and primary health

[12] Children are a large proportion of beneficiaries, lowering the average age of Beneficio de Prestação Continuada beneficiaries. This is often misunderstood in policy discussions as it is taken to imply laxed entry administration.

care providers. Some countries like Mexico enforced conditions with greater regularity and force, whereas in countries like Brazil non-compliance with conditions served as an indicator that further support was needed. Transfers are mostly fixed in value and are paid through financial providers. Transfer values are a fraction of the poverty line, with the implication that conditional transfers are intended as a contribution towards improving household finances. They are not intended to lift recipients out of poverty by themselves.[13] There are no labour supply restrictions associated with the receipt of the transfer.[14]

Programme designers paid more attention to entry conditions than to exit conditions. In fact, initially most programmes simply applied entry conditions to assess conditions for exit. This has not worked well (Barrientos & Villa, 2017). Changes in employment due to labour market volatility are perhaps the most significant factor pushing people into poverty. Consequently, the socio-economic conditions of a large proportion of low income families oscillate around the levels required by entry conditions. Families exiting the programme because they fail to meet entry conditions may soon find themselves meeting them. It makes sense to implement exit conditions to take account of labour market volatility. Brazil's *Bolsa Família* guarantees transfers for two years after entry. Colombia's *Más Familias en Acción* offers a reduced level of transfer support for families unable to meet entry conditions but remaining vulnerable. This support helps them smooth out exit from the programme (Barrientos & Villa, 2017).

The process of assessing entry conditions involves collecting data from current and potential participants. It led to the development of beneficiary databases available to programme agencies. There are two types of database. Participant registers collect information on current participants. Social registers collect information on current and potential participants. Governments in the region normally offer several public programmes supporting disadvantaged households including, for example, interventions in

[13] Conditional income transfers are around 20% of participant household income, Attuesta and Cecchini (2017) calculate that they deliver around US$ 150 per person per year on average for the region. Arenas de Mesa (2019) estimates that old age transfers are around 17.7% of GDP per capita on average for the region.

[14] This applies to old age and disability transfer too.

education, health, housing, etc. They used to involve separate registers and entry conditions. It made sense to consolidate these registers into a single social register, covering the population at risk of poverty. Colombia's SISBEN collects information on all households applying for any public programme. As the social registers grew, they provided governments with essential information on the target population for a variety of social policies. Social registers have been crucial to government policy addressing COVID19 (Berner & van Hemelryck, 2020).

Mexico's *PROGRESA* was introduced in the context of a financial crisis and against the opposition of pre-existing poverty programme (Levy, 2006). The designers of the programme included well-defined evaluation protocols to protect its initial development. By collecting a baseline, and follow up, household surveys and by exploiting a phased implementation, it became possible to compare outcomes for early and late entrants. Demonstrating the effectiveness of anti-poverty transfer programmes helped mitigate political opposition to the programme (Skoufias, 2005). Quasi-experimental impact evaluation studies have become the norm for conditional income transfers, generating valuable information on their effectiveness. They have contributed to the experimental turn in economic development (Banerjee & Duflo, 2011). Monitoring and evaluation protocols stand out as a very significant innovation in social assistance.

The evolution of conditional income transfer programmes over time in Latin America suggests three interesting trends.

First, conditional income transfers link programme agencies with the, often more powerful, ministries of education and health. Linking transfers in cash with access to basic services is central to the social investment orientation of these programmes (Barrientos, 2022). Inter-agency coordination can lead to improved access to a wider range of services and intermediation by conditional income transfer beneficiaries. Income transfers prove effective for most participant households, but some participants may require more specialised and direct forms of support. *Chile Solidario* was designed around dedicated household support (Barrientos, 2010). It has promoted the integrating income transfers and service provision to address inclusion barriers for poorest households.

Second, over time conditional income transfers have developed from fixed-term programmes into permanent government institutions.

Institutionalisation involves the establishment of social development agencies or ministries with parliament sanctioned budgets and legal oversight and operating frameworks (Székely, 2015). The evolution from interventions to institutions is not yet complete in less developed countries in the region (Cecchini & Madariaga, 2011b).

Third, conditional income transfers pose longer term policy dilemmas in need of future resolution. Some of these policy dilemmas have been covered in the discussion above: the definition of programme exits; the appropriate balance between protection and investment; their impact of growing social assistance institutionalisation on other parts of government; their linkages to occupational insurance. Conditional income transfers have unfolded against a sustained improvement in living standards and poverty levels in the region. The more developed countries in the region have evolved conditional income transfers into permanent support for less advantaged families with children. Argentina's *Asignación Unica por Hijo* is perhaps a case in point as it concluded a policy shift from emergency public works to conditional income transfers to child benefit (Gasparini & Cruces, 2010). On becoming President of Mexico, Lopez Obrador rescinded the long standing conditional income transfer (*Progresa, Oportunidades, Prospera*) are replaced it with scholarship programmes (Huesca Reynoso et al., 2020).[15] This pathway leans towards a stronger social investment orientation for social assistance.

4.4 Secondary Programmes

The discussion in this chapter has focused on the main programmes providing pension benefits and social assistance transfers. In practice, some countries have implemented a range of complementary programmes. A brief discussion of unemployment protection, family benefits and active labour market programmes follows.

With few exceptions, social protection in Latin American countries have not implemented large scale programmes against unemployment. Latin American countries have sought to protect jobs, not workers.

[15] The short-term distributional effects of replacing Mexico's *Prospera* with scholarship programmes are not progressive (INDESIG, 2021).

Severance pay regulations raise the costs of worker separation for employers by mandating compensation to affected workers. This is normally a lump sum reflecting years of service and other parameters. They are widely considered to be inadequate in terms of providing insurance for workers (Holzmann & Vodopivec, 2012). Because only a minority of workers are employed in firms that comply with employment regulations, severance pay is restricted in its application. Severance pay regulations "encourage stratified labor markets and impose barriers in employee's mobility and the firm's adjustment to changing labor market conditions" (Ferrer & Riddell, 2011, p. 1). They are consistent with import substitutions policies restricting competition in selected sectors. Severance pay regulations were always expected to apply selectively.

Unemployment insurance schemes are hard to implement successfully in labour market conditions such as those prevailing in Latin America. In conditions where a significant share of the labour force is self-employed or have weak and volatile employment relationships, programmes providing income protection for workers affected by unemployment are undermined by potential moral hazard. There are few examples of unemployment insurance programmes implemented early in the region (Velásquez Pinto, 2010). Argentina set up a scheme for construction workers in 1975. Panama introduced a scheme in 1972 for selected groups of workers. Brazil introduced the *Fondo de Garantia por tiempo de servicio* in 1967 and a second one, the *Fondo de Amparo al Trabajador*, in 1986. Other countries implemented partial unemployment insurance schemes in the 1990S. They include (start date): Ecuador (mixed 2001); Peru (1991); and Venezuela (1997). They have very limited coverage, as they exclude workers with weak job attachment, rural and urban informal workers, and public sector workers. In practice, they cover the workers least likely to experience unemployment. They are financed by a mix of employee and employer payroll contributions and attract government financial support.

Interest in unemployment insurance rose in the 2000s as individual retirement savings plans offered a ready-made infrastructure to collect workers' dedicated unemployment savings. Colombia (1990), Chile (2002) and Ecuador (2002) established unemployment savings plans solely on worker savings. Sehnbruch et al. (2020) offer an analysis of Chile's programme, using a sample of administrative records. They conclude that the programme has limited coverage among workers most likely to need it. Only 11.8% of workers with open ended contracts were entitled to make a claim and only 6.7% made a claim. Among fixed term contract workers, the relevant figures are 2.3% and 0.9% respectively. The low share of successful claims is due to the high level of job rotation (Gualavisi & Oliveri, 2016). An attempt to introduce an element of redistribution across participants did not fare well, "…the solidarity fund embedded in the system, which was originally supposed to redistribute funds towards lower income workers, does exactly the opposite" (Sehnbruch et al., 2020, p. 27).

As Bertranou and Maurizio (2011) conclude "…contributory-based unemployment insurance has not been fully developed in Latin America…This is mainly due to the high levels of informality (since these programmes have been designed to protect wage earners that hold a formal job, generally under a permanent contract) … and, to a lesser extent, to the occupational instability of workers in the formal market. Although these systems receive contributions from workers, they tend to depend on fiscal revenues, be it through regular contributions or indirectly when the State has to cover its operational deficits" (Bertranou & Maurizio, 2011, p. 17). Unemployment insurance schemes have not been successful in the region. They show the same limitations as the pension schemes their design is borrowed from, whether occupational pensions or individual retirement savings plans.

Active labour market policies are a component of social protection growing in significance in the region, albeit from a low base (Escudero et al., 2019). Active labour market policies consist of distinct main policies addressing unemployment: training programmes offering an upgrade in skills; public works and employment subsidies providing short term work to the unemployed; microenterprise development; and labour market intermediation. Their main objective is to raise employment. In the context of Latin America, active labour market policies are in the main oriented to low paid workers who are more likely to be affected by unemployment. While there are countries with large scale training infrastructure like Brazil financed from payroll taxes and with centralised governance, recent activation policies are more likely to complement participation in social assistance programmes (ECLAC/ILO, 2014) with which they share a social investment orientation (Barrientos, 2022).

Escudero et al. (2019) offer a meta-analysis of impact evaluations of active labour market policies in the region. They find that three quarters of the programmes studies focus on training. They are followed by initiatives to strengthen private sector incentives and labour market intermediation. Programmes have relatively short duration, less than 9 months. The impact of the programmes on employment is stronger for women and young workers, and for low-income workers. They find that activation programmes generally have stronger effects in the short-term.

Rossel (2013) offers a comprehensive review of family policies in Latin America. All countries in the region have regulations on maternity license and subsidies, but there is considerable variation across countries in the reach and generosity of their provision. The relevant legislation excludes several categories of workers so that in practice entitlements are only available to workers with permanent open ended employment contracts. Conditional income transfers reach low income and informal population groups, but their support for families is often limited to children and mothers.

Overall, this brief discussion of complementary social protection programmes confirms the main findings extracted from the examination of the main programmes as regards the structure and orientation of institutions in the region.

4.5 Conclusions

This chapter has examined the three main social protection institutions in Latin America countries: occupational pensions, individual retirement savings plans, and social assistance. It discussed the core features of each of these institutions, offering a perspective on their manifestation in each of the countries in the region as well as a more analytical assessment of their institutional scope and logic. This is necessary grounding for the study of their stratification effects to come in the next chapters.

In essence, social protection institutions can be arranged into two. Insurance-based institutions collect contributions from employees or citizens and compensate them in the event they are afflicted by pre-specified contingencies. Assistance based institutions funded from government revenues and providing income transfers to citizens affected by poverty and vulnerability. These two sets of institutions are involved respectively in horizontal redistribution, transferring income for the same people in different circumstances or stages of the line course, or alternatively vertical redistribution, transferring income from better off to worse off citizens. The bases of entitlements are respectively group membership and citizenship.

Current Latin America institutions show some adjustment to the two sets of institutions, and an addition.

Insurance-based institutions in Latin America are restricted to selected groups of workers, mainly skilled workers in large firms. They are also highly fragmented, despite governments attempts to streamline their governance. They are strongly dependent on public subsidies, although the level of subsidies is increasingly contested. If in their original designs, occupational insurance funds covered a wide range of contingencies, current occupational insurance is primarily focused on old age. This is in part due to the demographic transition, but it is also due to the politics of social protection, the fact that occupational insurance in Latin America is a stratification mechanism.[16] Recent trends in labour force participation in occupational insurance largely suggest stagnation during this century. Keeping in mind that participation rates significantly underestimate the share of participants who will secure adequate pension benefits at retirement, occupational insurance institutions in the region fail to guarantee income security in later age except for a selective group of workers. Occupational insurance is stronger in early industrialising countries and weak in the rest.

Social assistance greatly expanded in the new century. All Latin American countries implemented conditional income transfers, some countries did so to scale. Most countries have implemented large scale old age transfers or have strengthen pre-existing provision. By 2015, social assistance transfers reached around one third of the population in the region. The expansion of social assistance has involved a welcomed upgrade in institutional capacity. Conditional income transfers diffused rules-based programming, social registries, monitoring and evaluation, and evidence-based policy

[16] See Lynch (2006) for a discussion of the politics of pro-old welfare states. A discussion of the politics of occupational insurance in Latin America follows in the Incorporation chapter.

throughout the region. There is closer institutional harmonisation in social assistance than in occupational insurance in the region, bar outliers like Nicaragua and Venezuela. Argentina and Brazil provide contrasting examples of social assistance institutional transition.

Social protection institutions in Latin America contribute an additional set of institutions: individual retirement savings plans. They are neither grounded in insurance nor in assistance, but instead in individual saving capacity. They have not been implemented throughout the region. They show three distinct institutional settings. In Colombia and Peru, individual retirement savings plans compete with occupational insurance. In Costa Rica and Uruguay, they complement occupational insurance for advantaged workers. In the rest of the countries that have adopted them, a transition process will make them the sole mandated retirement income institution. Individual retirement savings plans have not proved successful in the region, and it is fair to say their institutional structures are in transition.

References

Altamirano Montoya, A., Berstein, S., Bosch, M., & García Huitrón, M. (2018). *Presente y futuro de las pensiones en América Latina y el Caribe*. Inter-American Development Bank.

Arenas de Mesa, A. (2019). *Los sistemas de pensiones en la encrucijada. Desafíos para la sostenibilidad en América Latina* (159; Libros de La CEPAL). Comisión Económica para América Latina y el Caribe.

Arenas de Mesa, A. (2020). *Los sistemas de pensiones en América Latina. Institucionalidad, gasto público y sostenibilidad financiera en tiempos de COVID-19* (Documento 212; Macroeconomía Del Desarrollo). Economic Commission for Latin America.

Arza, C. (2017). Non-contributory benefits, pension re-reforms and the social protection of older women in Latin America. *Social Policy and Society, 16*(3), 361–375.

Asociación Internacional de Organismos de Supervisión de Fondos de Pensiones. (2019). *Boletín Estadístico—December 2019* [Boletín Estadístico]. AIOS.

Asociación Internacional de Organismos de Supervisión de Fondos de Pensiones. (2022). *Boletín Estadístico—December 2021* [Boletín Estadístico]. AIOS.

Baldwin, P. (1990). *The politics of social solidarity. Class bases of the European welfare state 1875-1975*. Cambridge University Press.

Banerjee, A. V., & Duflo, E. (2011). *Poor economics. A radical rethinking of the way to fight global poverty*. Public Affairs.

Barrientos, A. (1998a). *Pension reform in Latin America*. Ashgate.

Barrientos, A. (1998b). Pension reform, personal pensions and gender differences in pension coverage. *World Development, 26*(1), 125–137.

Barrientos, A. (1999). The emerging pension fund management market in Latin America. *Journal of Pensions Management, 5*(1), 60–68.

Barrientos, A. (2010). Protecting capabilities, eradicating extreme poverty: Chile Solidario and the future of social protection. *Journal of Human Development and Capabilities, 11*(4), 579–597.

Barrientos, A. (2013). The rise of social assistance in Brazil. *Development and Change, 44*(4), 887–910.

Barrientos, A. (2018). *Social Assistance in Low and Middle Income Countries Dataset (SALMIC)*. Global Development Institute, University of Manchester. www.social-assistance.manchester.ac.uk

Barrientos, A. (2019). Conditional income transfers, social policy and development. In J. Midgley, R. Surender, & L. Alfers (Eds.), *Handbook of social policy and development* (pp. 373–392). Edward Elgar.

Barrientos, A. (2021). Inequalities in income security in later age in Latin America. *Pan American Journal of Public Health, 45*. https://doi.org/10.26633/RPSP.2021.85

Barrientos, A. (2022). Social investment and social assistance in Low- and Middle-income countries. In J. Garritzmann, S. Häusermann, & B. Palier (Eds.), *The world politics of social investment* (Vol. 1, pp. 173–193). Oxford University Press.

Barrientos, A., & Villa, J. M. (2017). *The impact of eligibility recertification on households excluded from an antipoverty programme* (Technical Note IDB-TN-1316). Inter-American Development Bank.

Berner, H., & van Hemelryck, T. (2020). *Sistemas de información social y registros de destinatarios de la protección social no contributiva en America Latina* (Documentos de Proyectos LC/TS.2020/140). CEPAL. https://www.cepal.org/es/publicaciones/46452-sistemas-informacion-social-registros-destinatarios-la-proteccion-social

Bertranou, F., Casalí, P., & Cetràngolo, O. (2018). *A mitad de camino entre Bismarck y Beveridge? La persistencia de los dilemas en el sistema previsional argentino* (OIT Cono Sur - Informes Técnicos 9). OIT.

Bertranou, F., & Maurizio, R. (2011). *The role of the labour market and social protection in reducing inequality and eradicating poverty in Latin America*. ILO.

Blinder, A. S. (1988). Why is the Government in the pension business? In S. M. Watcher (Ed.), *Social security and private pensions. Providing for Retirement in the 21st Century*. Lexington Books.

Bosch, M., Melguizo, A., & Pages, C. (2013). *Mejores pensiones, mejores trabajos*. Inter-American Development Bank.

CAF. (2020). *Los sistemas de pensiones y salud en América Latina. Los desafíos del envejecimiento, el cambio tecnológico y la informalidad*. Corporación Andina de Fomento.

Carnes, M., & Mares, I. (2015). Explaining the "return of the state" in middle-income countries: Employment vulnerability, incomes, and preferences for social protection in Latin America. *Politics and Society, 43*(4), 525–550.

Carrera, L., & Angelaki, M. (2021). Bringing back the state: Understanding varieties of pension re-reforms in Latin America. *Latin American Politics and Society, 63*(4), 22–44. https://doi.org/10.1017/lap.2021.36

Castiglioni, R. (2005). *The politics of social policy change in Chile and Uruguay*. Routledge.

Cecchini, S., & Atuesta, B. (2017). *Programas de transferencias condicionadas en América Latina y el Caribe* (Report 224; Series Politicas Sociales). CEPAL, División Desarrollo Social.

Cecchini, S., & Madariaga, A. (2011a). *Conditional cash transfer programmes. The recent experience in Latin America and the Caribbean* (Report LC/G.2497-P). ECLAC. https://papers.ssrn.com/sol3/papers.cfm?abstract_id=1962666

Cecchini, S., & Madariaga, A. (2011b). *La trayectoria de los programas de transferencia con corresponsabilidad (PCT) en América Latina y el Caribe* [Report]. CEPAL.

CEDLAS, & World Bank. (2012). *Socio-Economic Database for Latin America and the Caribbean*. CEDLAS.

CEPAL. (2020). *Base de datos de programas de protección social no contributiva en América Latin y el Caribe* [Database]. ECLAC, División de Desarrollo Social. https://dds.cepal.org/bpsnc/inicio

de Melo, G., Catiñeiras, N., Ardente, A., Montti, O., Zelko, B., & Araya, F. (2019). Eligibility for retirement and replacement rates in the Uruguayan multi-pillar pension system. *Revista Sociedad y Desarrollo, 83*, 105–144.

Dorlach, T. (2020). Business interests, Conservative economists, and the expansion of non-contributory pensions in Latin America. *Politics and Society, online*, 1–24.

ECLAC/ILO. (2014). *The employment situation in Latin America and the Caribbean. Conditional cash transfer programmes and the labour market* (10). ECLAC.

Edwards, S. (1996). *The Chilean Pension Reform: A Pioneering Program* (Working Paper 5811). National Bureau of Economic Research.

Escudero, V., Kluve, J., López Mourelo, E., & Pignatti, C. (2019). Active labour market programmes in Latin America and the Caribbean: Evidence from a meta-analysis. *Journal of Development Studies, 55*(12), 2644–2661.
Eslava, M., Meléndez, M., & Urdaneta, N. (2021). *Market concentration, market fragmentation, and inequality in Latin America* (Working Paper 11; UNDP LAC Working Paper). UNDP.
Fairfield, T., & Garay, C. (2017). Redistribution under the right in Latin America: Electoral competition and organized actors in policy making. *Comparative Political Studies, 50*(14), 1871–1906.
Ferrer, A. M., & Riddell, W. C. (2011). *Unemployment insurance savings accounts in Latin America: Overview and assessment* (Discussion Paper 5577; IZA Discussion Paper). IZA - Institute of Labor Economics.
Fiszbein, A., & Schady, N. (2009). *Conditional cash transfers. Reducing present and future poverty*. The World Bank.
Garay, C. (2021). Including outsiders in Latin America. In D. Kapiszewski, S. Levitsky, & D. J. Yashar (Eds.), *The inclusionary turn in Latin American democracies* (pp. 59–92). Cambridge University Press.
Gasparini, L. C., & Cruces, G. (2010). Las asignaciones universales por hijo en Argentina: Impacto, discusión y alternativas. *Económica, LVI*, 145–186. http://econpapers.repec.org/article/lapjournl/573.htm
Gill, I. S., Packard, T., & Yermo, J. (2004). *Keeping the Promise of Social Security in Latin America*. Stanford University Press and the World Bank.
Gualavisi, M., & Oliveri, M. L. (2016). *Antigüedad en el Empleo y Rotación Laboral en América Latina* (Nota Técnica IDB-TN-1072). Inter-American Development Bank. https://publications.iadb.org/publications/spanish/document/Antig%C3%BCedad-en-el-empleo-y-rotaci%C3%B3n-laboral-en-Am%C3%A9rica-Latina.pdf
Holzmann, R., & Vodopivec, M. (Eds.). (2012). *Reforming Severance Pay. An international perspective*. The World Bank.
Huesca Reynoso, L., Martínez-Martínez, O., & Velázquez Leyer, R. (2020). Reconfiguring social policy from the "left" in Mexico: So far, not so good? *Latin American Policy*.
Ibarrarán, P., Medellín, N., Regalia, F., & Stampini, M. (2017). *How conditional cash transfers work. Good practices after 20 years of implementation*. Inter-American Development Bank.
ILO. (2021). *World Social Protection Report 2020-22*. International Labour Office.
IMF. (2018). *Growing pains. Is Latin America prepared for population aging?* (Report 18/05). International Monetary Fund. https://www.imf.org/en/Publications/Departmental-Papers-Policy-Papers/Issues/2018/04/16/Growing-Pains-Is-Latin-American-Prepared-for-Population-Aging-45382

INDESIG. (2021). *Análisis preliminar de resultados de la Encuesta de Ingreso y Gasto de los Hogares (2020) desde un enfoque de desigualdad y redistribución*. Instituto de Estudios sobre Desigualdad. https://bit.ly/3zPq9ae

Kay, S. J., & Borzutzky, S. (2022). Can defined contribution pensions survive the pandemic? The Chilean case. *International Social Security Review, 75*, 31–50.

Levy, S. (2006). *Progress against Poverty. Sustaining Mexico's Progresa-Oportunidades Program*. Brookings Institution Press.

Lewis, C., & Lloyd-Sherlock, P. (2009). Social policy and economic development in South America: An historical approach to social insurance. *Economy and Society, 38*(1), 109–131.

Lynch, J. (2006). *Age in the Welfare State. The origins of social spending on pensioners, workers, and children*. Cambridge University Press.

Marx, I., & Nelson, K. (2012). *Minimum income protection in flux*. Palgrave.

Mesa-Lago, C. (1989). *Ascent to Bankruptcy: Financing social security in Latin America*. University of Pittsburgh Press.

Mesa-Lago, C. (2007). *Reassembling social security. A survey of pensions and healthcare reforms in Latin America*. Oxford University Press.

Mesa-Lago, C. (2020). *Evaluación de cuatro décadas de privatización de pensiones en América Latina (1980-2020): Promesas y realidades* [Report]. Fundación Friedrich Ebert en México.

OECD/IDB/The World Bank. (2014). *Pensions at a glance: Latin America and the Caribbean*. OECD Publishings.

Orszag, P. R., & Stiglitz, J. E. (1999). *Rethinking pension reform: Ten myths about social security systemes [Mimeo]*. The World Bank.

Ranaldi, M., & Milanovic, B. (2020). *Capitalist systems and income inequality* (Stone Center on Socio-Economic Inequality). [Working Paper]. City University of New York. https://stonecenter.gc.cuny.edu/research/capitalist-systems-and-income-inequality/

Rocha, S. (2013). *Transferencias de renda no Brasil. O Fim da pobreza?* Elsevier.

Rofman, R., Apella, I., & Vezza, E. (2013). *Mas alla de las pensiones contributivas. Catorce experiencias en America Latina* [Report]. The World Bank.

Rofman, R., & Oliveri, M. L. (2012). *Pension coverage in Latin America: Trends and determinants* (Social Protection & Labour Discussion Paper 1217). The World Bank.

Rossel, C. (2013). *Politicas para las familias en America Latina: Panorama de políticas de reduccion de pobreza y reconciliacion entre trabajo-familia* [Mimeo]. Universidad Catolica del Uruguay.

Sehnbruch, K., Carranza, R., & Contreras, D. (2020). *Unemployment Insurance in Chile: Lessons from a High Inequality Developing Country* (Working Paper 54; III Working Paper Series). London School of Economics.

Skoufias, E. (2005). *Progresa and its impacts on the welfare of rural households in Mexico*. International Food Policy Research Institute.
Székely, M. (2015). *Cambios en la institucionalidad de la política de protección social en América Latina y el Caribe: Avances y nuevos desafíos* (Nota Técnica 810). Inter-American Development Bank.
UNDESA. (2017). *Household Size and composition around the world 2017—Data Booklet* (Data Booklet ST/ESA/SER.A/405). United National Department of Economic and Social Affairs, Population Division.
Valdés-Prieto, S. (2009). *The 2008 Chilean pension reform to first pillar pensions* (Working Paper 2520). CESIFO.
Varian, H. R. (1980). Redistributive taxation as social insurance. *Journal of Public Economics, 14*, 49–68.
Velásquez Pinto, M. (2010). *Seguros de desempleo y reformas recientes en América Latina* (Working Paper LC/L.3144-P; Macroeconomía Del Desarrollo). CEPAL.
Villatoro, P., & Cecchini, S. (2018). *¿Cuál es el alcance de las transferencias no-contributivas en América Latina?* (Estudios Estadísticos 96; Serie Estudios Estadísticos). CEPAL, División de Desarrollo Social.
World Bank. (1994). *Averting the old age crisis: Policies to protect the old and promote growth*. Oxford University Press.

5

Employment

This chapter studies the stratification effects of social protection institutions on employment, the first of the three main causal effects identified.

The literature on social protection and employment has explored their linkages in detail in Latin America. Perhaps the salient characteristic of employment in the region is the large share of workers in informal employment. They include independent workers and dependent workers in small enterprises. Workers in informal employment lack access to pension schemes. In fact, common measures of informality are the residual of measures of participation in pension plans, whether in occupational insurance funds or in individual retirement savings plans. Informality is defined by the selective reach of social protection. There is broad consensus on the close correlation existing between employment status and participation in pension plans.

Consensus breaks down when the issue is to identify the direction of causality in the relationship between social protection institutions and the structure of employment. The conventional view is that the structure of employment places hard restrictions on the reach of pension schemes. Own account workers may have few incentives to participate in pension schemes if their pay flickers around a subsistence level and their

A. Barrientos, *Social Protection in Latin America*, Global Dynamics of Social Policy ,
https://doi.org/10.1007/978-3-031-49795-7_5

employment is precarious. Skilled workers with stable employment and good pay have strong incentives to participate in pension plans offering high and subsidised replacement rates on retirement. It is possible to turn the direction of causality around and make a case that social protection institutions contribute to the stratification of employment. Occupational insurance plans support skilled workers in good jobs. Large firms employing skilled workers might find it advantageous to offer occupational pension schemes for the purposes of enhancing productivity incentives as well as recruitment and retention. Proponents of individual retirement savings plans argued that removing the redistributive features of occupational pensions altogether would encourage job mobility and improve productivity. Levy argues that the overlap between insurance and assistance generates incentives for informality (Levy, 2008; Levy & Cruces, 2021). Arguments in favour of decoupling protection from employment status, as in social assistance or minimum guaranteed income proposals, aim to moderate the employment stratification effects of social protection institutions (Barrientos, 2009, 2012).

The framework developed in Chap. 3 distinguishes the period associated with the emergence of occupational insurance funds from the subsequent periods when social protection institutions are in place. The framework hypothesises that the process of industrialisation and the associated emergence of an urban working class was a causal factor in the eventual expansion of occupational insurance funds. The first incorporation led to the emergence of state-sanctioned occupational insurance funds. The direction of causality runs from changes in the employment structure to the emergence of social protection institutions. Research on social protection since has continued to assume the same direction of causality applies. Research and policy studies of social protection in Latin America often ascribes the perceived limitations of social protection institutions to primordial employment structures, e.g. the persistence of informality, the size of the middle class, reliance on primary production, scarcity of skilled work, or the size structure of firms (Bertranou &

Marinakis, 2020; Carnes & Mares, 2015; Eslava et al., 2021; Schneider, 2013). Social protection institutions are the dependent variable.[1]

The discussion in this chapter offers an alternative take on the direction of causality following the establishment of social protection institutions. Industrialisation did cause the emergence of social protection institutions in Latin America, and elsewhere. However, when these institutions are in place, they exert observable influence on the employment structure, as well on protection and incorporation. The discussion below focuses on an examination of the causal influence of social protection institutions on employment. As the materials discussed demonstrate, reversing the direction of causality is justified. Social protection institutions are a stratification mechanism. They influence the structure of employment, the pattern of employment relationships, and the productivity of employment. In fact, examining the influence of social protection institutions on employment adds to our understanding of both and provide new insights into the nature of social protection in the region.

The structure of the chapter is as follows. Section 5.1 discusses the direction of causality in more detail. Sections 5.2, 5.3, and 5.4 respectively on *Industrialisation*, *Limited Fordism*, and *Earnings* deals with occupational insurance funds. Sections 5.5, 5.6, and 5.7 respectively on *Tertiarisation*, the *Knowledge economy*, and *Global production networks* discuss the influence of neoliberal and post-neoliberal social protection reforms on changes in employment. A final section concludes.

5.1 Social Protection and Employment: Direction of Causality

Current theories of welfare institutions emphasise the distribution of employment and jobs as a dominant factor explaining the configuration of social protection institutions. This approach is rooted in the view that modern social protection institutions can be traced back to industrialisation. Compared to the diversified livelihoods experienced in rural areas

[1] Power resources and new institutional theories of welfare states share this approach (Korpi, 2006; Pierson, 2001), including when studying late industrialisers (Gough & Therborn, 2010).

with subsistence agriculture as a fallback, employment in urban industrialised economies is binary. Workers are either employed or unemployed. Unemployment has direct implications for their wellbeing (Atkinson, 1989). The emergence of mutual assistance and public assistance is therefore a consequence of industrialisation. From this perspective, social protection institutions move in lockstep with changes in employment, such that changes in the latter will inevitably bring about change in the former. Social protection policy debates often begin by examining changes to the structure of employment over time before moving on to identify policies appropriate to addressing the outcome arising from employment change (Bertranou & Marinakis, 2020; ILO, 1972).[2] From this perspective, the structure of employment, and associated socio-economic outcomes, can explain the dynamics of welfare institutions.

In practice, once institutions are in place, their weaknesses or resilience feedbacks into employment, raising the potentially autonomous role of institutions in reinforcing or preventing change. These approaches grant social protection some policy autonomy. A very influential approach can be traced to Polanyi's (1957) masterly analysis of capitalism. Polanyi argued that capitalism and social protection had distinct and conflicting logics. Capitalism is dominated by a logic of commodification. The forced extension of commodification to non-commodities like labour and land was essential to sustain the accumulation of capital. Social protection institutions emerged to address the resulting fractures: the impact of accumulation on the destruction of the environment and the threats to social reproduction enforced on workers because of a race to the bottom on wages. Polanyi argued that social protection was directed by the logic of solidarity, in contradistinction to the logic of commodification at the core of capital accumulation. Social protection institutions prevent the internal dynamics of capitalism from leading to its destruction. Polanyi described this process eloquently as a double helix, in which one, or the

[2] See Bertranou and Maurizio's assessment: "...contributory-based unemployment insurance has not been fully developed in Latin America...This is mainly due to the high levels of informality (since these programmes have been designed to protect wage-earners that hold a formal job, generally under a permanent contract) ... and, to a lesser extent, to the occupational instability of workers in the formal market. Although these systems receive contributions from workers, they tend to depend on fiscal revenues, be it through regular contributions or indirectly when the State has to cover its operational deficits" (Bertranou & Maurizio, 2011), p. 17.

other, logic came to dominate social processes at times. Social protection came to the forefront when capitalism was threatened by crises. Commodification, taken to its limits, results in crises and is rescued by a reassertion of social protection institutions. It is hard not to note the social-democratic overtones in this dualism. Note that in the Polanyi approach, social protection and commodification have independent dynamics, one is called to dominate only when the other has reached its (temporary) limits.

The present work proposes an alternative perspective. It supports the view that industrialisation gives birth to social protection. This is the case in Latin America. Industrialisation resulted in the spread of Bismarckian occupational insurance funds. However, the expansion of social protection institutions in the region does not originate in solidaristic values, independent of the structure of production and employment, as argued by Polanyi. Social protection institutions originate in changes in the employment structure associated with industrialisation. However, once social protection institutions are in place, they stand in a causal relationship with employment. Social protection institutions help regulate the very structure of employment, not just its consequential welfare outcomes.[3] They contribute to regulate the scale of available employment, the distribution of skills and productive quality of employment. Social protection institutions have observable effects on employment stratification. Now causality goes from social protection institutions to employment, not the other way around.

5.2 Industrialisation and Social Protection Expansion

The emergence of social protection institutions in Latin America in the middle of the twentieth century is explained by industrialisation. Figure 5.1 shows estimates of the ratio of gross value added in industry to gross value added in agriculture in the 'long' century. The data are sourced

[3] Social protection institutions effects in welfare outcomes and on political inclusion will be discussed in detail in the next two chapters.

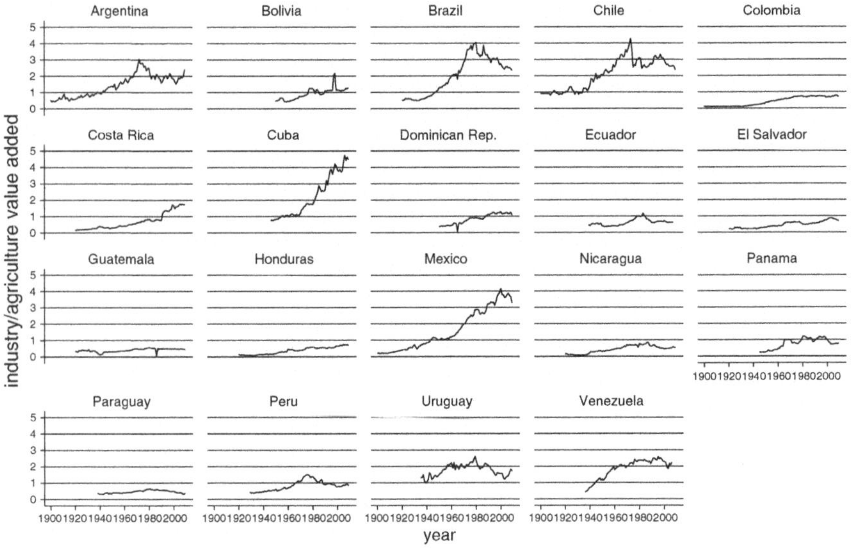

Fig. 5.1 Industrialisation in Latin America. Data source: MOxLAD (MOxLAD, n.d.)

from the Montevideo-Oxford Latin American Economic History database (MOxLAD, n.d.). The figure offers a visual perspective on the timing and intensity of industrialisation across countries in the region.

Taking Argentina as an example, the figure shows a gradual rise in the ratio beginning from the turn of the twentieth century, followed by an acceleration between the 1940s to the 1970s, with a decline and stagnation in the subsequent period. Brazil, Chile, Mexico, and Cuba show a roughly similar trend, rapid and deeper industrialisation in the mid-century period, followed by decline and stagnation. The decline after the 1970s peak has been attributed to premature de-industrialisation (Rodrik, 2016) but it also likely to reflect significant productivity improvements in agriculture, a measure of catch-up (Nin-Pratt & Valdés Conroy, 2020).

In Uruguay and Venezuela, and to some extent Panama, Peru, and Bolivia, the rise in industrial gross value added relative to agriculture is less pronounced, and peaks at a lower level. It is closer to an inverted 'U' than the inverted 'V' shown by the first group of countries. Central American countries, as well as Paraguay and Ecuador, show late and only very limited industrialisation. Costa Rica, on the other hand, shows a gradual but sustained rise in manufacturing value added relative to agriculture.

The Figure shows the ratio of industry to agriculture value added (in 1970 PPP USD). It captures the timing and depth of industrialisation across the countries in the region.

Comparison of industrialisation trends across the countries in the region point to three main country groupings: roughly a Central American cluster, an Andean cluster, and a Southern cone cluster plus Mexico and Costa Rica.[4] In broad terms, long-period trends in industrialisation across these three groups of countries match trends in the timing and depth of the expansion of occupational insurance funds. By the end of the 1970s, Argentina, Brazil, Cuba, and Chile had well developed occupational insurance funds covering a substantial share of the labour force in dependent employment. Central American countries together with Paraguay and Ecuador, on the other hand lagged some way behind them. The influence of industrialisation on social protection appears dominant, but there are some cases that buck the trend. Uruguay and Costa Rica reached comparable high rates of worker participation in occupational insurance funds by the 1970s, while Mexico's participation rates were significantly lower than predicted by its manufacturing value added relative to agriculture.

There is universal consensus in the literature in the central role of industrialisation and the associated development of state capacity in the expansion of social protection in the 1960s and 1970s (Mesa-Lago, 1978). Distinct industrialisation paths influenced the shape of emergent social protection institutions. In the literature on economic development in the region, a distinction is made between processes of industrialisation associated with implicit import-substitution in the earlier part of the twentieth century enforced by suspension of global trade, and the explicit state-led import-substitution policies embraced by some countries (Bértola & Ocampo, 2012). Industrialisation trends were evident in

[4] These country groupings will be studied in greater detail in Chap. 8 as they match country groupings based on social protection outcomes. Industrialisation paths have had a protracted influence on social protection institutional development in the region.

some countries in the region from the turn of the twentieth century (Williamson, 2011), a response to the suspension of world trade as a result of conflict. In some countries the state embraced a developmental model around import substitution policies (Astorga & Herraz-Loncán, 2020; Bértola & Ocampo, 2012). State-led import-substitutions policies reinforced and deepened the protection of favoured sectors in the economy. State-led developmental policies became central to the spread of occupational insurance funds for workers in these sectors. Social protection expansion through occupational insurance funds has important effects on employment. This is apparent from the fact that the initial focus on expanding social protection for urban workers and their dependants did not extend to other occupational groups such as informal or rural workers (Haggard & Kaufman, 2008). This became a feature of social protection in the region during the twentieth century. The sectoral affiliations of occupational insurance fund participants are fully consistent with state support for selected sectors in the economy. Occupational insurance funds lower competition in employment across and within the favoured sectors while raising competition for employment in the excluded sectors.

5.3 Limited Fordism and Social Protection

It is helpful to pay some attention to the qualitative as well as the quantitative quality of the employment effects of industrialisation.

Early industrialisation in the region involved a transformation of artisan manufacturing into larger-scale industrial production. This can be observed for selected countries from data collected for a 1966 Report on Industrialisation by ECLAC (ECLAC, 1966) which distinguishes between artisan and factory employment. Figure 5.2 shows the share of artisan employment and the share of factory employment in total employment in selected countries for the period 1925–1950, the early industrialisation expansion. In countries with a larger share of the labour force in industrial employment, like Argentina and Chile, expansion of factory employment reaches one half of manufacturing employment by 1950. In the other countries, starting from a lower share of employment in

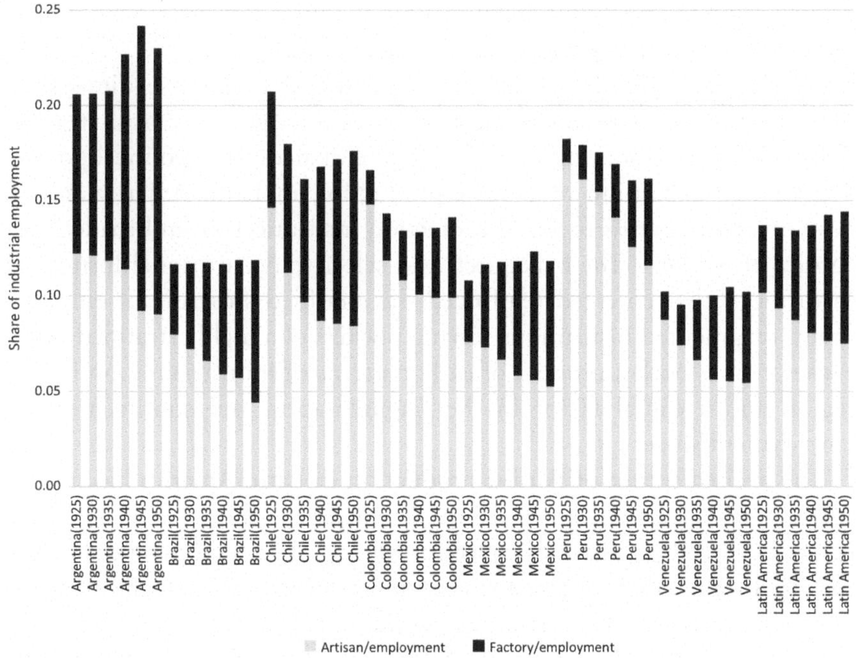

Fig. 5.2 Artisan vs factory employment in selected countries 1925–1950. Data source: Statistical Annex to ECLAC Report on Industrialisation (ECLAC, 1966)

industry, factory employment is rising at a much lower pace and remained a minority in the later years. It is apparent from these data that employment in small enterprises was a feature of early industrialisation.[5] In Latin America, industrialisation did not result in the agglomeration of employment in large Fordist enterprises to a significant extent.

The Figure shows the artisan and factory shares of industrial employment for selected countries in Latin America. It shows the rise in factory employment against dominant artisan employment.

Fordist production has direct implications for social protection institutions. It relies on agglomerating workers with different skills within large integrated production processes. In combination with labour organisation and collective bargaining, fordist production can rapidly extend

[5] This remains the case (Eslava et al., 2021).

participation in social protection to a broad range of workers with different skill levels within enterprises (Rueda et al., 2015). In the social protection literature, Fordist production has a further, qualitative, dimension of interest, as the agglomeration of workers in large firms facilitates the development of labour organisations and enhances their political power. The limited expansion of Fordist production in Latin America might have prevented access to social protection institutions from broader categories of workers. The balkanised and selective occupational insurance institutions that emerged reinforced the stratified structure of employment. Fragmented institutions serving pockets of a highly stratified wage earner class is both a product of early patterns of industrialisation in the region and a causal factor in the fragmentation and stratification of employment since.

The limited spread of Fordist production in Latin America has been a constant in discussions on economic development and social protection. Eslava et al. (2021) provides a recent review of the literature and data on the significance of firm size for economic development in the region.[6] They estimate that 18 percent of workers in the region are currently employed in firms with more than 100 employees, 14 percent in firms with 11–100 workers, and 36 percent in firms employing 10 workers or less. Own account workers account for a further 32 percent of employment.[7] Firm size is also positively correlated with worker earnings and education levels and higher productivity when compared to smaller firms.

The small share of employment in large firms encourages a concern that the incidence of small firms and self-employment in Latin America, compared to other regions, is detrimental to productivity and might be a central explanatory factor in economic development outcomes (Levy & Cruces, 2021). This is presented as an issue of a 'missing middle': "…the size distribution of productive units in Latin America reveals a combination of massive excess fragmentation of production in the extreme left tail and an additional mass in large corporations, with a notable missing

[6] See also a McKinsey Report on the topic (McKinsey, 2019).

[7] This is based on estimates from household survey data for 2019 except for Chile (2017) and Mexico (2018). The figures are a weighted average of 11 countries: Argentina, Bolivia, Brazil, Chile, Colombia, Costa Rica, Dominican Republic, Mexico, Paraguay, Peru and Uruguay (Eslava et al., 2021, p. 21).

middle" (Eslava et al., 2021, p. 8). The connotation is that the distribution of productive units is also responsible in some way for structural inequality in the region and, by extension, its employment and social stratification. Hsieh and Olken (2014) dispute the 'missing middle' argument in development concerning firms size and employment. Whilst confirming the low absolute number of large firms, they demonstrate that the full distribution of firms in three middle income countries including Mexico is not unusual, it is well populated in the middle, and fails to show significant gaps.

The association with social protection participation is straightforward. Participation in occupational pensions is positively correlated with firm size, while participation in social assistance is negatively correlated with firm size. Social assistance programmes were explicitly designed to provide some protection to households dependent in informal employment while occupational pension plans were explicitly designed to include workers in larger firms and permanent employment relationship and exclude self-employed and rural workers.

The issue of causality is crucial to interpret these associations. It is a received view from the literature on this issue that changes in the structure of employment, and in legislation regulating the employment relationship, will be needed to secure a more comprehensive and inclusive social protection (Bertranou & Maurizio, 2011; Bosch et al., 2013). This is also a received view on the extensive literature in informality and the formalisation of informality. It is implicit in these views that causality runs from the structure of employment to social protection institutions.

On the other hand, Levy (2008) places the emphasis on the influence of social protection design on employment choices. In his view the combination of occupational insurance and social assistance undermines incentives for workers to opt for formal employment in larger firms. To the extent that workers can access health care and income protection from budget financed social assistance, the incentives to move to larger and more productive firms, forced to deduct pension fund contributions from their workers, are mitigated. Levy's argumentation assumes a causal path going from social protection institutions to the distribution of employment across firms. Levy and Cruces (2021) develop a more sophisticated model in which the design of social protection institutions and firm growth are endogenous to multiple economy wide factors, via the incentives faced by economic agents. The causal links implied by Levy, from social protection design to firm size employment incentives, are now replaced by multiple cross-determining factors.

Their contribution raises a crucial policy dilemma, whether changes in the structure of employment are required to secure more inclusive and comprehensive social protection institutions (Martínez-Franzoni & Sánchez-Ancochea, 2017) or whether reforms to social protection institutions are required to reduce the stratification in employment (Levy, 2008). Proposals for delinking employment status and social protection participation suggest an alternative route to reducing employment stratification.

5.4 Earnings

Astorga (2017) constructs wage data for the 'long century' for three occupational groups (based on an ILO classification) for six countries. The occupational groups are: (i) relatively skilled workers (technicians and administrators); (ii) semi-skilled workers (semi-skilled blue collars workers and other urban workers in relatively low productivity sectors such as retailing and transport, and artisans); and (iii) unskilled workers (rural and urban unskilled workers, including domestic servants and street vendors). Figure 5.3 shows trends for monthly earnings in US$ at 1970 PPP for each of the countries and a simple regional average (LA6). Unfortunately, the countries included in Astorga's dataset exclude Central American and Andean countries. Vertical dashed lines divide the 'long century' into three main periods 1900–1940, 1940–1980, and 1980–2011. These periods reflect early industrialisation, state-led development, and the neoliberal and post neo-liberal periods.

The Figure shows long period monthly earnings of skilled, semiskilled, and unskilled workers for selected countries and a Latin America simple average, in 1970 PPP USD.

The 1900–1940 period shows only gradual improvements in earnings for the three occupational groups. Differentials across these groups are

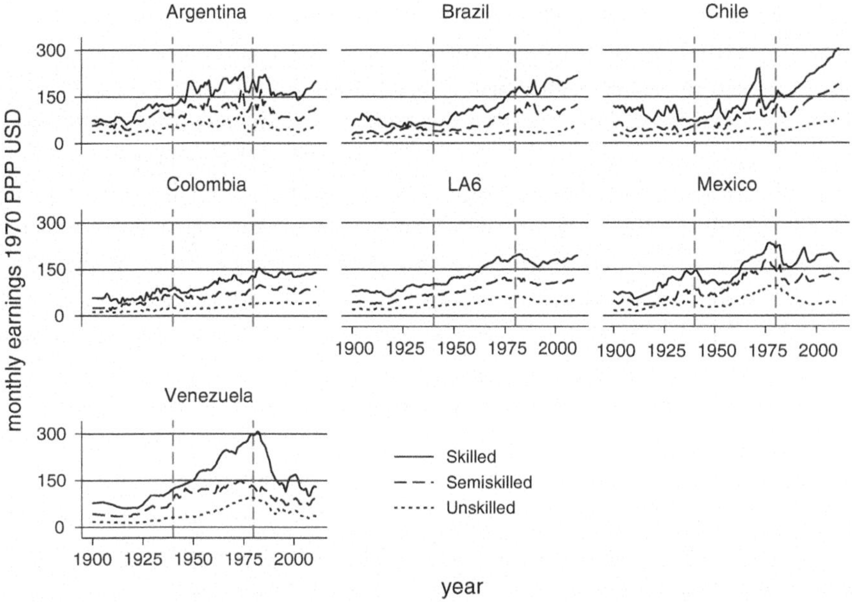

Fig. 5.3 Skilled, semi-skilled, and unskilled wage growth for selected countries 1900–2012. Data source: Astorga (2017)

not marked. Frankema (2010) finds that inter-industry wage inequalities in Latin American countries were muted until the middle of the twentieth century. These findings are consistent with moderate differentials across workers grouped by skill. In the 1940–1980 period, the state-led developmental period in the selected countries, earnings rise sharply, although the rise is more moderate in Colombia, and to an extent Brazil. The post 1980 period is characterised by stagnation in labor earnings for all countries except Chile. There are cross-country differences in the intensity of the trend, but they share similar period patterns. Labour earnings show a marginal increase in the early industrialisation period, a sharp rise in the state-led development period, and stagnation in the neoliberal and post-neoliberal period.

Regarding differentials across the three skill groups, they show a relatively stable pattern in the early period, a sharper differentiation in the state-led industrialisation period, and some stability in skill differentials in the neoliberal period, apart from Chile who shows widening skill earnings differentials. The timing of industrialisation could explain variations in the pattern across countries. Earlier industrialisation in Argentina would probably explain the greater intensity of the earnings growth for the skilled group. The state-led development period shows a rapid increase in skilled and semi-skilled earnings reflects rapid industrialisation in protected sectors. Venezuela in particular shows a very significant rise in earnings for the skilled group. The last period is one of wage stagnation for all workers in all countries except Chile and to a lesser extent Brazil.

For the full period, and focusing on the LA6 data, wage earnings growth can be observed for all groups of workers with a widening in differentials. According to Astorga, the wages of the unskilled group rose in the full period by 147 percent while the average wage growth was 257 percent. The growth in earnings appears to have petered out in the neoliberal period. The average earnings for the LA6 countries at the end of the data period in 2011 are lower in PPP terms than at the end of the state-led period in 1980.

The expansion of occupational insurance funds in the industrialisation period will have contributed to the rise in earnings differentials, through a relatively stronger rise in earnings of skilled workers. Occupational insurance funds restricted competition within the sectors privileged by import-substitution-industrialisation. The exclusion of rural and unskilled workers expanded competition among these workers. Occupational insurance funds reinforced sectoral stratification. The fragmentation and selectivity associated with occupational insurance funds in Latin America enforced significant intra-wage earner divisions, as shown by growing skill differentials.

Efforts to undermine workers organisations and minimise their influence over social protection policies and institutions in the neoliberal period together the acute economic and financial crises that accompanied structural adjustment helped moderate earnings differentials but reinforced employment stratification. The expansion of social assistance and the rise in real minimum wages in the new century led to a relative improvement in the earnings of low income workers and raised reservation wages. These policies led to a reduction in wage earner stratification.

Duality in social protection provision contributed to sustain wage earners stratification by skills.

The sustained reduction in labour earnings inequality in Latin America since the turn of the century has attracted considerable attention. Messina and Silva (2018) find that labour earnings inequality decrease sharply in the first decade of the 2000s in 16 out of 17 countries they study. Faster rise in the earnings of lower paid workers is the main driver for the overall reduction in wage inequality. The extensive literature seeking to identify the causal factors responsible for the relative improvement in the earnings of less skilled workers has explored a wider range of possibilities. They range from supply side factors associated with education expansion; demand side changes in global demand and improvement in the terms of trade; and policy factors such as improvements in the minimum wage (Firpo & Portella, 2019). Supply side explanations emphasise the expansion of secondary and tertiary education in the last quarter of the twentieth century which might have reduced the skill premia observed in the 1980s and 1990s. The commodity boom brought about by the integration of China in the world economy and its rapid growth could have raised demand for workers in primary and tertiary sectors, with positive implications for their earnings. A widespread rise in real minimum wages and the expansion of conditional income transfers could have lifted reservation wages among less skilled workers. The literature has not reached agreement. Interestingly, Messina and Silva conclude that "most of the decline is explained by falling intra-group wage inequality" (Messina & Silva, 2018, p. 61), effectively discounting the influence of changes in worker characteristics or sectoral employment.

5.5 Tertiarisation and Social Protection: Driver or Consequence?

In the second half of the twentieth century tertiarisation trends began to dominate the structure of employment. Secular reductions in the share of employment in agriculture and stagnation in industrial employment resulted in a rising share of employment in services as shown in Fig. 5.4.

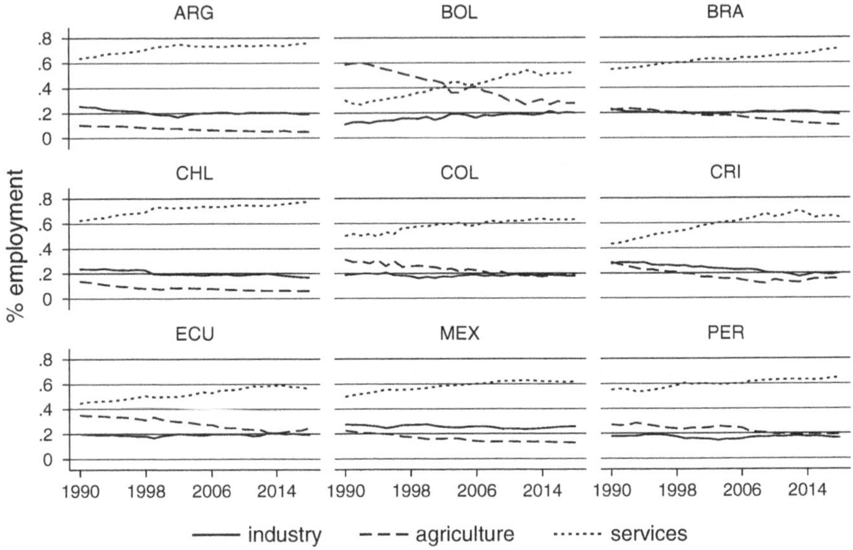

Fig. 5.4 Share of employment by industry sector. Data source: Economic Transformation Database (de Vries et al., 2021)

What are the implications for the link between social protection and employment?

The Figure shows trends in employment shares by main industrial sectors: agriculture, industry, and services from 1950 to 2014. It captures the secular decline in the share of employment in agriculture, and the rise in the share of employment in services. The share of employment in industry has retained stability through the period.

Taking for granted that the direction of causality goes from employment to social protection, researchers have argued that the expansion of tertiary employment was in part responsible for the stagnation of social protection in the neoliberal period. Compared to industrial employment, tertiary jobs outside public services are less likely to agglomerate large numbers of skilled workers. They are less likely to rely on firm specific skills and therefore long-term employment relationships. Most firms in the tertiary sector rely largely on general skills and are not dependent continuous employment. They likely see the costs of occupational pension funds as non-recoverable expense. Researchers have noted the more volatile nature of services employment is ill suited to occupational insurance funds, which sustainability and resilience relies on more permanent working relationship. Tertiarisation is, from this perspective, an explanation for the stagnation of participation in occupational insurance funds.

Approaching this from the perspective that social protection influences employment provides a different, and perhaps more robust, reading of tertiarisation. Social protection reforms are capable of driving change in the nature of the employment relationship itself. The introduction of individual retirement savings plans supports a more flexible approach to employment relationships. Shifting social protection to individual retirement savings plans would encourage firms and workers to restructure their employment relationship.

Occupational insurance funds require active management on the part of employers with associated costs. The economic literature has examined the recruitment and retention effects of occupational insurance funds (Lazear, 1983). Pension provision designed for the armed forces is a good example. Occupational pension plans in the armed forces require many years of continuous contribution before allowing access to entitlements. This is intended to incentivise recruits to work through the costs of training. Occupational pensions with long vesting periods select workers with long-term horizons, prepared to trade off current pay for future pension income. Firm-specific skills training is unlikely to be attractive to workers who move jobs, while general skills can provide such workers with substantive benefits.

Shifting social protection to individual retirement savings plans enables firms and workers to restructure their employment relationship (Barrientos, 1998b, 1998a; Barrientos & Firinguetti, 1995). Individual retirement savings plans could more easily accommodate a measure of volatility in employment, due to their portability across jobs and the individualised entitlement rules. Participants get what they save, plus the returns on their savings. Volatility of employment is unlikely to undermine the operation of savings plans, especially where fees are extracted on a regular basis form the balances of the plans.

Occupational insurance funds can help firms deploy productivity incentives for workers in activities with costly monitoring. The fragmented nature of tertiary employment and the large share of small firms in the private sector implies that the monitoring of worker productivity is costless for employers. A shift to individual retirement savings plans enables changes in the employment relationship in firms benefiting from costless monitoring of worker effort. In sum, pension reforms facilitate tertiarisation.

The stagnation in industrial employment also bears some consideration. Discussing trends in industrialisation in low and middle-income countries, Rodrik (2016) argues that premature de-industrialisation is likely to have a stunting effect on the economies and institutions of these countries. Late and weak industrialisation in Latin American countries, compared to early industrialisers, might help explain the relative weaknesses and fragmentation of early welfare institutions. Taking the argument forward in time, Rodrik argues that de-industrialisation, associated with the shift to export-led growth in the last quarter of the last century, has further undermined the emergence of strong and unified welfare states. Rodrik is perhaps over-pessimistic about the extent to which weak and late industrialisation might permanently affect late industrialisers. He writes: "Historically, industrialisation has played a foundational role in creating modern state and democratic politics. Its relative absence in today's developing societies could well be the source of political instability, fragile states, and illiberal politics" p. 24. His argument relies explicitly on applying the trajectory of early industrialisers to countries in Latin America and elsewhere. He takes it for granted that the direction of causality goes from employment to social protection.

However, data on selected countries in the region shown in Fig. 5.4 do not fully support the de-industrialisation argument. The data confirm that the share of industrial employment has been relatively stable through the period. At any rate, relatively higher productivity in industry than in services or agriculture is consistent with a moderate fall in industrial employment over time, as productivity gains materialise.

5.6 The Knowledge Economy and Skill Polarisation

There is growing interest on the likely impact of the 'knowledge economy' on employment in the region. Undoubtedly, the spread of information technology and of innovations in automation and communications have had a significant impact on the way we work and on workers skills set requirements. In early industrialisers, research centres around occupational polarisation caused by off shoring and automation. Off shoring describes the relocation of economic activity to emerging economies and consequent effects on job demand. Automation describes the spread of computer assisted machine production as a complement or replacement of workers. The combination of off shoring and automation in early industrialisers has affected particularly routine occupations because they are more susceptible to automation. This has resulted in a hollowing out of the employment structure, particularly in manufacturing and clerical jobs. The implications for labour demand are a polarisation of employment, sustained demand low skill and high skill workers contrasting with a collapse in demand for routine blue and white collar employment (Autor & Dorn, 2013).[8]

This issue is relevant for countries in Latin America. First, research into off shoring and automation in early industrialisers has generated new insights and perspectives on the relationship between skills, capital, and employment. It has led to the development of a novel task approach to employment (Acemoglu & Autor, 2011; Autor, 2013). Second, off-shoring and automation raise an interesting set of questions around the potential consequences for employment in the region. Are Latin American countries likely to benefit from the jobs off shored to the periphery. Will this raise demand for routine employment? Will demand for highly skilled, and low skilled jobs drain our economies of their employment? Are there any new investment opportunities that could impact on

[8] Palier (2019, p. 117) draws out the implications for the social structure in early industrialisers" "Along with the polarization of the labour market, a new social polarization is thus emerging, and a new social divide is forming between very highly-paid "productive" workers and "non-productive" workers, whose jobs are concentrated in personal services; this new form of polarization is leading to a new form of social domination of the "brains" over the "servants", a relationship that is becoming typical of the knowledge economy."

employment structures in the region? And what is the contribution of social protection to this change?

Research on the empirical effects of off shoring and automation on the employment structure in Latin America has not reached clear-cut conclusions. One strand of research has focused on assessing the exposure of occupations to potential routinisation. Gasparini et al. (2021) study the routine content of jobs in six countries in the region to establish how open they are to job polarisation. They find that unskilled occupations have a higher routine content compared to semi-skilled occupations and are significantly higher than for skilled occupations. They conclude: "[A]lthough there is considerable heterogeneity across countries, the general result holds: in all six countries employment has increased less, or even decreased, in occupations with high routine task content. As a result of the asymmetric changes in employment, the overall degree of routinization has mildly decreased in the Latin American economies over the last two decades. The fall was more marked in the 2000s than in the 2010s. Between and within-sector changes are relevant to understand these patterns." (Gasparini et al., 2021, pp. 2–3). This finding is confirmed by research in Bonavida et al. (2021) for a range of Latin American countries and Nogueira (2015) for Brazil.

Instead of working out the potential scope for change, we could attempt to measure actual changes in employment by occupation using ISCO08 data from the ILO covering 11 Latin American countries.[9] This classification distinguishes occupations according to their skill content (Ospino Hernandez, 2018). The nine one-digit occupational ISCO groups can be further consolidated into three: routine (clerical support workers, skilled agricultural, forestry and fishing workers, craft and related workers, plant and machine operators and assemblers); non-routine manual (services and sales workers and armed forces); and non-routine cognitive (Managers, Professionals and Technician and associate professionals). Figure 5.5 shows the ratio of the share of workers in each

[9] Data for Panama (4 years) and Peru (1 year) were available but not included due to the short time span.

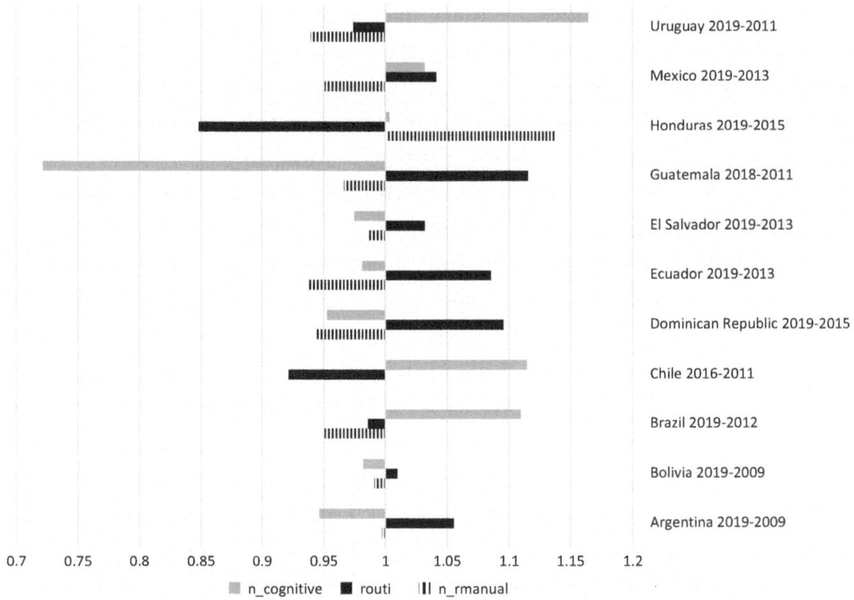

Fig. 5.5 Job Polarisation? Share ratios of cognitive, routine, and non-routine manual occupations for selected countries. Data source: Own analysis of ILO ISCO08 data file accessed 21/9/21

The Figure shows the ratio of the shares of employment in non-routine cognitive, non-routine manual and routine occupations for selected countries. Ratios greater (less) than 1 show growth (decline) in occupations. It captures potential employment polarisation between the first and last available in the data.

of the three categories in the last year that data is available for the relevant countries compared to the initial year.

Job polarisation of employment due to automation would be consistent with growth in the share of employment in non-routine cognitive jobs and possibly some growth in the share of non-routine manual jobs (to the extent that high skill workers need complementary ancillary workers, e.g., home deliveries and take away meals). In contrast, the effect of a transfer of routine jobs from early industrialisers due to off shoring would be consistent with a rise in the share of routine jobs.

Central American countries and Ecuador show an increase in the share of routine jobs as well as declines in the job shares of both non-routine manual and non-routine cognitive jobs. The same trend can be observed in Bolivia, but the changes are marginal. Argentina is an intriguing case because of the large increase in the share of routine job share. This places Argentina closer to the trend for Central American economies. Mexico shows a rise in both routine and non-routine cognitive job shares, together with a decline in the share of non-routine manual jobs.

Uruguay, Chile, and Brazil exhibit some signs of job polarisation due to the growth in the share of non-routine cognitive job share. However, this is combined with some decline in the share of routine and non-routine manual job share. Perhaps more appropriately, these countries demonstrate the impact of the' knowledge economy', un upgrade in the share of workers performing skilled jobs.[10]

It is hard to see a common trend across the Latin American economies included. Southern cone countries, less Argentina plus Mexico, show signs of the 'knowledge economy' restructuring employment, in the rise of non-routine cognitive job share. For Central American and Andean countries, occupational changes are in line with off shoring of routine jobs from early industrialisers.

The off shoring and automation narratives emphasise demand side factors in explaining occupational change in early industrialisers. In the context of Latin America, it is interesting to consider supply conditions. In the last quarter of the twentieth century Latin American countries upgraded their education provision (Lindert, 2010, 2021).

How well positioned are Latin American countries to meet the coming knowledge economy? Figure 5.6 cross tabulates the share of the relevant population group enrolled in tertiary education with the share of non-routine cognitive jobs across several Latin American countries. Paying attention to supply conditions does not change the findings from the examination of occupational employment changes in significant ways. Countries that experienced a rise in non-routine cognitive jobs also show higher than average share of tertiary enrolments in the relevant age group. Aside from Argentina, countries showing increases in the share of routine jobs also have lower than average share of tertiary enrolments in the

[10] These changes are more marked if the analysis is replicated for female employment only.

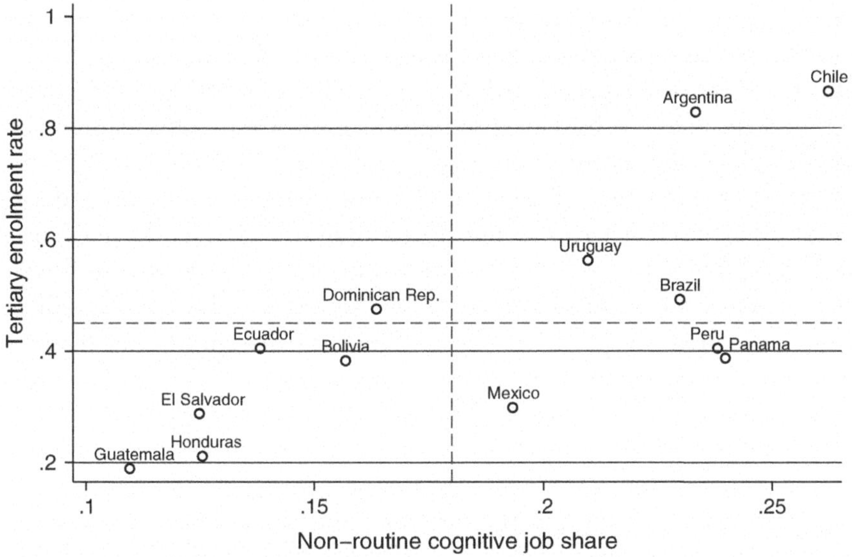

Fig. 5.6 The coming 'knowledge economy'? Data source: Tertiary enrolment from Our World in Data; Non-routine cognitive share of employment from own estimation using ILO ISCO08 data file accessed 21/9/21. Data points are for 2014, except non-routine cognitive share for Chile and Dominican Rep. in 2015 and for Peru in 2010

relevant population. Among these countries, supply side constraints match weak demand trends.

The Figure shows a crosstabulation of the share of tertiary enrolments and the share of non-cognitive jobs in employment for selected countries. It offers a graphical summary description of supply and demand conditions in preparation for the 'knowledge economy'.

Individual retirement savings plans and social assistance have features that will contribute to the changes in employment associated with automation and with job relocation. As discussed in Chap. 3, both individual retirement savings plans and social assistance expansion are associated with a shift in dominant stratification from sectors to skill. Changes in employment due to automation and job relocation are part of this shift.

Occupational insurance funds provided incentives for employment in the favoured sectors of the economy. They reduced competition within these sectors and restricted job mobility across sectors. High replacement rates for stayers in occupational pensions were dependent on limited benefits for lower paid workers with low probability of meeting vesting periods and on public subsidies. The introduction of individual retirement savings plans and recent reforms to occupational pensions (Altamirano Montoya et al., 2018) will have the effect of raising competition and job mobility within and across sectors. Deterioration or scaling down of subsidised replacement rates in occupational insurance funds, due to financial pressures and reduced levels of public subsidies or internal subsidies, will further reduce incentives for employment in routine non-manual jobs, their core constituency.

Social protection reforms in Latin America since the beginning of the neoliberal period have supported a shift to skill stratification. As occupational insurance funds stagnated or declined, individual retirement savings plans were pushed into the forefront. Individual retirement savings plans are not sector specific or sector selective. Individual retirement savings plans lack redistributive features with entitlements based on capacity to save rather than group membership. Individual retirement savings plans replace sector stratification with skill stratification.

From the turn of the century, social assistance has expanded its reach of low-income groups often dependent on informal or unprotected employment. The fact that social assistance entitlements are not dependent in employment status removes any sector stratification bias. At the same time, their social investment orientation, if effective, raises education and skill levels among younger cohorts and will upgrade the skill composition of the labour force (Parker & Vogl, 2018).[11] Social assistance transfers, and recent minimum wage upgrades, have the effect of raising the reservation wage of lower skilled workers, especially in routine manual occupations. The expansion of social assistance can offer support for changes in the employment structure associated with automation and job relocation.

Given conditions in the region, a 'knowledge economy' scenario is consistent with current social protection trends: the stagnation and decline of occupational insurance funds; a realignment of social protection and skill stratification through individual retirement savings plans,

[11] Social assistance outcomes will be covered in more detail in Chap. 6.

and the expansion and institutionalisation of social assistance supporting non-routine manual workers.

5.7 New Forms of Integration with the World Economy

Global production networks have far-reaching implications for employment in Latin America, especially in the context of the commodity boom (Ocampo, 2017; Pérez, 2010). Global production networks, also referred to as global value chains, describe agreements involving firms in different countries to contribute specific components of a production line. They involve the subdivision of production processes and the allocation tasks across national borders. A key characteristic of global production networks is that component firms are not vertically integrated with the dominant firms, their collaboration is based on mutual advantage not ownership. This process is the reverse of multinational corporations' vertical ownership and command. Component firms are in a network but retain a measure of autonomy and are fully inserted in their domestic economy.

This is related to off shoring in early industrialisers where firms relocate the production of components to locations where conditions are more favourable (say due to labour supply or natural resources), or at least less unfavourable (say locations with less costly environmental and labour regulations).

The first issue to explore is the extent of Latin American countries' participation in global production networks. A measure of global production network participation can be constructed using UNCTAD-Eora data (Casella et al., 2019). It estimates flows of value added in exports, extracted from country level input-output matrices, aggregated for the global economy. A measure of global production network participation subtracts backward value added from forward export value added. Forward export value added is the value added in goods and services used as intermediate inputs in third countries and excluding value added in goods exported for direct consumption. Backward value added is the value added in imports associated with global production network in the

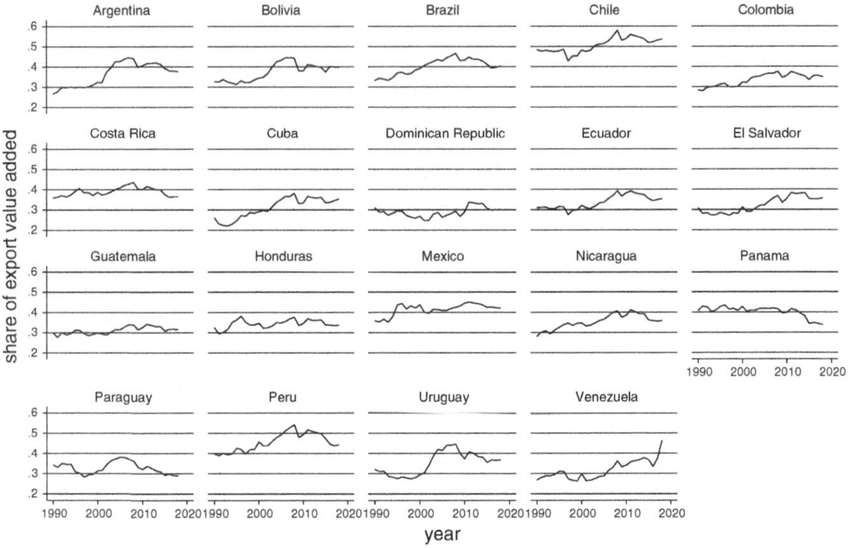

Fig. 5.7 Global Production Networks participation index. Data source: UNCTAD-Eora data (Casella et al., 2019). Index adds forward and backward linkages

home economy (Casella et al., 2019). Figure 5.7 shows the trend in global production network participation as fraction of exports for Latin America countries in the database 1990–2018.

The Figure shows the Global Production Networks participation index for Latin American countries. The index is the share of export value added accounted for by forward and backward linkages.

The general trend is concave over time, with participation rising in the 2000s but showing a gentle stagnation or decline after 2010. Global value network participation grew in significantly in the 2000s. The 2008 global financial crisis, with a delayed impact in Latin American countries, appears to have arrested the rise in global production network participation.[12] Among the largest economies of the region, global production network participation remains at significant levels. The fraction of export

[12] Contemporaneous accounts of labour market trends suggested rapid recovery in Latin America (Marinakis, 2011), but trends deteriorated in mid-2010s (ECLAC/ILO, 2020). Hence possible delayed effects from the 2008 crisis. It is likely that COVID19 might have undermined global production networks.

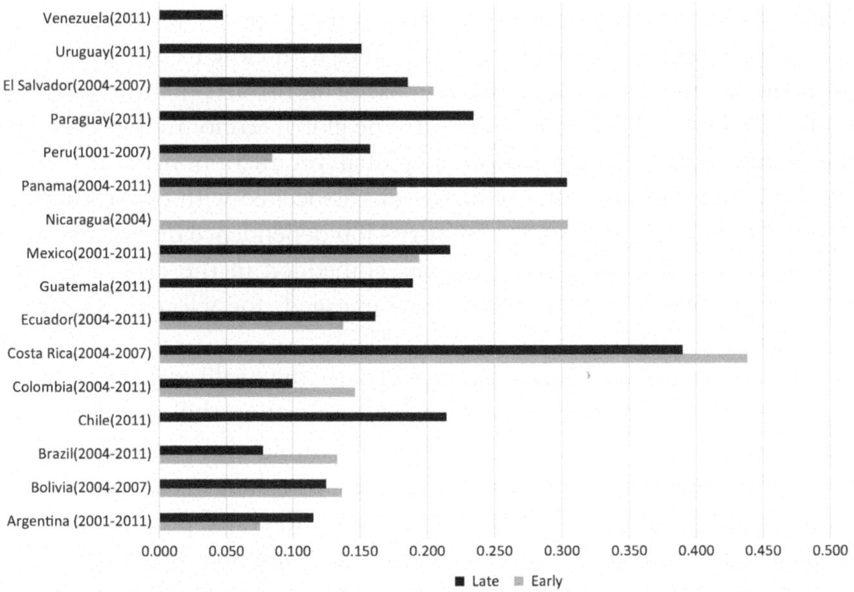

Fig. 5.8 Share of direct and indirect jobs embedded in export sector. Data source: LACEX database (Cali et al., 2016)

value added accounted for by participation in global production networks peaked at around 0.5 for the countries with the highest levels of participation, namely Chile and Peru. For Argentina, Bolivia, Brazil, Costa Rica, and Uruguay global production network participation peaked around 0.4.

The next issue is to assess the contribution of participation in global production networks in employment. LACEX jobs data supports measures of the direct number of jobs engaged in exports (forward linkages) as well as the indirect number of jobs (backward linkages) associated with domestic inputs into the sector exports (Cali et al., 2016).

Figure 5.8 shows the share of jobs estimated to be associated with global production networks as a share of employment. Where data are available, the Figure compares early and late observations for each country. Care should be exercised in interpreting the figures for 2011 as they probably reflect the delayed effect of the 2008 global financial crisis on the region. A rough average for the region suggests that around one sixth of all jobs are associated the global production networks integration into the global economy. Costa Rica is an outlier with close to one half of all jobs contributing to exports. This exercise demonstrates that the integration of Latin American economies into the global economy, and perhaps the significance of participation in global production networks goes much further than measures of direct jobs associated with exports alone. They substantially understate a country's job dependence on exports.

The Figure shows the share of jobs embedded in the export sector, including those directly and indirectly engaged, for selected countries and years.

Social protection reforms in the region since the neoliberal period have facilitated global production networks by supporting skill stratification. The discussion in the previous section regarding the contribution of social protection to changes in employment applies here in full. Individual retirement savings plans facilitate participation in global production networks due to their flexibility with regards to job mobility and reliance on individual savings capacity. Social assistance provision also facilitates employment in global production networks by lower skilled workers. The limited role and responsibility of employers in the management and financing of individual retirement accounts and in the budget-financing of social assistance minimise the costs associated with compliance with social protection labour regulations and enhances their competitive position. Social protection reforms support the temporal and changing nature of firms' global production networks commitments.

5.8 Conclusions

This chapter examined the association existing between social protection institutions and employment. Researchers have paid a great deal of attention to the close connection between social protection institutions and employment. The definition of informal employment in common use, namely workers who lack social protection, underlines the close association between them.

Consensus over the significance of this association breaks down when the issue becomes to establish the direction of causality. The conventional approach, supported by current theories of welfare institutional development, is to assume that the structure of employment shapes social protection institutions. This makes sense when researching the origins of welfare institutions. Social protection institutions in Latin America emerged with changes in employment imposed by industrialisation. The emergence of an urban working class for whom employment was binary posed large risks to the wellbeing of workers and their dependents in the event of unemployment, sickness, or old age. Government supported occupational insurance funds emerged with the incorporation of urban industrial workers in mass politics. However, once social protection institutions are in place, they exercise considerable influence on employment. The direction of causality is now from social protection to employment. The discussion in the chapter explored the stratification effects of social protection institutions on the structure of employment. Adopting this approach new insights into social protection.

Occupational insurance funds expanded in the region with state-led import-substitution-policies. They reinforced the dominance of sectoral stratification by enhancing worker incentives for employment in the protected sectors are reducing competition within selected sectors. Occupational insurance funds strengthened recruitment and retention within these sectors. They also excluded workers from outside these sectors. Core features of occupational insurance funds, like vesting periods, redistributed entitlements away from low skilled workers with discontinuous employment and towards skilled workers with continuous, long tenured, employment.

Pension reform in the 1990s, including individual retirement savings plans, and the growth of social assistance represent a shift towards skills stratification. Individual retirement savings plans are not directed to sustain favoured economic sectors, but instead aim at enhancing competition within and across sectors, job mobility, and to minimise redistributive features that weaken the association between entitlements, skills, and savings capacity.

The expansion of social assistance in the new century further reinforces a shift towards skill stratification. In this case, they are directed at low paid workers in informal employment. Social assistance entitlements are independent of employment status and sectoral affiliation. Conditional income transfers' social investment orientation is aimed at upgrading educational attachment and at promoting the acquisition of skills among participant children. Conditional income transfers seek to improve the productive capacity of low income groups in the medium and longer term.

The chapter discussed social protection contribution to three changes in employment in the region: tertiarisation, job polarisation and relocation, and participation in global production networks. It argued that social protection reforms, individual retirement savings plans and social assistance, have contributed to these changes in the employment structure. Approaching the association between social protection and employment as a causal path brings new insights on social protection institutions in the region.

References

Acemoglu, D., & Autor, D. H. (2011). Skills, tasks and technologies: Implications for employment and earnings. In *Handbook of Labor Economics* (Vol. 4b, pp. 1043–1171). Elsevier B.V.

Altamirano Montoya, A., Berstein, S., Bosch, M., & García Huitrón, M. (2018). *Presente y futuro de las pensiones en América Latina y el Caribe*. Inter-American Development Bank.

Astorga, P. (2017). Real wages and skill premiums in Latin America, 1900-2011. *Revista de Historia Económica, 35*(3), 319–353. https://doi.org/10.1017/S021261091700009X

Astorga, P., & Herraz-Loncán, A. (2020). Latin America. Stalled catching up. In S. Broadberry & K. Fukao (Eds.), *The Modern World. Volume II: 1870 to the present* (pp. 251–275). Cambridge University Press.

Atkinson, A. B. (1989). Social insurance and income maintenance. In A. B. Atkinson (Ed.), *Poverty and social security*. Harvester Wheatsheaf.

Autor, D., & Dorn, D. (2013). The growth of low-skilled service jobs and polarization of the US labour market. *American Economic Review, 103*(5), 1553–1597.
Autor, D. H. (2013). The "task approach" to labor markets: An overview. *Journal of Labour Market Research, 46*, 185–199.
Barrientos, A. (1998a). Pension reform, personal pensions and gender differences in pension coverage. *World Development, 26*(1), 125–137.
Barrientos, A. (1998b). Supplementary pension coverage in Britain. *Fiscal Studies, 19*(4).
Barrientos, A. (2009). Labour markets and the (hyphenated) welfare regime in Latin America. *Economy and Society, 38*(1), 87–108.
Barrientos, A. (2012). Dilemas de las políticas sociales latinoamericanas ¿Hacia una protección social fragmentada? *Nueva Sociedad, 239*, 65–78.
Barrientos, A., & Firinguetti, L. (1995). Planes de Pensión de Capitalización Individual y Beneficios Previsionales para Trabajadoras de Bajos Ingresos. *Estudios de Economía,* 22(1), 17–44.
Bértola, L., & Ocampo, J. A. (2012). *The economic development of Latin America since independence*. Oxford University Press.
Bertranou, F., & Marinakis, A. (Eds.). (2020). *Reflections on work. Perspectives from the Southern Cone of Latin America on the occasion of the ILO Centenary*. ILO.
Bertranou, F., & Maurizio, R. (2011). *The role of the labour market and social protection in reducing inequality and eradicating poverty in Latin America*. ILO.
Bonavida, C., Brambilla, I., & Gasparini, L. (2021). *Automation and pandemic: Threats to employment in Latin America* (Covid-19 and Labor Markets) [Working Paper]. Future of work in the Global South. https://fowigs.net/automation-and-pandemic-threats-to-employment-in-latin-america/
Bosch, M., Melguizo, A., & Pages, C. (2013). *Mejores pensiones, mejores trabajos*. Inter-American Development Bank.
Cali, M., Francois, J., Hollweg, C. H., Manchin, M., Oberdabernig, D. A., Rojas-Ramagosa, H., Rubinova, S., & Tomberger, P. (2016). *The labour content of exports database* (Policy Research Working Paper 7615; Policy Research Working Paper). The World Bank.
Carnes, M., & Mares, I. (2015). Explaining the "return of the state" in middle-income countries: Employment vulnerability, incomes, and preferences for social protection in Latin America. *Politics and Society, 43*(4), 525–550.

Casella, B., Bolwijn, R., Moran, D., & Kanemoto, K. (2019). Improving the analysis of global value chains: The UNCTAD-EORA database. *Transnational Corporations, 26*(3), 115–142.

de Vries, G., Arfelt, L., Drees, D., Godemann, M., Hamilton, C., Jessen-Thiesen, B., Ihsan Kaya, A., Kruse, H., Mensah, E., & Woltjer, P. (2021). *The Economic Transformation Database*. UNU World Institute for Development Economic Research.

ECLAC. (1966). *The process of industrialization in Latin America. Statistical Annex* [Report]. Economic Commission for Latin America.

ECLAC/ILO. (2020). *Employment situation in Latin Amertica and the Caribbean. Work in times of pandemic: The challenges of the coronavirus disease (COVID19)* (22). and the International Labour Office.

Eslava, M., Meléndez, M., & Urdaneta, N. (2021). *Market concentration, market fragmentation, and inequality in Latin America* (Working Paper 11; UNDP LAC Working Paper). UNDP.

Firpo, S., & Portella, A. (2019). *Decline in wage inequality in Brazil. A survey* (Policy Research Working Papers 9906). The World Bank.

Gasparini, L. C., Brambilla, I., Falcone, C., & César, A. (2021). *Routinization and Employment: Evidence for Latin America* (Working Paper 276; Documentos de Trabajo Del CEDLAS). CEDLAS, Universidad Nacional de La Plata. https://www.cedlas.econo.unlp.edu.ar/wp/no-276/

Gough, I., & Therborn, G. (2010). The global future of welfare states. In F. G. Castles, S. Leibfried, & J. Lewis (Eds.), *Oxford handbook of comparative welfare states* (pp. 703–720). Oxford University Press.

Haggard, S., & Kaufman, R. R. (2008). *Development, democracy, and welfare states. Latin America, Asia and Eastern Europe*. Princeton University Press.

Hsieh, C.-T., & Olken, B. A. (2014). The missing "Missing Middle.". *Journal of Economic Perspectives, 28*(3), 89–108.

ILO. (1972). Social Security in Latin America: Evolution and prospects. *International Social Security Review, 305–356.*

Korpi, W. (2006). Power resources and employer-centered approaches in explanations of welfare state and varieties of capitalism: Protagonists, consenters, and antagonists. *World Politics, 58*(2), 167–206.

Lazear, E. P. (1983). *Incentive effects of pensions. NBER.*

Levy, S. (2008). *Good intentions, bad outcomes. Social policy, informality and economic growth in Mexico*. The Brookings Institution.

Levy, S., & Cruces, G. (2021). *Time for a New Course: An essay on social protection and growth in Latin America* (Working Paper 24; UNDP LAC Working Paper). UNDP.

Lindert, P. H. (2010). The unequal lag in Latin American schooling since 1900: Follow the money. *Revista de Historia Económica, 28*(2), 375–405.

Lindert, P. H. (2021). *Making social spending work*. Cambridge University Press.

Marinakis, A. (2011). *Explaining Latin America's robust recovery from the crisis* [Conference Presentation]. ILO.

Martínez-Franzoni, J., & Sánchez-Ancochea, D. (2017). *The quest for universal social policies in the South*. Cambridge University Press.

McKinsey. (2019). *Latin America's missing middle. Rebooting inclusive growth*. McKinsey & Company. www.mckinsey.com/mgi

Mesa-Lago, C. (1978). *Social security in Latin America: Pressure groups, stratification, and inequality*. University of Pittsburgh Press.

Messina, J., & Silva, J. (2018). *Wage inequality in Latin America. Understanding the past to prepare for the future*. The World Bank.

MOxLAD. (n.d.) *Montevideo-Oxford Latin American Economic History Data Base* [Database]. Montevideo-Oxford Latin American Economic History Data Base. http://moxlad.cienciassociales.edu.uy/en#

Nin-Pratt, A., & Valdés Conroy, H. (2020). *After the boom: Agriculture in Latin America and the Caribbean* (Technical Note IDB-TN-0208; IDB Technical Notes). Inter-American Development Bank.

Nogueira, V. (2015). *Is that where you work or what you do? Understanding job polarization in Brazil* [PHD thesis]. Simon Fraser University.

Ocampo, J. A. (2017). Commodity-led development in Latin America. In G. Carbonnier, H. Campodónico, & Tezanos Vázquez (Eds.), *Alternative Pathways to Sustainable Development: Lessons from Latin America* (pp. 51–76). https://www.jstor.org/stable/10.1163/j.ctt1w76w3t.11

Ospino Hernandez, C. G. (2018). *Occupations: Labor market classifications, taxonomies, and ontologies in the 21st century* (Technical Note IDB-TN-1513; Labor Markets Division). Inter-American Development Bank.

Palier, B. (2019). Work, social protection and the middle classes: What future in the digital age? *International Social Security Review, 72*(3), 113–133.

Parker, S., & Vogl, T. (2018). *Do conditional cash transfers improve economic outcomes in the next generation? Evidence from Mexico* (Working Paper 24303; NBER Working Paper). National Bureau for Economic Research.

Pérez, C. (2010). Dinamismo tecnológico e inclusión social en América Latina: Una estrategia de desarrollo productivo basada en los recursos naturales. *Revista de La CEPAL, 100*(1), 123–145.

Pierson, P. (2001). *The new politics of the welfare state*. Oxford University Press.

Polanyi, K. (1957). *The great transformation*. Beacon Press.

Rodrik, D. (2016). Premature deindustrialization. *Journal of Economic Growth, 21*, 1–33.
Rueda, D., Wibbels, E., & Altamirano, M. (2015). The origins of dualism. In P. Beramendi, S. Hausermann, H. Kitschelt, & H. Kriesi (Eds.), *The politics of advanced capitalism* (pp. 89–111). Cambridge University Press.
Schneider, B. (2013). *Hierarchical capitalism in Latin America. Business, labor and the challenges of equitable development*. Cambridge University Press.
Williamson, J. G. (2011). *Industrial catching up in the poor periphery 1870-1975 [Mimeo]*. Harvard University.

6
Protection

This chapter studies the main protection outcomes of social protection institutions in Latin America. Following the approach in the book, the discussion concentrates on the main protection institutions: occupational insurance funds, individual retirement savings plans, and social assistance. Data and space constraints recommend a streamlined approach in which the aggregate protection effects of these institutions on poverty and inequality take a central place. Historical data are not available on a consistent basis for the period prior to the 1970s (Mesa-Lago, 1978), with the implication that the findings from the analysis are more reliable the closer they are to the present day.

The analysis of the protection effects of pensions will naturally focus on the reach and distribution of pension benefits from occupational insurance funds and individual retirement savings plans where applicable. Pension benefits are to be distinguished from old age transfers, i.e., budget financed transfers based on age. Old age transfers will be considered in more detail in the context of social assistance. Regarding pensions, the main finding is that the reach of pension benefits has improved since the 1970s. This is to be expected as the funds implemented in the 1970s or earlier have gradually matured. Income support for older people, pension benefits and old age transfers, has risen fast in the region, but

A. Barrientos, *Social Protection in Latin America*, Global Dynamics of Social Policy,
https://doi.org/10.1007/978-3-031-49795-7_6

mainly because of the rapid expansion of old age transfers. Large inequalities in the size of the pension benefits remain and contribute to the high levels of income inequality present in the countries of the region.

The recent expansion of social assistance programmes in the region has had a positive effect on poverty reduction. The employment and labour earnings compression effects of the commodity boom, together with increases in the real minimum wage, have also contributed to the decline in poverty in the new century. Social assistance transfers have had a sustained effect on poverty reduction, sustained after the end of the commodity boom and through the 2007 financial crisis.

Taking account of the fact that public subsidies to pension benefits are in all countries many times higher than budgetary support for social assistance, the overall effect of social protection institutions is not everywhere positive. Analysis of available data on tax-transfer systems in the region indicate limited impact on income inequality. The persistence of inequality-raising social protection institutions in the region is explained by their role as a stratification mechanism.

The chapter is organised as follows: Section 6.1 discusses protection outcome indicators. Section 6.2 examines the reach and distribution of pension benefits: occupational insurance funds and individual retirement savings plans. Section 6.3 focuses on the protection outcomes from social assistance, including conditional income transfers and old age transfers. Section 6.4 assesses the available evidence on the distributional effects of tax-transfer systems. Section 6.5 discusses gender outcomes. A final section concludes.

6.1 Assessing Effects of Social Protection

There is a variety of methods available to assess the protection outcomes of social protection institutions. They are briefly described here to get a sense of their strengths and weaknesses and to help interpret their results.

First, a direct approach can be employed to assess the incidence of transfers. Where programmes provide direct income transfers to households, a straightforward approach is to consider the change in household income before and after receipt of the transfer. The observed change in household income is taken as the outcome of the transfer programme (Barrientos & Mase, 2012). Aggregating changes in income across all households provides a measure of the economy-wide change in income poverty or inequality. Paying attention to the taxes that support them provides information on the effects of tax-transfer system.

The direct approach to measuring the effects of transfers on poverty or inequality suffers from several shortcomings. The direct approach might under/over-estimate the amount of the actual transfer. Administration costs and compliance costs will ensure that disposable income associated with the transfer received by households is lower than the gross transfer amount. Consumption taxes will ensure that the welfare effect of a transfer is less than the gross value of the transfer. Behavioural responses to the transfer might reduce the effectiveness of the transfer. This is typically associated with concerns that social assistance recipient households might not use the transfer to raise their consumption, might redistribute some of the transfer to their families or neighbours, or might opt to reduce their labour earnings.

Changes in economic conditions in response to the social assistance transfer might work to mitigate the effects of the transfer. If the social assistance budget is tax financed, rises in consumption taxes to finance them will reduce recipients' disposable income and, over the medium-term taxes might lower consumption and employment.

Potential concerns regarding the disposable income from transfers could be addressed by assessing administrative and compliance costs directly. Concerns associated with behavioural responses to the transfers are addressed through impact evaluations of social assistance programmes measuring outcomes net of behavioural effects. In the Latin American context, the example of *Progresa*'s approach to impact evaluation has led to a large empirical literature assessing the outcomes of conditional income transfers and the impact of old age transfers. Comparing household consumption before and after the implementation of a social assistance programme and across a treatment group and a control group (Difference-in-difference) provides a measure of the impact of transfers net of behavioural responses (Skoufias, 2005). In contexts where transfer incidence depends on personal identifiers, like age, that are out of the control of potential beneficiaries, comparing household consumption just below the age of entitlement and just above it provides a reliable measure of the effect of the transfer. This approach takes advantage of an observable discontinuity separating beneficiaries from non-beneficiaries (Regression discontinuity design) (Barrientos & Villa, 2015a). This approach is commonly applied to the study of the impact of old age transfers (Canavire-Bacarreza et al., 2017).

Regarding the last set of concerns, the possibility that taxes introduced to finance transfers might reduce their impact in beneficiary households, they can be addressed by examining the joint effects of taxes and transfers. This is the focus of a literature combining household survey samples, administrative data, and national income accounts (Lustig, 2011). In the context of Latin American countries, survey limitations in sampling the very poor and the very rich calls for supplementing this information with administrative data. Detailed income stocks and flows associated with economic and fiscal activity can be tracked in the household survey data and aggregated in line with administrative data and national income accounts. This literature offers valuable insights on the income effects of particular social protection programmes in the context of the tax-transfer system.

There are four main sources of data discussed in this chapter: administrative data from social protection agencies, household survey responses question on participation and transfer receipt, social expenditure and national income accounts data, and programme evaluation surveys. Chapter 4 drew attention to disparities emerging from comparisons of household survey and administrative data on participation in social protection programmes (Cecchini & Atuesta, 2017). They are especially relevant to social assistance but also apply to occupational insurance funds data (Arenas de Mesa, 2019). Disparities emerging from comparison of aggregated household survey data and national income accounts data are relevant to studies of tax-transfer systems (Lustig, 2018). The implementation of quasi-experimental programme evaluations in social assistance programmes is making a large contribution to our knowledge of the impact of these programmes and has advanced the use of causal inference in social protection. Meta studies of impact evaluations help overcome the external validity restrictions of experimental data and provide harmonised data on programme outcomes (Araújo, 2021; García & Saavedra, 2022).

6.2 Pensions

The protection effects of pensions are best observed in the reach and distribution of pension benefits. This section will examine the incidence and value of pension benefits in the population over 65. The focus is on pension benefits, from occupational pensions and individual retirement savings plans, as opposed to old age transfers. Regarding individual retirement savings plans, it is important to keep in mind the distinction made in Chap. 4 between countries with transitioning reforms, where individual retirement savings plans are in the process of replacing occupational pension schemes; countries with competing individual retirement savings plans and occupational pensions; and countries where individual retirement savings plans complement occupational pensions. In terms of reach, complementary individual retirement savings plans are not additive, but in terms of the value of pension benefits they are so. Some reference to old age transfers will be provided where relevant to help complete a picture of old age income support, but the focus at this point is on pension benefits.

6.2.1 The Reach of Pension Benefits

Figure 6.1 shows the share of the population aged 65 and older in receipt of pension benefits, including from occupational pensions and individual retirement savings plans, and the share in receipt of old age transfers. The values are sourced from administrative data reported in Arenas de Mesa (2019) for the period 2000 to 2019. They show the protective effects of pensions in each of the countries in the region and simple regional average.

The average for Latin America indicates that less than one half of the age group are in receipt of a pension benefit. This figure is relatively stable for the period in question. The old age transfer receipt regional average share shows a doubling in reach in the period, from around 10 percent of the age group to over 20 percent. This reflects the rapid expansion of social assistance in the region.

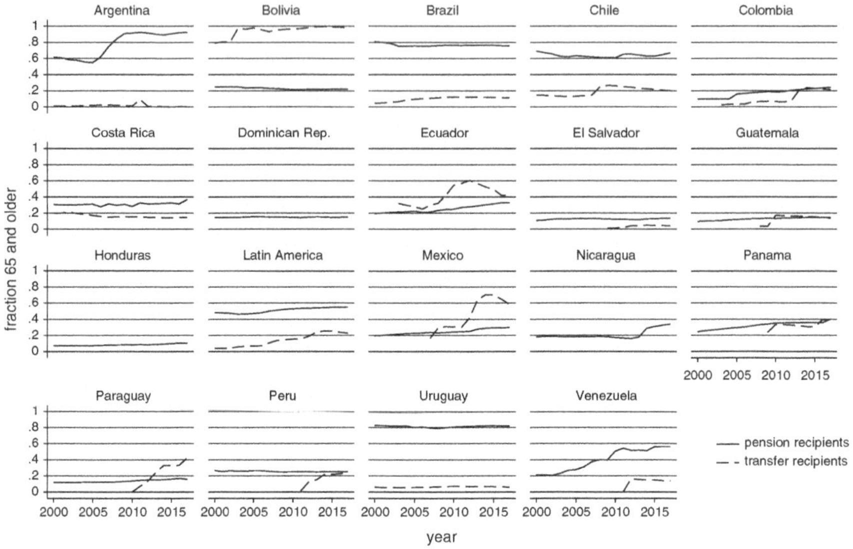

Fig. 6.1 Pension benefits and old age transfers among individuals 65 and older. Data source: Administrative data reported in Arenas de Mesa (2019)

The Figure shows the share of the population aged 65 and over who are in receipt of a pension benefit, from occupational pension or individual retirement savings plan, and those who are in receipt of an old age transfer.

In Central American countries pension receipt is the exception, reaching around 20 percent of the demographic group. Protection is restricted to high level public sector workers and highly paid private sector workers. The reach of pensions is relatively stable over time. Panama is an exception with rising pension receipt share over the period, from around 20 percent of the age group to around 40 percent towards the end of the period. It is worth noting that Costa Rica is not an outlier, pension receipt shares are stable at around 30 percent. In Mexico, pension receipt is steadily rising reflecting the maturing of individual retirement savings plans.

Andean countries show contrasting trends, gently rising pension receipt share in Ecuador and Colombia in contrast to falling or stagnant pension receipt share in Paraguay, Peru, and Bolivia. The expansion of old age transfers is important for these countries and will be discussed in more detail in the social assistance sub-section.

Atlantic South American countries and Chile show stable or marginally declining pension receipt share, from a high baseline. The marginal decline can be observed in Brazil and Chile. Argentina merits special attention due to the significant expansion of pension receipt associated with the 'moratoria'. The step change in pension receipt share is the result of an explicit intervention, as opposed to an underlying trend. There is a measure of uncertainty over the medium- and longer-term financing of the expansion of pension benefit receipt.

Venezuela is the only country in the region with a marked and sustained rise in pension receipt share, belying its political and economic crisis.

Overall, the protection effects of occupational pensions and individual retirement savings plans, as measured by pension receipt share, fail to show any consistent improvement in the region since the turn of the century. There is a 'glass-half-full' interpretation, sustaining that pension schemes in the region have proved resilient and relatively stable in the period in question. Their resilience can be taken as confirmation that social protection institutions for better off workers have weathered changes in the economy and society relatively well, including the 2008 financial crisis for example. The 'glass-half-empty' interpretation would emphasise that the economic growth associated with the commodity boom, leading to rising fiscal revenues, together with repeated pension reforms have not resulted in any observable strengthening of the protection effects of pensions, as indicated by the share of pension receipt among the relevant age group. There is no firm evidence to argue that structural and parametric reforms, the restoration of democracy and workers' rights, left governments, and improved state capacity as observed in this period, has led to improved protection outcomes.

6.2.2 Pension Benefit Replacement Rates

The analysis of reach provides a binary picture of the distribution of pension benefits, receipt, or no receipt. An examination of replacement rates is essential to assessing the protection effects of pensions for pensioners.

In the pensions literature the conventional approach is to construct measures of the replacement rate of pension benefits as the ratio of pension benefits at retirement to labour earnings in the period prior to retirement. The replacement rate provides information on the extent to which withdrawal from the labour market will result in a significant cut in living standards for workers. The selection of a benchmark labour earnings for this calculation has an important bearing on assessing protection effects of pension benefits. Skilled workers show earnings rising steeply over their working life—due to experience, skills premia, or firms' structuring of lifetime earnings. This suggests that some average of earnings over the working life might constitute a more appropriate measure of reference labour earnings. Average lifetime earnings are also a reasonable indicator of households' permanent income, a measure of longer-term standard of living. In practice the calculation of pension replacement rates relies on a measure of labour earnings averaged over several years prior to retirement.[1] Taking on board these provisos,[2] pension replacement rates add an important dimension to the assessment of the protection effects of pensions.

Due to the scarcity of long-term longitudinal data on labour earnings and pension benefits in Latin America, studies have largely relied on simulations with fixed parameters for an average or standard worker (Altamirano Montoya et al., 2018; Arenas de Mesa, 2019; IMF, 2018; OECD/IDB/The World Bank, 2014).

Figure 6.2 shows simulated pension replacement rates for a selection of pension schemes in Latin America constructed by Altamirano Montoya et al. (2018). The parameters assume that workers start work at age 20 and retire at the scheme designated retirement age. The representative worker has complete labour and contribution histories over this period. Earnings are assumed to rise at a constant 2 percent per year. For the purposes of calculating replacement rates the reference labour earnings are earnings in the last year prior to retirement. Males have a spouse who is 3 years younger, the reverse is the case for females.[3] Pension benefits are

[1] Less skilled workers have flatter life-earnings profiles (Ljungqvist, 1995).

[2] The pension replacement rate is not a consistent or a reliable measure of income adequacy. The ILO recommends a pension replacement rate of at least 40 percent of preretirement earnings, but 40 percent of the minimum wage implies a very different standard of living than 40 percent of the labour earnings in the top decile.

[3] The study relies on country and gender specific mortality tables.

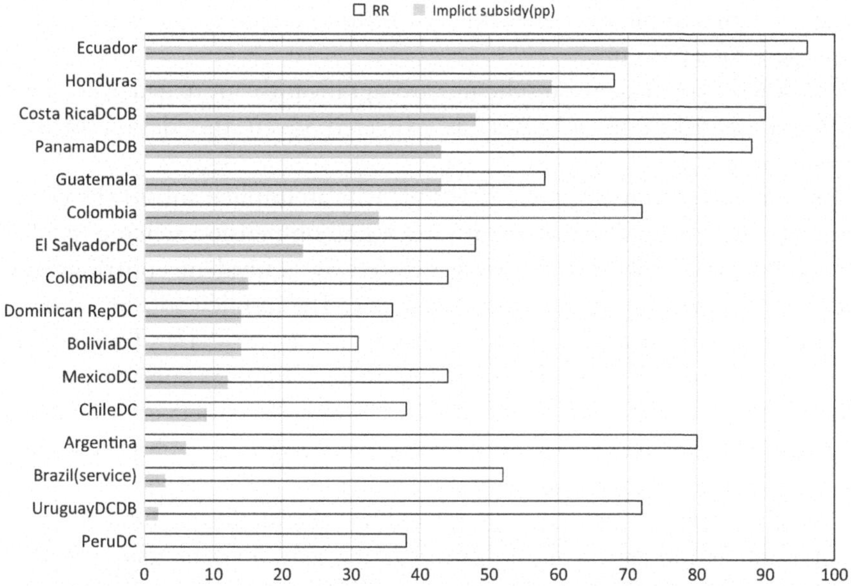

Fig. 6.2 Simulated replacement rates and implicit subsidy for selected pension schemes. Data Source: Altamirano Montoya et al. (2018). DC stands for defined contribution or individual retirement savings plans; DB stands for defined benefit occupational pensions

defined by their respective pension scheme regulations. In defined contribution schemes, an annual interest rate of 3.5 is applied to pension savings.[4]

The Figure shows simulated replacements rates and implicit subsidies for selected pension schemes in Latin America.

The pension retirement rate simulations offer several interesting findings.

Overall, most pension schemes in the region would exceed by some distance ILO recommendations on replacement rates. The schemes failing to achieve this benchmark are all individual contribution savings plans, those in Chile, Dominican Republic, and Peru. The representative

[4]The authors provide an excel file enabling researchers to change these parameters (Altamirano Montoya et al., 2018).

worker with complete labour and contribution histories stands to receive very generous pensions.[5]

Defined benefit pension schemes are significantly more generous than defined contribution schemes, as expected given the design of the schemes.

Altamirano Montoya et al. (2018) identify an implicit subsidy by comparing the simulated replacement rates based on pension scheme regulations with the replacement rate generated by equivalent contributions accumulated at the 3.5 percent interest rate. The implicit subsidy, shown as percentage points of the replacement rate, is very large for defined benefit schemes. The sources of the simulated implicit subsidy are the funds redistributed from workers who fail to collect their entitlements, because of short lives and short working lives, and from public subsidies as in guaranteed minimum pensions.

Whilst replacement rates generated by simulations under perfect employment and contribution histories suggest more than adequate protection effects of pensions, this is an unrealistic expectation when considering what we know about these histories in practice. Studies based on administrative data for Latin America find workers have significant gaps in their employment and contribution histories (Bertranou, 2001; Bosch et al., 2013; CAF, 2020; Ferrer & Riddell, 2011; Gualavisi & Oliveri, 2016). The gaps are larger for women and low-income groups. Estimates based on administrative data of the share of work spells without contributions indicate they are as high as 65 percent in Argentina, 49 percent in Brazil, 53 percent in Ecuador, and 50 percent in Uruguay (CAF, 2020). This study finds that "…in Argentina only 7 percent of women and 13 percent of men would have accumulated 30 years of contributions at the current retirement age. Equivalent figures are 8 and 12 percent for Brazil, 21 and 6 percent in Ecuador, and 15 and 20 percent in Uruguay." (CAF, 2020, p. 119).[6]

---

[5] Vastly more generous than the OECD average at 54 percent (OECD/IDB/The World Bank, 2014).

[6] Figures reported in OECD (2014) indicate the share of male workers expected to achieve less than 50 percent contribution density for Chile, Peru, and El Salvador was estimated at 40, 75, and 67 percent respectively. The figures for female workers for the three countries plus Mexico ranges from 70 percent to 87 percent.

One of the few replacement rate studies based on a random sample of administrative data for Uruguay confirms these findings. This is an important study because Uruguay has one of the region's most stable and robust pension schemes, with individual retirement savings plans complementing the occupational pension scheme. As the authors put it, "[O]ur results suggest that while 51% would be eligible for retirement at age 60, 28% would not be able to retire from the contributory system even at age seventy. We expect that 34% of those retiring at age 60 will receive a minimum pension while the average replacement rate is estimated to be 52% relative to the previous year's wage"(de Melo et al., 2019, p. 106).

The findings from this literature make two significant points for our understanding of the protection effects of pensions.

First, the employment and contribution engagement of workers over their working lives is an important factor in determining replacement rates. High vesting periods make it impossible for a large share of current workers to access their pension entitlements at retirement. Given the volatility of employment in the region, vesting periods enforce redistribution of funds from low contribution density workers to high contribution intensity workers. Occupational pensions encourage sustained worker contribution density and penalise workers with low contribution density. This is another example how social security institutions influence employment and protection.

Second, occupational pensions favour high-income and high contribution density workers, essentially those with high levels of skill. Pension schemes are highly responsive to earnings inequality and are not designed to reduce income inequalities among pensioners. This is transparently the case with individual retirement savings plans that lack inequality-reducing redistributive effects. Redistributive effects in the shape of solidarity funds, minimum guaranteed pensions, and subsidies to low-income pensioners are commonly regulated for and financed by governments. Consequently, pension schemes are not inequality reducing and could well be inequality enhancing with direct implications for their protection effects. As demonstrated by studies simulating and estimating replacement rates, pension schemes generate large stratification effects in the older population in Latin America.

6.2.3 Inequalities in Old Age Income Support

Inequality in income support for older people is a primary indicator of the protection effects of pension provision. Figure 6.3 reports on the distribution of pension benefits and old age transfers combined, a measure of income support in old age, estimated from household survey data for the countries in the region.[7] The fact that pension benefits and old age transfers might not be reliably reported in survey data provides a strong justification for measuring them jointly. Because old age transfers are fixed in value, the inclusion of old age transfers is unlikely to distort the observed protection effects of pension benefits. The focus is therefore on all pension and transfer income for centiles of the population aged 65 and over.[8] To get a sense of the adequacy of income protection in later age, the panels include the level of the US$ 4 poverty line, denoted by the broken line. The moderate poverty line is more appropriate to Latin American countries (Castañeda et al., 2016).

All the panels show a consistent picture, beginning with a large group of older people without any income support, followed by another group with relatively constant income support in the middle of the distribution, and a small number of older people in receipt of very generous pensions. Roughly 85 percent of the population over 65 have no access to income security or receive basic levels of income from retirement benefits and transfers. Income security climbs steeply for the richest 15 percent of the population aged 65 and over. This exercise demonstrates that income support in late age is hugely unequal in the countries of the region. The effects of social protection stratification effects on income security in later age are not hard to discern from the panels.

It might be helpful to get a sense of the occupational background of the three main groups. The groups on the right-hand side of the panels,

---

[7] It is worth keeping in mind that survey and administrative data on pension receipt can be subject to large discrepancies (Arenas de Mesa, 2019).

[8] Pen (1971) described income inequality by imagining a procession in which people's height would be proportional to their income. The procession would open up with the smallest people, with the lowest income, followed by increasingly taller people, and ending with a few giants. This device helps to represent the acute inequalities in income security among people aged 65 and over.

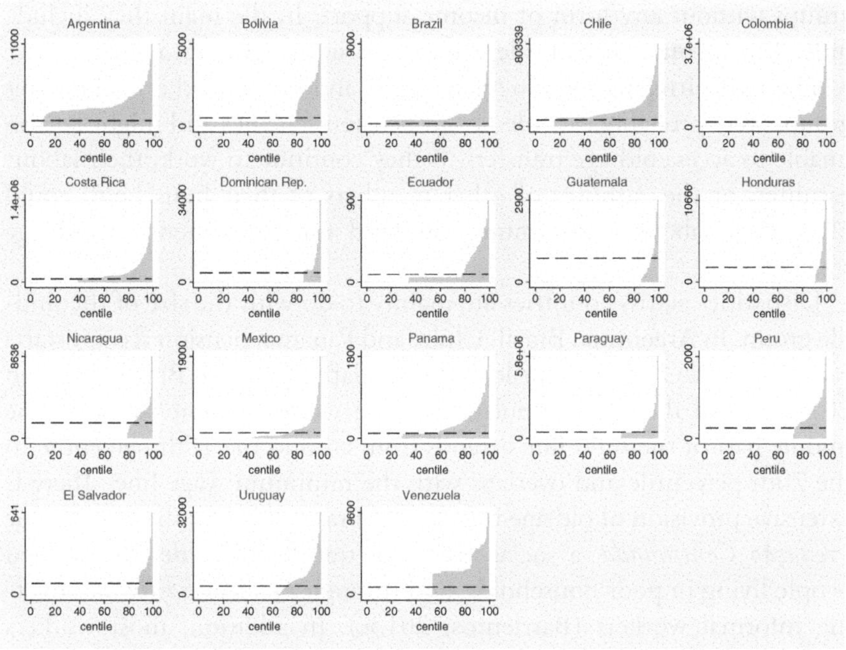

Fig. 6.3 Pension benefits and old age transfers by centile of population 65 and over. Data Source: Own elaboration based on household survey data from around 2012. Dash indicated $4 a day PPP USD poverty line. Amounts in local currency.

The Figure shows pension benefits plus old age transfers by centile of population aged 65 and over. It captures the distribution and level of income support in later age in Latin America.

roughly from the 85th-90th percentile, show rapidly rising pension benefits (measured in local currency). They include pensioners from the high ranks of the civil service, the military or police, judges, and former parliamentarians. In countries with individual retirement savings plans, pensioners from highly paid jobs in the private sector will be found among them. The flat section in the middle of the panels is populated by older groups able to access old age transfers or in receipt of minimum retirement benefits from occupational insurance funds or individual retirement savings plans. The left-hand side of the panels is populated by older groups without any form of income support. In the main they include older low-income workers dependent on informal employment, older women with irregular employment spells and home workers. The latter groups were probably excluded from pension schemes and might be also unable to access old age transfers. If they continue to work, their labour earnings, or the earnings of other members of their household, could place them above a minimum threshold for entitlement to old age transfers.

Disparities across countries are mainly to do with the size of the middle group. In Argentina, Brazil, Chile, and Panama, pension receipt starts earlier after the 20th percentile, but it is relatively flat. In Brazil, less than 20 percent of the older population cannot access income support. The middle part of the solid line extends from around the 18th percentile to the 70th percentile and overlaps with the minimum wage line. There is extensive provision of old age transfers in Brazil, through the *Beneficio de Prestação Continuada*, a social assistance transfer for older or disabled people living in poor households, and through *Previdência Rural*, targeting informal workers (Barrientos, 2013c). In addition, most workers affiliated to the private sector pension scheme retire with only a minimum guaranteed benefit. All these groups receive income support equivalent to the minimum wage and explains the extended flat middle part of the distribution (Mesquita et al., 2010). In Argentina, only around 10 percent of older people have no access to income support. Old age transfers and minimum retirement benefits from occupational pensions explain the gently rising bars in the middle of the distribution (Bertranou et al., 2011). Uruguay is an interesting case. The relevant panel show limited income support below the 60th percentile, in contrast to the information coming from administrative data. Legislation in 2012 relaxed the conditions for accessing pension benefits (de Melo et al., 2019).

Some Andean countries have extended income support through the provision of old age transfers. Bolivia and Ecuador show the effects of the large expansion of old age transfers on protection among older people. In contrast, the absence of large-scale old age transfer programmes in Peru and Colombia explains the limited protection effects of income support, although old age transfers have been strengthened in both countries since 2012.

Central American countries show very limited income protection for older groups. In Guatemala, El Salvador, Honduras, Nicaragua, and the Dominican Republic, pension receipt is limited to the top two deciles. Costa Rica has extended income support further down to the top four deciles but only the top two deciles receive pensions above the poverty line. Mexico has rapidly expanded old age transfers since 2012, but there remain large groups of older people with no income support.

The analysis of the distribution of pension benefits and old age transfers for the countries in the region revealed large inequalities in income protection in later life. The tails of the distribution underline the main findings. In most countries, a substantial group of people aged 65 and over are excluded from income support in old age. At the other extreme, a minority, around 15 percent of the population aged 65 and over, capture very high retirement benefits. In between, older people are supported by old age transfers and minimum pension guarantees, in the main publicly funded. Broadly, the protection effects of occupational pensions and individual retirement accounts are limited to the top two deciles of the older population. The main outcome of institutions providing income support in later age is a sharply stratified older population (Barrientos, 2021).

6.3 Social Assistance

The analysis of the protection effects of pension benefits focused mainly on the incidence and distribution of the transfers, relying on a direct approach. Assessing the protection effects of social assistance has the additional challenge of accounting for behavioural responses to the transfers. Researchers have sought to address this challenge by developing and implementing experimental and quasi-experimental methods of evaluation (Angrist & Pischke, 2008; Imbens & Angrist, 1994; Ravallion, 2005).

Three main strategies to reliably identify programme outcomes have been employed in the literature researching transfers. First, a difference-in-difference strategy constructs equivalent treatment and control groups prior to the intervention and measures changes in target indicators before and after implementation. This strategy has been applied to study the impact of conditional income transfer programmes (Skoufias, 2005). Second, regression discontinuity design is a strategy identifying factors outside the control of potential transfer recipients that could help separate out treatment and control groups. This has been applied to assess the impact of old age transfer programmes with a qualifying age and to conditional income transfers implementing changes in programme design (Barrientos & Villa, 2015a; Canavire-Bacarreza et al., 2017). Third, a matching strategy is employed in evaluation studies identifying ex post a control group among non-recipients sharing the same characteristics than recipient households or individual (Glewwe & Kassouf, 2012; Kassouf et al., 2011). Matching strategies have the disadvantage that matching can only be based on observed variables.[9]

6.3.1 Conditional Income Transfers

Conditional income transfers normally have strong impact evaluation protocols and are significantly more likely to be evaluated than any other social protection programmes (Barrientos & Villa, 2015b). Outcomes are often estimated using dedicated quasi-experimental evaluation datasets able to identify the causal relation between programme participation and outcomes. The canonical example for the region is PROGRESA in Mexico (Skoufias, 2005). PROGRESA was implemented in 1997, in the context of a budgetary squeeze and competing antipoverty programmes. A strong evaluation protocol was required to provide incontrovertible evidence that the programme would work to make sure its budget would be protected (Levy, 2006). Designers relied on a census to identify potential recipients and implemented the programme in 1998 in stages. Subsequent evaluation surveys in 1999 and 2000 provided information on the households in locations included in the programme from the start and those in locations where entry was delayed. It was then possible to compare the two groups of households and identify the outcomes of the programme (Skoufias, 2005). The findings revealed a rise in consumption among recipients and a reduction in poverty, in conditions where

[9] Unobserved variables measuring effort or commitment, for example, might be central to the outcomes of interventions.

consumption was generally declining because of a financial crisis. Evaluation protocols became de rigueur in the subsequent spread of conditional income transfers in the region.

The fact that the evaluation datasets from PROGRESA were made available to academic researchers, an example followed by other conditional income transfer programmes, facilitated the exponential growth of impact evaluation studies focused on intended and unintended effects (Fiszbein & Schady, 2009; Stampini & Tornarolli, 2012). The growth in programme studies encouraged the emergence of meta-analysis harmonising and comparing the findings from individual studies (Araújo, 2021; Baird et al., 2014; García & Saavedra, 2022; McGuire et al., 2022). This section will rely primarily on meta studies.[10]

Conditional income transfers have two main objectives: to raise the consumption of households in poverty and to facilitate investment in human capital, a social investment objective (Barrientos, 2013b). The former is expected to reduce poverty in the short run while the second is expected to improve future productive capacity, and therefore earnings, of participant children thus reducing the probability of poverty in the future. Impact evaluations have focused on whether programmes achieve these objectives.

As regards consumption, it is a no brainer that consumption rises after transfer receipt. How much does it rise will depends on households' allocation of the transfer. As a rough average, around 80 per cent of the value of the transfers is accounted for by higher consumption among participant households (Fiszbein & Schady, 2009). Conditional income transfers reduce poverty measured in terms of consumption or income.[11] They are not designed to take households above the poverty line. As a rough average, transfer values are around 20 per cent of average participant

[10] There is an interesting and apposite debate on the limitations of impact evaluation studies and by extension on the limitations of meta-analysis (Banerjee & Duflo, 2011; Deaton & Cartwright, 2017; Ravallion, 2005). The issue is that the findings from quasi-experimental studies (comparing treatment and control groups) have validity only in the specific context in which they are set. Their causal findings cannot be directly extrapolated to other contexts, conditional income transfers programmes in this case. Meta-analysis can mitigate these limitations through exacting protocols, but cannot eliminate them (Ravallion, 2012).

[11] Bastagli et al. (2016) surveyed all cash transfer programmes and were only able to find one example of a programme that did not reduce poverty in Albania, due to mitigating labour supply effects.

household consumption, so that households with incomes below 80 per cent of the poverty line will remain in poverty (Barrientos, 2013b). The main impact of transfers will be on the poverty gap of participant households, not the poverty headcount. An early impact evaluation of Progresa concluded that after two years of programme participation, from October 1997 to November 1999, poverty headcount in participant households fell by 17.36 per cent compared to a control group, while the reduction in their poverty gap was estimated at 36.13 per cent (Skoufias, 2005).

Assessing social investment outcomes in conditional income transfers is more complicated as they are expected to roll out in time and to involve income and behavioural responses (Molina Millán et al., 2019; Parker & Vogl, 2018). The heavy lifting is done by the conditions in the programme design. These vary in terms of both design and implementation. A critical issue is whether the effects from programme participation are mainly due to the income transfer lifting financial constraints on recipient households, or whether they are mainly due to the conditions encouraging behavioural change. This is critical, because if the change is due solely to the income transfer, an equal-sized transfer without conditions attached could deliver the same outcomes.[12] This will be considered further below.

It is straightforward to identify immediate outcomes in terms of school enrolment and attendance by children in participant households. The rise in enrolments is smaller for primary school age participants than for secondary school participants. This is explained by relatively high primary school enrolment rates in middle income countries, compared to secondary school enrolment rates. Saavedra and Garcia (2017) provide a meta-analysis of 42 conditional income transfer programme, including programmes in other developing regions. They calculate that the programmes examined generated on average a 3 percentage points (3.4 per cent) improvement in primary school enrolment rates and a 5 percentage points (9 per cent) improvement in secondary school enrolment rates. They conclude that conditional income transfers by themselves are

[12] There are numerous studies and policy papers on the merits and de-merits of conditions. Even the late bishop Tutu of South Africa contributed a view. An excellent account of the relationship existing between conditions and domestic politics can be found in Borges (2019).

unlikely to ensure full enrolment rates in the absence of supply-side improvements.

Hard evidence on the separate effectiveness of conditions is scarce. Baird et al. (2014) conducted a meta study of the schooling effects of conditional and unconditional income transfers, identifying 35 such studies. The authors were particularly interested in identifying differences in schooling effects between programmes with and without conditions. They found that variations in the intensity of conditions have a measurable influence on programme impact. Using children not receiving a transfer as a control group they find that, for the set of programmes included in the study, children in households receiving a transfer show 1.36 higher odds of school enrolment. Compared to the control group, recipients of transfers without conditions show 1.23 higher odds of school enrolment, whereas recipients of transfers with conditions show 1.41 higher odds of school enrolment. Taking programme conditions as a range—including programmes providing transfers without conditions; programmes providing transfers with some conditions that are not implemented or are implemented lightly; and programmes with conditions that are explicit, monitored and implemented strictly—suggests that changes in school enrolment are positively related to the intensity of conditions. In programmes providing transfers with explicit conditions, children show 1.60 higher odds of school enrolment than children in the control group.

The study also considered school attendance outcomes and found that transfer receipt raises the odds of children attending regularly. Children in receipt of transfers with no conditions have a 1.42 higher probability of attending regularly compared to the control group; while children in receipt of a transfer with conditions show a 1.65 higher probability of attending regularly compared to a control group (Baird et al., 2014). The probability of regular attendance rises with the intensity of conditions.

A crucial issue with the social investment outcomes of transfers is the extent to which conditional income transfers could improve the future productive capacity of children from low-income households. Early simulations suggested measurable and positive effects. Glewwe and Kassouf (2012) estimated the schooling effects of participation in Bolsa Escola, one of the earliest conditional income transfer programmes and the core component of today's Bolsa Família. They found that improvements in school enrolment and attendance among children participating households were equivalent on average to an 18 per cent increase in their education cycle or 1.5 additional years of education. From 2004 PNAD data they calculated that an additional year of education raised wages in Brazil by around 11 per cent, implying an increase in labour earnings of 16–17 per cent among the poorest third of the population, or around 1.5 per cent for the labour force taken as a whole. This is equivalent to an additional 0.8 per cent of gross domestic product (GDP). Programme costs are 0.4 per cent of GDP. Spreading the benefits over 40 years from the expected lifetime labour force participation in Brazil, and applying a 6 per cent discount rate, would yield a net present value for the investment at 0.3 per cent. They conclude that while 'it is unclear whether the benefits exceed the costs' (Glewwe and Kassouf 2012, p. 516), their rough calculations suggest that well-designed and implemented conditional income transfer programmes could pay for themselves.

Comparative studies of impact evaluation studies, to distinguish them from meta-analysis, have considered labour supply effects of transfers. The motivation of labour supply studies is to establish whether conditional income transfers are mitigated by adverse employment decisions by recipient households. In general, the literature confirms reductions in the labour supply of children, especially where conditions on schooling or market employment are included in the design of the programme (de Hoop & Rosati, 2014). Labour supply outcomes associated with adults tend to be more heterogeneous but small and in most cases not statistically significant (Barrientos & Malerba, 2020). Using a regression discontinuity design applied to administrative data, Barrientos and Villa (2015a) find a positive and significant labour supply effect for women, suggesting that large samples and further disaggregation of programme participants could reveal labour supply effects that net out at the aggregate level. Labour supply effects from old age transfers will be covered in the next section.

Gradually, studies focused on medium- and long-term social investment effects of conditional income transfers are beginning to draw a tentatively positive picture (Parker & Vogl, 2018). The paucity of research on these outcomes is largely explained by data and methodological constraints. Impact evaluations grounded on quasi-experimental data are extremely effective in assessing short term effects of interventions but deploying these techniques to assess long term effects is particularly challenging. Typically, evaluation surveys are collected in the first few years following the implementation of a conditional income transfer programme. As more households are included in the programme, control groups disappear. Changing households, social and economic conditions also make it harder to identify appropriate control groups. Families are not expected to remain unchanged over time. Migration is an issue in rural areas affected by worsening economic conditions and housing generates geographical mobility areas in rural areas. In Mexico, programme eligibility was established in 1997 prior to implementation, with some communities integrated into the programme in 1999 acting as a control group. By 2000, all communities were in the programme. Further evaluation rounds in 2003 and 2007 involved, in each case, the construction of a new control group. Each time, the control group was eventually integrated into the programme, precluding treatment control group comparisons. Attrition among the original participants was very high, reflecting the incidence of migration in rural Mexico. In 2007, the evaluation survey round registered attrition among children in the 1997 original group as high as 60 per cent.

Quasi-experimental evaluations of long-term effects are hugely challenging, to the extent that alternative approaches and data might be required. Kugler and Rojas (2018) rely in data from PROGRESA evaluation surveys 2003–2015 using the length of potential exposure to the programme to identify effects in 2015. Their findings are positive, programme participants show additional years of education (0.8 years if 3 year exposure rising by 0.5 years with extra years of exposure), higher rates of employment among women (7–11 pps increase from a 26 percent baseline) and 50% rise in monthly labour earnings for women. Parker and Vogl (2018) rely on 2010 census data for Mexico and compare 7–11 year olds in 1997 with 15+ year olds as a means of identifying programme effects. They find additional completed years of education, more likely to be employed with higher earnings for persons with average exposure.

Molina-Millan et al. (2016) provide a careful assessment of the longer term effects of participation in conditional income transfers in Mexico,

Nicaragua and Colombia, countries with available longer-term evaluation surveys. They review both experimental and non-experimental studies. They focus on the transition to school of children exposed to the programme *in utero* or in early childhood, and on the transition to adulthood of programme participant children while at school. They find clear results for schooling and attendance but mixed results for other learning outcomes. They acknowledge that data limitations might be responsible for the latter. In an enlarged and updated meta-analysis of education, García and Saavedra conclude: "The existing evidence on CCTs long-term impacts is clearer for some than for other outcomes. The experimental literature provides consistent evidence of impacts on schooling, as well as some evidence of impacts on cognitive skills and learning, socioemotional skills, and improved labor market outcomes. Yet many studies also find a fair share of results that are not statistically different from zero. Unsurprisingly, it is often difficult to discern whether this is due to a lack of impact or other methodological concerns. The non-experimental literature provides a similarly mixed picture, along with greater concerns about internal validity." (García & Saavedra, 2022, p. 152)

6.3.2 Old Age Transfers

A growing literature estimates the outcomes of old age transfers using quasi-experimental methods. Old age transfers pose some additional challenges to the identification of transfer outcomes. Conditional income transfers are designed as household transfers and therefore outcomes are measured on households. Old age transfers are individual transfers that are normally shared within households (Lloyd-Sherlock, 2006) and therefore it makes sense to consider household outcomes of old age transfers. As households are not static, attention has been paid to potential household changes in response to old age transfer (Edmonds et al., 2001). Studies have also shown that households recompose themselves in response to economic crises (D'Elia, 2007).

In Latin America, conditional income transfers have a relatively uniform design but old age transfers are more heterogeneous. Old age transfers in Latin America have been designed (i) to reach all people above a particular age (categorical); or (ii) older people without a pension (complementary); or (iii) older people in poverty (targeted), or as a first pillar of a multi-pillar pension system (basic or minimum pension).[13] Heterogeneity in design complicates assessment of outcomes.

Meta-analysis studies of old age transfer impact evaluations are lacking in the region. This section will therefore aim to provide a synthesis of findings from existing studies. Data limitations apply to the assessment of the protection effects of old age transfers as household surveys commonly sample a small number of older people, due to demographic factors, limiting the reliability of statistical analysis on these groups. Ad hoc surveys of older people are relatively new in the region, but they are becoming more common.

All impact evaluation studies measuring household consumption effects find a rise in consumption expenditure associated with the transfer and consequently a fall in measured income poverty (Bando et al., 2021; Decancq et al., 2018; Galiani et al., 2014; S. Martínez, 2004; Martínez et al., 2020). A set of studies focus on potential labour supply effects of old age transfers. Their findings, taken together, suggest a reduction in the labour supply of older recipients (Bosch & Guajardo, 2012; Elizondo et al., 2018; Hernani-Limarino & Mena, 2015; Juarez & Pfutze, 2015). Measured outcomes on the labour supply of co-residents are mixed. Generally, changes in labour supply of co-residents are found to be marginally positive, especially for women. Studies examining at the impact of transfers on co-resident children found positive effects on schooling and education related expenditures (Juarez & Pfutze, 2015; Martínez et al., 2020; Yañes-Pagans, 2008). Regarding potential household changes that could mitigate the positive effect of transfers on household consumption, study findings fail to confirm this hypothesis.

The main conclusion is that social assistance transfers have positive and significant protection effects on the consumption of recipient households and their resilience. Social assistance transfers reach population groups with low incomes. Social assistance transfer programmes do not require recipients to withdraw from employment and their entitlements are independent from the type of employment or occupation. This opens

[13] Argentina provides budget financed pension to persons of merit.

the possibility that transfers could support existing employment and encourage employment for particular types of workers (Barrientos & Villa, 2015a). Old age transfers do lead to reductions in employment among older groups, although these reductions in employment could be compensated for by co-residents. The reduction in child labour associated with social assistance will positively impact on their personal development.

A feature of social assistance in Latin America is a focus on social investment (Barrientos, 2022). Research on the protection effects of social assistance in the medium and longer term suggests positive results. To date, reported findings are mixed but support an expectation that conditional income transfers will be shown to contribute to an improvement in the skills and productive capacity of younger generations. Conditional income transfers have evolved in ways that strengthen their social investment features.[14]

On a less positive note, and from a regional perspective, the limitations of current social assistance programmes in terms of reach and adequacy are significant. Social assistance institutions are less developed and have weaker governance in precisely the countries which need them most.

6.4 Tax-Transfer Systems

Previous sections considered protection outcomes separately from the core social protection institutions: pension benefits, conditional income transfers, and old age transfers. The estimates of incidence and outcomes offer an instructive perspective on the protection effects of social protection institutions in Latin America. There remains a further issue to consider, whether protection effects of social protection institutions are strengthened or weakened by taxation. To address this issue, this section will review the available literature on the broader protection effects of fiscal policy in the countries in the region.

[14] Mexico's replacement of Prospera with a range of education subsidies and debates on the future of conditional income transfers in Argentina and Brazil suggest their social investment orientation will be strengthened in future reforms (Barrientos, 2013a).

This is an important issue. Take social assistance transfers for example, they are financed from domestic revenues which themselves have implications for poverty and inequality. Impact evaluations of conditional income transfer programme can generate a reduction of poverty but, if financed by a regressive indirect tax, poverty and inequality reduction effects could be partially mitigated (Lustig, 2017). Along the same lines, it is feasible that unequally distributed pension benefits may nevertheless work to reduce the primary inequality in market income. Tax expenditures are in fact social protection interventions for the better off (OECD/CIAT/IDB, 2023). A brief discussion of the protection effects of social protection institutions within the tax-transfer system will provide a welcomed additional perspective on the findings so far.

The Commitment to Equity CEQ initiative has produced estimates of the distributional effects of fiscal policies, including estimates of poverty and inequality outcomes from social protection transfers (Lustig, 2018). They can throw light on the issue at hand. CEQ estimates identify household income flows from household survey data and arrange them to identify four income concepts. Market income is all income from the factors of production plus private transfers plus imputed rent and own production. Disposable income adds all direct taxes and transfers. Consumable income accounts for all indirect taxes and transfers. Final income includes monetised value of in-kind transfers and related fees and co-payments. For our purposes we are particularly interested in the distributional changes associated with moving from market income to disposable income, as the latter incorporates the outcomes from social protection taxes and transfers.

There are advantages from to this approach. Income flows from national income accounts are reported in aggregate, offering very limited information on the incidence of taxes and transfers in the population and consequently on their distribution. Household survey data can throw light on both these issues. At the same time, household survey data suffers from sampling restrictions, limited coverage of economic activities, and reporting errors, to name those most relevant in our context. In the Latin American context, household surveys often fail to reach the very rich and the very poor in sufficient numbers. There is limited time allocated for household survey interviews. It is inescapable that the household surveys might leave out requests for information on income flows of interest, for example respondent participation in smaller social protection programmes. Few household surveys in Latin America collect information on factor income flows in full. Corporate taxation, for example, does not directly apply to households, so the relevant information is not available from household surveys. Further limitations relate to the cross-section nature of survey data, with restricted information on intertemporal income flows, and limited ability to capture behavioural responses to taxes and transfers. However, taking these limitations on board, CEQ estimates provide very useful information on the outcomes from social protection institutions.

The treatment of pension income and contribution, from occupational insurance funds or individual retirement savings plans, merits a brief discussion. It illustrates the limitations of this approach in respect to intertemporal income flows. There are two ways in which we could account for pension income flows: as a government transfer or as deferred compensation. If pensions benefits are accounted for as deferred compensation, that is as a share of wages kept by pension institutions and disbursed to the worker after retirement, it makes sense to include pension benefits and pension contributions as market income. The relevant counterfactual here is a situation in which workers set part of their income aside, invest them in return yielding asset and translate them into an annuity at retirement. Alternatively, accounting for pension benefits as government transfers, perhaps financed in part from payroll taxes, would suggest pensions should be included under disposable income, not market income. Whilst it is the case that governments in the region provide significant subsidies to mandated pension schemes, treating pension benefits and contributions as direct transfers is problematic. The counterfactual in this case is the absence of pension schemes. Effectively workers' pay taxes and will be pleasantly surprised to receive transfers at retirement. Accounting for pensions as government transfers is likely to overestimate the redistribution effects of fiscal policies as relatively advantaged workers without savings at retirement would report zero incomes before the transfer.[15] CEQ estimates are implemented separately for these two cases. In the discussion below, the focus will be on pensions as a government transfer, with market income including pension benefits net of pension contributions.

6.4.1 Poverty and Inequality Outcomes

Figure 6.4 compares poverty rates before and after direct taxes and transfers for Latin American countries. The focus is on the poverty headcount rate with the poverty line set at US$5.5 2011 PPP. In all countries direct taxes and transfers reduce the poverty rate. However, and aside from a handful of countries, the change in poverty headcount is very small. This applies especially to countries with high headcount poverty rates. In Chile, Argentina, Uruguay and Panama, direct taxes and transfers have stronger effects on the poverty headcount rate. They halve the headcount rate in Argentina. Poverty reduction outcomes are mainly the consequence of direct transfers. In most countries in the region, direct taxes apply at best to households in the top four deciles of income and are unlikely to include groups in poverty.

Tax and transfer systems in Latin America have only limited effects on inequality. Figure 6.5 highlights changes in the Gini index associated with moving from market income to disposable and consumable income. Countries are arranged from left to right in the Figure according to the size of the effect of tax and transfers on income inequality. Where data is available for more than one year, an earlier and a later year are shown.

A handful of countries show relatively larger drops in inequality associated with direct taxes and transfers. Argentina and Uruguay top the list. As we move from left to right in the Figure, the inequality reduction

[15] This applies to superficial comparisons of the redistribution of income in countries with generous welfare states and Latin American countries. Sweden's tax-transfers can halve the Gini of market income, but they lump together horizontal redistribution, the same people at different points in time, and vertical redistribution, from the rich to the poor. Studies indicate that the reduction in the Gini is neatlyd divided in half, vertical distribution and half horizontal redistribution each contribute one half (Bengsston et al., 2012). In Latin American countries with truncated pension schemes most of the fiscal redistribution is horizontal.

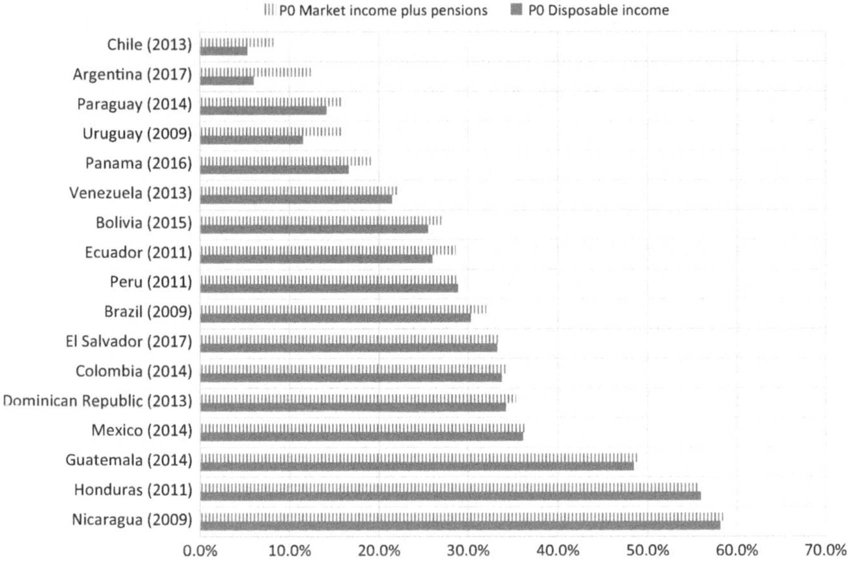

Fig. 6.4 Poverty headcount effects of direct taxes and transfers. Data source: Lustig et al. (CEQ Institute, 2022). $5.5 a day PPP USD poverty line

effects decline in size. Overall, the reduction in inequality from direct taxes and transfers is disappointing for most countries in the region. Changes in the Gini index moving from disposable income to consumable income, that is incorporating indirect taxes and subsidies, are generally in an equalising direction. But the absolute changes are very small. Venezuela stands out due to generous energy subsidies. The top level conclusion from this exercise is that fiscal policy in Latin America has very limited effects on market inequality.

6.5 Gender

Gender is a dimension cross cutting the issues discussed in this chapter.

Occupational pension schemes reproduce and reinforce gender differentials in employment and pay (Arza, 2017). By the same token, occupational pension schemes reinforce gender differentials in access to pension benefits. The redistribution effects in pension funds from workers with

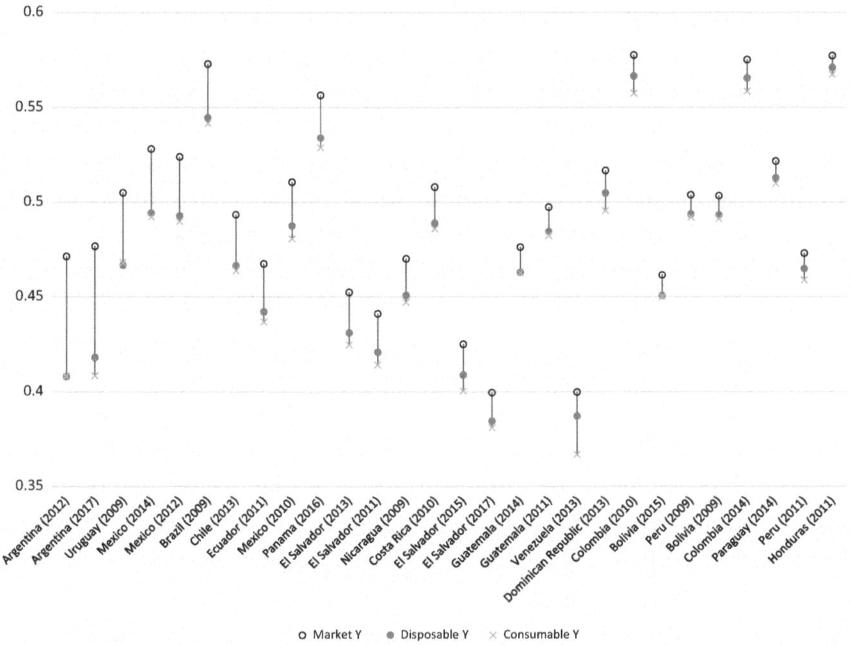

Fig. 6.5 Gini index for income categories—CEQ estimates. Data source: Lustig et al. (CEQ Institute, 2022)

The Figure shows the change in the Gini index estimated with market income, disposable income, which includes direct transfers and taxes, and consumable income, which includes all indirect taxes and subsidies, for selected countries and years.

low earnings and interrupted employment records to workers with high earnings and long tenures have an obvious gender dimension as women are more likely to be found among the former. Survivor provision regulations in occupational pension are highly relevant for women. However, this underlines their access to pension entitlement as dependants.

Individual retirement savings pension plans also reproduce and reinforce gender differentials in employment and pay (Barrientos, 1998) and survivor benefit provision are also highly relevant. But there are additional issues to consider. The accumulation period in individual retirement savings plans replicates directly gender disparities in pay and employment. Decisions concerning retirement arrangements will bring to the fore potential gender discrimination in the contracting of an annuity, depending on whether insurance companies are legally allowed to use sex-specific mortality tables.

Social assistance transfers, on the other hand, are in theory gender neutral, in so far as they are household based and fixed in value as in conditional income transfers, or individual and fixed in value as in old age transfers. In practice, social assistance protection arguably has a positive gender bias. Conditional income transfers are designed to be received by mothers, a feature that has encourage research into the implications for women's roles in the implementation of the programmes and into the effect of acting as the income recipient in their autonomy (Barber & Gertler, 2010; Borges Sugiyama & Hunter, 2019; Molyneux, 2006, 2008; Schady & Rosero, 2008). Demographically, women are overrepresented in late age, with the implication that in practice old age transfers have an unintended gender bias (Kassouf et al., 2011). Old age transfers contribute to reducing gender inequality in later age (Barrientos, 2021).

6.6 Conclusion

This chapter has examined the protection effects of social protection institutions. This involved examining the main outcomes of the core institutions and of tax and transfer systems. The most significant outcome of social protection provision in Latin America is its stratification. Occupational pension schemes and individual retirement plans reach better off sections of the population while social assistance supports low-income groups dependent on informal employment.

A detailed analysis of the incidence of pension benefits, from occupational pensions and individual retirement savings plans, confirmed they reach less than half the population aged 65 and over. The reach of pension benefits is significantly higher in the Southern countries, a legacy of longstanding occupational insurance funds. However, reach is stable or declining in most of these countries, including countries like Chile, that implemented far reaching structural pension reform. In Central American countries the reach of pension benefits is very limited and show little improvement over time. In Andean countries plus Mexico, the expansion of old age transfers has outpaced the reach of pension benefits. An analysis of old age income support, combining pension benefits and old age transfers, reveal large inequalities in income security. Tracking income support for the population aged 65 and over reveals a 'hockey stick' picture, with most people in this group lacking income support or receiving at best a minimum level, and with a small proportion of pensioners receiving very generous pension benefits.

Assessing the protection effects of social assistance has been greatly facilitated by the spread of quasi-experimental evaluation studies. The evidence base on the outcomes of social assistance offer a very positive picture. Conditional income transfer programmes have measurable effects in improving the consumption of participant households. They reduce poverty in the short term and facilitate investment in schooling and health with implications for the productive capacity of participants in the longer term. Evaluation studies largely confirm the short term positive effects of conditional income transfers. Research on the longer term impact of conditional income transfers has important gaps to date, in part because of the need to develop appropriate methods of investigation. Recent work offers a more positive account of longer term outcomes. Studies evaluating the protective effects of old age transfers find reductions in poverty and vulnerability among recipients and their households.

Taking a joint perspective on social expenditure and taxation confirms the findings from the analysis of the outcomes of core social protection institutions. It finds that tax-transfer systems in the countries in the region have limited effects of poverty and inequality.

References

Altamirano Montoya, A., Berstein, S., Bosch, M., & García Huitrón, M. (2018). *Presente y futuro de las pensiones en América Latina y el Caribe*. Inter-American Development Bank.

Angrist, J. D., & Pischke, J.-S. (2008). *Mostly Harmless Econometrics: An Empiricist's Companion*. Princeton University Press.

Araújo, V. (2021). Do anti-poverty policies sway voters? Evidence from a meta-analysis of Conditional Cash Transfers. *Research and Politics*, 1–9. https://journals.sagepub.com/doi/10.1177/2053168021991715

Arenas de Mesa, A. (2019). *Los sistemas de pensiones en la encrucijada. Desafíos para la sostenibilidad en América Latina* (159; Libros de La CEPAL). Comisión Económica para América Latina y el Caribe.

Arza, C. (2017). Non-contributory benefits, pension re-reforms and the social protection of older women in Latin America. *Social Policy and Society, 16*(3), 361–375.

Baird, S., Ferreira, F., Ozler, B., & Woolcock, M. (2014). Conditional, unconditional and everything in between: A systematic review of cash transfer programs on schooling outcomes. *Journal of Development Effectiveness, 6*(1), 1–43.

Bando, R., Galiani, S., & Gertler, P. (2021). *Another brick on the Wall: On the effects of non-contributory pensions on material and subjective well being* (NBER Working Paper 28318). National Bureau of Economic Research.

Banerjee, A. V., & Duflo, E. (2011). *Poor Economics*. Public Affairs.

Barber, S. L., & Gertler, P. J. (2010). Empowering women: How Mexico's conditional cash transfer programme raised prenatal care quality and birth weight. *Journal of Development Effectiveness, 2*(1), 51–73.

Barrientos, A. (1998). Pension reform, personal pensions, and gender differences in pension coverage. *World Development, 26*(1), 125–137.

Barrientos, A. (2013a). *Human development income transfers in the longer term* (IPC Working Paper 116). International Policy Centre for Inclusive Growth.

Barrientos, A. (2013b). *Social assistance in developing countries*. Cambridge University Press.

Barrientos, A. (2013c). The rise of social assistance in Brazil. *Development and Change, 44*(4), 887–910.

Barrientos, A. (2021). Inequalities in income security in later age in Latin America. *Pan American Journal of Public Health, 45*. https://doi.org/10.26633/RPSP.2021.85

Barrientos, A. (2022). Social investment and social assistance in low- and middle-income countries. In J. Garritzmann, S. Häusermann, & B. Palier (Eds.), *The world politics of social investment* (Vol. 1, pp. 173–193). Oxford University Press.

Barrientos, A., & Malerba, D. (2020). Social assistance and inclusive growth. *International Social Security Review, 73*(3), 33–53.

Barrientos, A., & Mase, J. (2012). Poverty transitions among older households in South Africa and Brazil. *European Journal of Development Research, 24*(4), 570–588.

Barrientos, A., & Villa, J. M. (2015a). Antipoverty transfers and labour force participation effects. *Journal of Development Studies, 51*(9), 1224–1240.

Barrientos, A., & Villa, J. M. (2015b). Evaluating antipoverty transfer programmes in Latin America and Sub-Saharan Africa. Better policies? Better politics? *Journal of Globalization and Development, 6*(1), 147–179.

Bastagli, F., Hagen-Zanker, J., Harman, L., Barca, V., Sturge, G., & Schmidt, T. (2016). *Cash transfers: What does the evidence say? Annex 1 Overview of existing cash transfer reviews* [Report]. Overseas Development Institute. https://www.odi.org/publications/10505-cash-transfers-what-does-evidence-say-rigorous-review-impacts-and-role-design-and-implementation

Bengsston, N., Holmlund, B., & Walderstrom, D. (2012). *Lifetime versus Annual tax Progressivity: Sweden 1968-2009* (IZA Discussion Paper 6641). IZA.

Bertranou, F. (2001). *Empleo, Retiro y Vulnerabilidad Socioeconómica de la Población Adulta Mayor en Argentina* [Mimeo] (p. 21). Universidad Siglo

Bertranou, F., Cetràngolo, O., Grushka, C., & Casanova, L. (2011). *Encrucijadas en la seguridad social argentina: Reformas, cobertura y desafíos para el sistema de pensiones*. CEPAL/OIT.

Borges, F. A. (2019). Adoption and evolution of cash transfer programs in Latin America. In *Oxford Research Encyclopedia*. Oxford University Press. https://doi.org/10.1093/acrefore/9780190228637.013.1521

Borges Sugiyama, N., & Hunter, W. (2019). Do conditional cash transfers empower women? Insights from Brazil's Bolsa Família. *Latin American Politics and Society, 62*(2), 53–74.

Bosch, M., & Guajardo, J. (2012). *Labor Market Impacts of Non-Contributory Pensions. The Case of Argentina's Moratorium* (IADb Working Paper IDB-WP-366). Inter-American Development Bank.

Bosch, M., Melguizo, A., & Pages, C. (2013). *Mejores pensiones, mejores trabajos*. Inter-American Development Bank.

CAF. (2020). *Los sistemas de pensiones y salud en América Latina. Los desafíos del envejecimiento, el cambio tecnológico y la informalidad*. Corporación Andina de Fomento.

Canavire-Bacarreza, G., Chong, A., Rios-Avila, F., & Yanes-Pagans, M. (2017). *Will elders provide for their grandchildren? Unconditional cash transfers and educational experiences in Bolivia* (Policy Research Working Paper 8176). The World Bank.

Castañeda, A., Doan, D., Newhouse, D., Nguyen, M. C., Azevedo, J. P., & Uematsu, H. (2016). *Who are the poor in the developing world?* (Policy Research Working Paper 7844). The World Bank.

Cecchini, S., & Atuesta, B. (2017). *Programas de transferencias condicionadas en América Latina y el Caribe* (Report 224; Series Politicas Sociales). CEPAL, División Desarrollo Social.
CEQ Institute. (2022). *CEQ Standard Indicators Web version 4.0*. Tulane University.
D'Elia, V. (2007). *Pobreza en hogares con adultos mayores: Un análisis a partir del Plan de Inclusión Social* [Report]. ANSES.
de Hoop, Jacobus & Rosati, Furio C. (2014). *Cash transfers and child labor* (Policy Research Working Paper 6826). The World Bank.
de Melo, G., Catiñeiras, N., Ardente, A., Montti, O., Zelko, B., & Araya, F. (2019). Eligibility for retirement and replacement rates in the Uruguayan multi-pillar pension system. *Revista Sociedad y Desarrollo, 83*, 105–144.
Deaton, A. S., & Cartwright, N. (2017). *Understanding and misunderstanding randomized control trials* (NBER Working Paper 22595). National Bureau of Economic Research.
Decancq, K., Olivera, J., & Schokkaert, E. (2018). *Program evaluation and ethnic differences: The Pension 65 program in Peru* (Working Paper DPS18.14). Department of Economics KE Leuven.
Edmonds, E., Mammen, K., & Miller, D. (2001). Rearranging the family? Household composition responses to large pension receipts. *Journal of Human Resources, 40*(1), 186–207.
Elizondo, H., Flores, S., & de Quinto, A. (2018). *The impact of non-contributory pensions. A case study for Costa Rica*.
Ferrer, A. M., & Riddell, W. C. (2011). *Unemployment insurance savings accounts in Latin America: Overview and Assessment* (Discussion Paper 5577; IZA Discussion Paper). IZA - Institute of Labor Economics.
Fiszbein, A., & Schady, N. (2009). *Conditional cash transfers. Reducing present and future poverty*. The World Bank.
Galiani, S., Gertler, P., & Bando, R. (2014). *Non-contributory pensions* (NBER Working Paper w19775). NBER.
García, S., & Saavedra, J. (2022). *Conditional Cash Transfers for Education* (NBER Working Paper 29758). National Bureau for Economic Research. http://www.nber.org/papers/w29758
Glewwe, P., & Kassouf, A. L. (2012). The impact of Bolsa Escola/Bolsa Familia conditional cash transfer program on enrollment, dropout rates and grade promotion in Brazil. *Journal of Development Economics, 97*, 505–517.
Gualavisi, M., & Oliveri, M. L. (2016). *Antigüedad en el Empleo y Rotación Laboral en América Latina* (Nota Técnica IDB-TN-1072). Inter-American

Development Bank. https://publications.iadb.org/publications/spanish/document/Antig%C3%BCedad-en-el-empleo-y-rotaci%C3%B3n-laboral-en-Am%C3%A9rica-Latina.pdf

Hernani-Limarino, W., & Mena, G. (2015). *Intended and unintended effects of unconditional transfers* [Working paper]. Inter American Development Bank.

Imbens, G., & Angrist, J. D. (1994). Identification and estimation of local average treatment effects. *Econometrica, 142*, 615–635.

IMF. (2018). *Growing pains. Is Latin America prepared for population aging?* (Report 18/05). International Monetary Fund. https://www.imf.org/en/Publications/Departmental-Papers-Policy-Papers/Issues/2018/04/16/Growing-Pains-Is-Latin-American-Prepared-for-Population-Aging-45382

Juarez, L., & Pfutze, T. (2015). *The effects of a non-contributory pension program on labour force participation: The case of 70 y mas in Mexico* [Mimeo]. ITAM.

Kassouf, A. L., Rodrigues de Oliveira, P., & de Aquino, J. M. (2011). *Impact Evaluation of the Brazilian Pension Program Beneficio de Prestacão Continuada (BPC) on Gamily Welfare* [Report]. Universidade de Sao Paulo.

Kugler, A. D., & Rojas, I. (2018). *Do ccts improve employment and earnings in the very long-term? Evidence from Mexico* (NBER Working Paper 24248). National Bureau of Economic Research.

Levy, S. (2006). *Progress against Poverty. Sustaining Mexico's Progresa-Oportunidades Program*. Brookings Institution Press.

Ljungqvist, L. (1995). Wage structure as implicit insurance on human capital in developed versus underdeveloped countries. *Journal of Development Economics, 46*, 35–50.

Lloyd-Sherlock, P. (2006). Simple transfers, complex outcomes. The impacts of pensions on poor households in Brazil. *Development and Change, 37*(5), 969–995.

Lustig, N. C. (2011). *Fiscal policy and income redistribution in Latin America: Challenging the conventional wisdom* [Mimeo]. Tulane University.

Lustig, N. C. (2017). El impacto del sistema tributario y el gasto social en la distribución del ingreso y la pobreza en América Latina. Una aplicacion del marco metodológico del proyecto Compromiso con la Equidad (CEQ). *El Trimestre Económico, 84*(3), 493–568.

Lustig, N. C. (Ed.). (2018). *Commitment to Equity Handbook. Estimating the impact of fiscal policy on inequality and poverty*. CEQ Institute at Tulane University and Brookings Institution Press. https://commitmentoequity.org/publications-ceq-handbook

Martínez, S. (2004). *Pensions, poverty and household investments in Bolivia* [Mimeo]. University of California at Berkeley.

Martínez, S. W., Pérez, M., Tejerina, L., & Yarygina, A. (2020). Pensions for the poor: The effects of non-contributory pensions in El Salvador. *Journal of Economics, Race, and Policy, 3*, 96–115. https://doi.org/10.1007/s41996-019-00032-2

McGuire, J., Kaiser, C., & Bach-Mortensen, A. M. (2022). A systematic review and meta-analysis of the impact of cash transfers on subjective well-being and mental health in low- and middle-income countries. *Nature Human Behaviour, 6*, 359–370. https://doi.org/10.1038/s41562-021-01252-z

Mesa-Lago, C. (1978). *Social security in Latin America: pressure groups, stratification, and inequality*. University of Pittsburgh Press.

Mesquita, A. C. S., Jaccoud, L., & dos Santos, M. P. G. (2010). *Garantia de Renda na Política Social Brasileira: Entre a Proteçao aos Riscos Sociais e o Alivio à Pobreza [Mimeo]*. IPEA.

Molina Millán, T., Barham, T., Macours, K., Maluccio, J. A., & Stampini, M. (2019). Long-term impacts of conditional cash transfers: Review of the evidence. *World Bank Research Observer, 34*(1), 119–159. https://doi.org/10.1093/wbro/lky005

Molina-Millan, T., Barham, T., Macours, K., Maluccio, J. A., & Stampini, M. (2016). *Long-term impacts of conditional cash transfers in Latin America* (Technical Note IDB-TN-923). Inter-American Development Bank.

Molyneux, M. (2006). Mothers at the service of the new poverty agenda: Progresa/Oportunidades, Mexico's conditional transfer programme. *Social Policy and Administration, 40*(4), 425–449.

Molyneux, M. (2008). *Conditional cash transfers: A 'Pathway to Women's empowerment'?* Pathways of Women's Empowerment RPC-University of Sussex.

OECD/CIAT/IDB. (2023). *Revenue Statistics in Latin America and the Caribbean 1990-2021* [Report]. OECD. https://doi.org/10.1787/a7640683-en

OECD/IDB/The World Bank. (2014). *Pensions at a glance: Latin America and the Caribbean*. OECD Publishings.

Parker, S., & Vogl, T. (2018). *Do conditional cash transfers improve economic outcomes in the next generation? Evidence from Mexico* (Working Paper 24303; NBER Working Paper). National Bureau for Economic Research.

Pen, J. (1971). *Income distribution*. Penguin Books Ltd..

Ravallion, M. (2005). *Evaluating anti-poverty programs* (World Bank Policy Research Working Paper WPS3625). The World Bank. https://papers.ssrn.com/sol3/papers.cfm?abstract_id=922915

Ravallion, M. (2012). Review: Fighting poverty one experiment at a time: a review of Abhijit Banerjee and Esther Duflo's "Poor Economics: A Radical Rethinking of the Way to Fight Global Poverty.". *Journal of Economic Literature, 50*(1), 103–114. https://www.jstor.org/stable/23269972

Saavedra, J. E., & Garcia, S. (2017). *Educational impacts and cost-effectiveness of conditional cash transfer programs in developing countries: A meta-analysis* (Working Paper 23594; NBER). National Bureau for Economic Research.

Schady, N., & Rosero, J. (2008). Are cash transfers made to women spent like other sources of income? *Economics Letters, 101*, 246–248.

Skoufias, E. (2005). *Progresa and its impacts on the welfare of rural households in Mexico*. International Food Policy Research Institute.

Stampini, M., & Tornarolli, L. (2012). *The growth of conditional cash transfers in Latin America and the Caribbean. Did they go too far?* (IZA Policy Paper 49). IZA.

Yañes-Pagans, M. (2008). *Culture and human capital investments: Evidence of an unconditional cash transfer programme in Bolivia* (Discussion Paper 3678). IZA.

7

Incorporation

This chapter focuses on the incorporation effects of social protection.[1] An alternative title is the politics of social protection in Latin America and indeed much of the literature to be discussed here carries the word politics in the title. The term incorporation has the advantage of signalling a perspective in which the political incorporation of wage earners takes centerstage and where the analysis is focused on the influence of social protection institutions on that incorporation.

The term has the additional advantage of setting out a more eclectic approach to what politics entails in this context than that enforced by a political science approach. A primary concern in the politics literature is to examine how political processes and institutions help define the institutions of social protection. Research questions include, for example, the

[1] I borrow the term incorporation from Collier and Collier (1991). They define it thus: "During a relatively well-defined period in most countries, a historic change took place in the relationship between the state and the working class. An earlier pattern—in which repression was generally a far more central feature of the state response to worker organization and protest—gave way to state policies that launched the 'initial incorporation' of the labor movement. State control of the working class ceased to be principally the responsibility of the police or the army but rather was achieved at least in part through the legalization and institutionalization of a labor movement sanctioned and regulated by the state. In addition, actors within the state began to explore far more extensively the possibility of mobilizing workers as a major political constituency." (Collier & Collier, 1991, p. 3).

A. Barrientos, *Social Protection in Latin America*, Global Dynamics of Social Policy,
https://doi.org/10.1007/978-3-031-49795-7_7

extent to which democratic political regimes facilitate the expansion of social protection, or whether authoritarian regimes are more likely to lead to fragmented occupational insurance than open competitive regimes. More recently, political science has focused on policy decisions with a political market perspective, examining a 'demand' for social protection policies and an elite response or 'supply'. From these perspectives, social protection is the dependent variable. In this chapter the focus is instead on causal explanations of the influence of social protection on wage earner incorporation or exclusion.

The discussion in the chapter pursues two intertwined elements in the study of the influence of social protection on incorporation. Attention is paid to 'critical realignments' which yield a periodisation of the evolution of social protection institutions: industrialisation and the emergence of occupational insurance funds; retrenchment and the spread of individual retirement savings pension plans; and the expansion of social assistance. They describe a first incorporation, an exclusionary period, and a second incorporation. A second element is provided by the theoretical approaches available to study the evolution of social protection institutions: inter alia, the power resources approach, neo institutionalism, and varieties of capitalism. The chapter will assess their contribution to our understanding of social protection and incorporation. The analysis in the chapter connects these two elements in the context of assessing the incorporation effects of social protection institutions.

The chapter is divided into three main sections. Section 7.1 covers the first incorporation in the middle of the last century. Section 7.2 discusses the retrenchment period. Section 7.3 examines the second incorporation. The approach is not historical but analytical.[2] Theoretical perspectives and political institutions and processes will be referred to where relevant.

7.1 First Incorporation

Research on social protection in Latin America has paid close attention to the relationship existing between the second wave of industrialisation in the middle of the twentieth century, the emergence of an urban working

[2] The confluence of diachronic, synchronic, and analytical dimensions in Latin American social protection institutions discussed in Chap. 3 enables this approach.

class, and the expansion of occupational insurance funds (Borzutzky, 2002; Dion, 2010; Huber & Stephens, 2012; Malloy, 1979; Mesa-Lago, 1978; Segura-Ubiergo, 2007). There is consensus in the literature on the causal relationship linking industrialisation to social protection expansion in the same period. Countries that industrialised early and more deeply—Southern cone countries—are also the countries that experienced early and more extensive development of occupational insurance funds (Mesa-Lago, 1978). It is important to avoid economic determinism, such as that associated with the 'logic of industrialism' in welfare states, and to pay attention to the political dimension.[3] The mediating factor here is the political incorporation of the emergent industrial working class. Collier and Collier (1991) explore incorporation in this period through a comparative study of eight countries in Latin America but omit any reference to social policy. This sub-section explores the expansion of occupational insurance funds in this context.

7.1.1 Two Waves of Industrialisation

In twentieth century Latin America, industrialisation advanced in two distinct phases coinciding with periods of rapid globalisation in the world economy. The first phase runs from the turn of the twentieth century up until the Great Crisis (Bénétrix et al., 2012; Gómez Galvarriato & Williamson, 2008). The second wave covers the period between the Great Depression and the 1973 oil crisis.

The first industrialisation wave geared to supply rising world demand ensured rapid urbanisation and growing industry in the more advanced countries in Latin America. It created an emergent urban working class clustered around commodity production, transport, and banking. Gómez Galvarriato and Williamson (2008) find that, at the turn of the twentieth century, the manufacturing share of employment was as high as 25 percent in Chile and Argentina and around 11 percent in Mexico. The surge in industrialisation was not accompanied by significant political change.

[3] Collier and Collier's version is this: "The pattern of links between socioeconomic change and politics…is one in which a major economic and social transformation sets into motion processes of political change which later achieve a certain margin of autonomy in relation to the socioeconomic context" (Collier & Collier, 1991, p. 770).

Fledging worker organisations did not prioritise participation in domestic politics relying instead on direct action to improve pay and conditions and on self-administered occupational insurance funds for protection (Coppedge, 1989; Dix, 1989). It was a realistic strategy in a context in which the franchise was highly restricted and elections were rigged in favour of dominant elites (Carnes, 2009). Even in countries where legislation had formally extended the franchise to males, informal restrictions applied to electoral registration. In the countryside, landowners prevented rural workers from voting (Dix, 1989). In Chile, for example, only 5 percent of the population were eligible to vote in 1915 and by 1958 this share had reached only 10 to 19 percent (Coppedge, 2001, p. 170). Elections, where and when they took place at all, were rigged in favour of dominant elites whose principal response to the emerging worker organisations was to outlaw and repress them (Collier & Collier, 1991).

The first wave of industrialisation generated demand for agricultural exports from Central America, principally coffee and bananas (Bielchowsky et al., 2022). The concentration of land ownership ensured the economic and political domination of landowning elites. The latifundista elites kept a firm control of labour through legislation and repression. The coexistence of large landholding with a mass of subsistence farmers ensured constant oversupply of (largely male) labour. In Central American countries, industrialisation was delayed by the resilience of the agro-export model until the middle of the twentieth century (Segovia, 2022). In addition, the export focus implied that profits were realised in the USA, restricting domestic demand. Central American elites faced few pressures to incorporate labour as did the countries in South America and Mexico.

The second industrialisation wave accelerated in the post-WWII period. In Latin America, the second phase shows important differences with the first phase. Latin American economies' disengagement from early industrialisers caused by the Great Crash and WWII meant that import-substitution- industrialisation strategies emerged endogenously, with diverse timing and intensity across countries. Some domestic governments in the region embraced state-led import-substitution-industrialisation (ISI) development strategies. Proponents of this model argued that long term terms of trade move against commodity exporters. Their

Table 7.1 Political regime reforms—key dates

Country	Male suffrage (2)	Female suffrage (1)	Literacy test lifted (1)	Third wave democracy (3)
Argentina	1857	1947	1912	1983
Bolivia	1956	1952	1952	1982
Brazil	1891	1932	1985	1985
Chile	1888	1949	1970	1990
Colombia	1936	1954	1936	1958
Costa Rica	1949	1949	1913	1949
Dominican Rep.	1865	1942	1865	1978
Ecuador	1861	1929	1978	1979
El Salvador	1883	1950	1945	1984
Guatemala	1879	1946	1946	1986
Honduras	1894	1955	1894	1982
Mexico	1857	1953	1857	1988
Nicaragua	1893	1955	1893	1984
Panama	1904	1945	1904	1990
Paraguay	1870	1961	1870	1989
Peru	1931	1955	1979	1980
Uruguay	1917	1932	1918	1985
Venezuela	1946	1946	1947	1959

Notes: Male suffrage is date last restrictions were lifted. Female suffrage is date of legal extension of the franchise. Third Wave Democracy is year a competitive political regime was first established post-1978. Colombia, Costa Rica, and Venezuela had theirs established prior to 1978

Sources: (1) (Aidt & Eterovic, 2011); (2) (Negretto & Visconti, 2018); (3) (Pérez-Liñan & Mainwaring, 2013)

policy prescriptions supported the protection of nascent industry through high tariffs on manufacturing imports and state support for domestic industrial investment and technology. Multiple exchange and interest rates intended to accelerate industrial development in favoured sectors became the norm.[4] Import-substitution-industrialisation also involved policies to divert resources from agriculture to support industrialisation with implications for the linkages between town and country.

By the time the second industrialisation wave took hold in the region, political institutions were undergoing important change. Table 7.1 shows

[4] Some recent scholarship questions the effectiveness, and therefore significance, of ISI policies in the region (Gómez Galvarriato & Williamson, 2008).

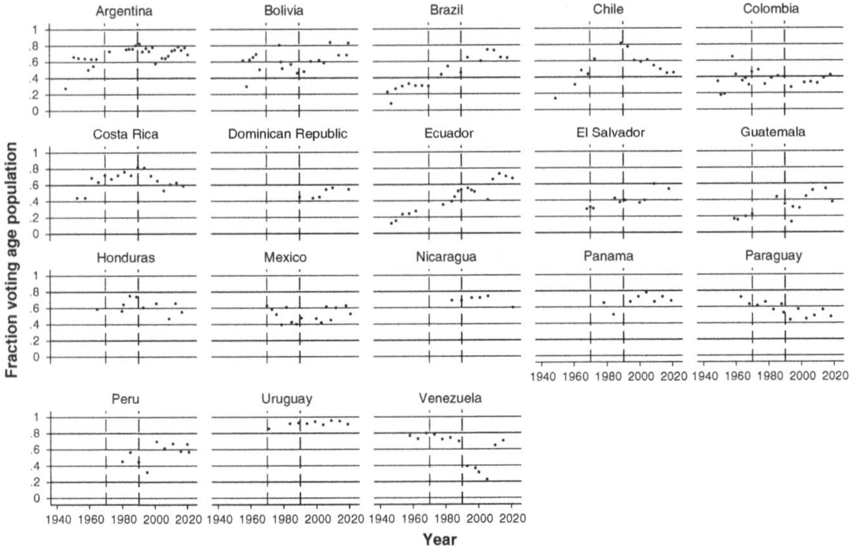

Fig. 7.1 Net voter turnout at parliamentary elections. Notes: Net voter turnout at parliamentary elections, turnout minus invalid votes, as a share of the voting age population. Vertical dash marks 1970 and 1990. Data source: Voter turnout database (IDEA, 2022)

key dates. In Latin America, the legal extension of the franchise proceeded by incorporating males, then females and finally illiterates (Aidt & Eterovic, 2011). The formal elimination of property, income or tax qualifications for males was achieved early for some countries: Argentina and Mexico (1857), Chile (1888), Brazil (1891). In other countries it was secured in the middle of the twentieth century: Costa Rica (1949), Colombia (1936), Peru (1931) (Negretto & Visconti, 2018). Most countries extended the franchise to women around the middle of the twentieth century. The removal of literacy qualifications is also country specific. Colombia, Mexico, Nicaragua, Panama, and Paraguay never had literacy qualifications. In other countries, literacy qualifications were removed very late: Chile (1970) Peru (1979), Brazil (1985).

In practice, dominant elites successfully managed to restrict electoral registration to a minority of supporting groups up until the second industrialisation phase. Thereafter, electoral participation rose rapidly. Figure 7.1 shows the turnout for parliamentary elections as a share of population for Latin American countries.[5] The Figure shows, for most countries, a very rapid increase in turnout during the middle of the twentieth century, from a very low base.

The lifting of legal restrictions to the franchise was accompanied by related changes to the political regime. They included a shift to proportional representation and the secret ballot. The shift to proportional representation for the election of legislators was pioneered by Costa Rica (1913), Uruguay (1918), Chile (1924) and Brazil (1932), but did not materialise in other countries until the 1950s. By the 1960s, all Latin American countries had embraced proportional representation for parliamentary elections. This change in the political regime left Latin American countries with hybrid majoritarian electoral systems for the executive and proportional representation systems for the legislature. Negretto and Visconti (2018) argue that the move to proportional representation in Latin America is explained primarily as a strategy of dominant elites aimed at retaining power in the face of increasing opposition from within. Except for two countries, Chile and Peru, proportional representation was introduced by authoritarian governments. Over time, the shift to proportional representation for the election of legislators created the conditions for greater political competition. A broader range of civil society groups now had incentives to engage electorally. Dion (2010) notes the growing role of the Mexican parliament in budgetary processes strengthened the links exiting between civil society organisations and legislators.

The adoption of secret ballots in the 1950s (Coppedge, 2001) shored up confidence among workers and their families that participation in elections would not be subject to manipulation by employers or *latifundistas* or led to repression by the police or the armed forces. The growing participation of the population in elections reflected to a greater extent a change in working class expectations of the political system and government policy. Combined with growing engagement of governing coalitions in social protection, to be discussed in the next section, changes in the political regime delivered stronger incentives for worker organisations to engage in the political process.

[5] This measure is more informative for our purposes than turnout as a share of the population registered to vote.

7.1.2 The Top-Down Character of the First Incorporation

Collier and Collier (1991) comparative study of eight countries in Latin America distinguish four main types of incorporation: state incorporation in Chile and Brazil represented an attempt at depolitisation through forceful legalisation and institutionalisation of labour organizations and enforcing their legal separation from political parties. The other six countries are examples of party incorporation, with some variation. Colombia and Uruguay show incorporation by old traditional parties, where labour organisations are mobilised electorally. Peru and Argentina are examples of labour populism in which labour organisations are mobilised through efforts to link them to political parties or movements. Mexico and Venezuela are presented by Collier and Collier as examples of radical populism in which, in addition to the incorporation of workers in the modern sector, agrarian reforms help to extend this electoral and partisan incorporation to include the peasantry.

The modalities of incorporation in Latin America share a top-down character. Elites sought to integrate or mobilise workers to gain advantage in intra-elite competition and conflict. Aside from the cases of Mexico and Venezuela in Collier and Collier, incorporation was restricted to urban workers in the modern sector and excluded workers in the traditional sector and agriculture (Haggard & Kaufman, 2008). This tallies with the restricted expansion of the franchise and the nature of its exclusions shown in Table 7.1 above.

7.1.3 Occupational Insurance Funds

The first occupational insurance funds emerged in Latin American during the first industrialisation phase. Self-administered funds were established in a piecemeal fashion by professionals and worker organisations in the modern sector. The piecemeal nature of the funds and their self-administered status explains in part why there is very limited systematic information on coverage from before the 1950s. Information on the rapid growth of funds during this period in Brazil indicates the number of funds doubled between the start of the series in 1923 and the end of that decade. By 1936 the number of funds exceeded 180 (IBGE, 1951). After that, a process of consolidation starting in 1937 reduced the number of funds back to below 40 and remained stable thereafter. This was purely a process of consolidation of the funds as the total number of active contributors rises consistently through the whole period. At the same time, governments established occupational insurance funds for the military, police, and high level officials (Mesa-Lago, 1978). Available information on funds is skewed towards government supported funds because they required legislation.

The second industrialisation wave and the incorporation of workers and their organisations into the political systems encouraged the expansion of Bismarckian type funds.[6] With variation in timing, all Latin American countries took steps to introduce and/or extend insurance coverage to selected groups of workers (Mesa-Lago, 1978). In countries with existing insurance funds, governments took active steps to incorporate new groups of workers. The piecemeal and occupational basis of the early funds replicates the fragmentation of worker organisations and is a consequence of their limited political participation and influence. The Bismarckian feature of the funds was a direct response to these conditions. Governing coalitions supported the establishment of funds for selected groups of workers as a mechanism of incorporation and as an electoral strategy (Mesa-Lago, 1989). Malloy observes that the expansion of social insurance "reflected an attempt to use paternalistic public policies to defuse labour agitation, not by responding to generalized class demands, but by co-opting specific key groups through concrete particularized programs of social protection" (1979, p. 150). In effect, the stratified expansion of coverage helped reinforce the Bismarckian orientation of social protection.

Occupational insurance funds began life as fully funded providing an additional incentive for government involvement. Whereas governments committed to import-substitution-industrialisation policies at first benefited from balance of payments surpluses accumulated during the WWII

[6] Bismarck's social insurance laws mandated worker participation in Germany, but actual participation was very limited. Labour force coverage of the old age and disability pension was 12% in 1889; 43% in 1911; 61% in 1931; 85% in 1956. Comprehensive coverage only came after 1950s. The emergence of Bismarckian type occupational funds was endogenous to Latin America. It paralleled, not followed, similar developments in European countries.

period, these proved insufficient to sustain large investments in infrastructure and industry. Taxation provoked resistance from wealth owners and workers. The occupational funds accumulated over time became hugely attractive to governments to finance investment projects. Government involvement led to change in the funding of social insurance funds from fully funded to pay-as-you-go. The switch in the financing modality left the funds open to rising deficits, especially as governments were committed to extending their scope and coverage. Over time, the funds dependence on government funding increased, a key justification offered for structural pension reform in the 1990s. Governments sought to consolidate the governance of the occupational funds, although not necessarily to consolidate their design and entitlements. In fact, the stratification of entitlements continued through this process of governance consolidation (Mesa-Lago, 2007).

7.1.4 Power Resources

The received view on the links between industrialisation, incorporation, and occupational insurance funds suggests a sequential causal process. Industrialisation creates a working class which demands social protection and, in increasingly democratic regimes, forces elites to respond. The linkages are well noted in the literature and have become a reference point for all subsequent research. The relevance of the power resources approach developed to explain the emergence of welfare states in early industrialisers is apparent. This approach argues that welfare states are the outcome of industrialisation processes via the emergence of an industrial working class able to exercise significant influence over government policy (Esping-Andersen, 1990; Korpi, 1980; Stephens, 1979). Fordist industrialisation is an important component. In combining workers of different skill levels within a single production unit, Fordist production enables broad coalitions in support of inclusive welfare institutions.[7]

[7] Korpi and Palme (1998) highlight the role of overlapping 'social risks' experienced by blue- and white- collar workers as the driving force behind their electoral coalition in support of welfare state development. Fordist production enables the emergence of cross-skill and inclusive worker organisations.

Democracy fosters labour organisations and left parties sustaining these institutions.[8]

Cross-national research finds a positive correlation between social protection spending, the strength of trade unions and left parties, and the persistence of democratic institutions (Haggard & Kaufman, 2008; Huber & Stephens, 2012; Segura-Ubiergo, 2007). They offer confirmation of the relevance of the power resources approach to explain the expansion of occupational insurance funds in Latin America.[9] Countries where labour organisations were weak or non-existent failed to develop strong and inclusive social protection institutions. Power resources is also relevant to the divergent course of social protection in Latin America compared to the universalistic welfare states in early industrialisers. The inequality and underdevelopment characterising welfare institutions in Latin America can be explained by reference to its fragmented class structures. As Huber and Stephens write, "… the class structure of Latin America is inhospitable to class organization and class political mobilization compared to that of Western Europe…the scope for union organization is much more limited in Latin America … These same features of the class structure have not been favourable to democracy, … weaken the density of civil society and this the potential for autonomous (i.e. non-clientelistic) political mobilization of lower class groups" (Huber & Stephens, 2012, pp. 25–25).

The precise specification of the association between incorporation and occupational insurance funds could benefit from further clarification. The issue is to do with the direction of causality, whether occupational insurance funds are the outcome of labour demands from newly incorporated workers or whether they are themselves an instrument of stratified incorporation. The line of argument developed in this book suggests that causality runs from social protection to the political

[8] Esping-Andersen (2014) argues that European welfare states are not egalitarian but are in fact designed to preserve differential status among workers. In his view the egalitarian achievements of Nordic welfare states might be explained by a 'wage earner' coalition seeking to reduce gender differentials and egalitarian services.

[9] Huber and Stephens (2012) adapt the power resources approach to Latin America. They add an international dimension and recast power resources as a 'power constellations' approach. They pay attention to three clusters of power: (i) domestic class power and parties; (ii) state-society balance (constitutional dispersion of political power, veto players); (iii) international organisations.

incorporation of wage earners. Social protection institutions reinforce sectoral segmentation in the labour market and facilitate the political incorporation of workers in those sectors.

Participation in occupational pension funds was restricted to urban workers in medium to large firms, the modern sector. It applied especially to workers in sectors benefiting from substantial government protection under import-substitution-industrialisation policies. They constituted a minority of the labour force. The fact that small firms and own account workers are the plurality of employment in urban areas and an unorganised rural labour force dominate employment in rural areas, set definite limits to the coverage of occupational insurance funds. Collier and Collier did not connect the processes of worker incorporation to the expansion of occupational pension funds, in part because they focused on the onset of incorporation around the 1940s. However, their description of the incorporation of workers in the modern sector is revealing. Distinguishing 'specific sectors of the working class' with 'special capacity for collective action', they go on to argued that the "...formal sector emerged as the product of the political demands of these segments of the working class and of state policies that responded to, or sought to pre-empt, these demands...Thus, the formal sector was created by politics and public policy" (Collier & Collier, 1991, p. 45).

The power resources approach has considerable explanatory power when applied to the origins of occupational insurance funds in Latin America. Industrialisation processes in Latin America shaped the emergence of an urban industrial working class and constitute the main causal factor in the emergence of occupational insurance funds. However, when social protection institutions are in place, they influence the stratified character of incorporation.

7.2 Retrenchment

By the 1970s, the import-substitution-industrialisation model in the more industrialised countries of the region was showing signs of exhaustion. Their Achilles heel was the need to accumulate sufficient foreign exchange to pay for imports of consumer goods and capital equipment.

The need to sustain foreign exchange reserves led to recurrent financial crises. The 1973 Oil Crisis and its impact in world trade accelerated financial crises in the region and forced economic and trade liberalisation. Governments began to discard import-substitutions-industrialisation strategies in favour of export-led growth policies, opening their economies to a new wave of globalisation. The immediate consequences of this structural adjustment were a rise in unemployment, poverty and vulnerability (Altimir, 1997). Governments in the region managed social unrest by repressing worker organisations and restricting political participation.

Fiscal pressures encouraged governments to reduce expenditure. Occupational insurance funds whose governance and financing had been partially consolidated in the 1960s in several countries provided a prominent target for reform (Mesa-Lago, 1989). The reforms came in two stages. In a first stage, governments intervened to streamline the occupational insurance funds restricting the range and generosity of the transfers and services they provided. In effect, reformed occupational insurance funds focused on pension income transfers: old age, retirement, and sickness and disability pensions. Parametric reforms were aimed at improving the governance and financing of occupational insurance funds.

In a second stage, some countries chose to go further and implemented structural reforms through the introduction of individual retirement pension plans. Authoritarian governments in Chile and Argentina pushed for radical social protection reforms. They involved mandating savings, as a share of labour earnings, invested by ad-hoc private financial providers, with the balance of the accounts made available at retirement (Barrientos, 1998). Twelve countries in the region legislated to replace or complement existing pay-as-you go pension schemes with individual retirement accounts. Eventually only ten countries implemented them, starting with Chile in 1981.[10]

[10] Encouraged by the Chilean pension reform, the World Bank became an ardent advocate of individual retirement savings plans subsequently helping transfer know-how on pension reform to countries in Eastern Europe, Africa and Asia (Gill et al., 2004).

7.2.1 Individual Retirement Savings Plans

The introduction of individual retirement savings plans is the most salient feature of social protection retrenchment in the neoliberal period in Latin America. Following the discussion in Chap. 4, it is helpful to distinguish three modalities of implementation of individual retirement savings plans: as a complement to occupational pensions for better off participants; as a competing alternative to occupational pensions; and as a replacement for occupational pensions. In the latter modality, a protracted period of transition is necessary to transfer participants to savings plans. As regards incorporation effects, there are some differences across the three modalities. Overall, individual retirement savings have contributed to a reversion in the earlier incorporation of workers and their organisations. There are several strands of evidential support for this claim.

Individual retirement savings plans were introduced without meaningful participation of labour organisations. Mesa-Lago and Müller (2002), later updated by Mesa-Lago (2020), discussed the political process leading to their adoption in a comparative perspective. Their research documented deficits in meaningful participation by labour organisations and left parties in the process of formulating and adopting individual retirement savings plans. In some countries, Chile is the exemplar, the introduction of individual retirement savings plans was facilitated by the suspension of political rights and the repression of labour organisations and left parties. The limited participation of labour and civil society organisations, and their explicit exclusion in some cases, provide support for the view that structural pension reforms sought a reversal in worker incorporation.

Addressing the perceived macroeconomic problems that were supposed to be solved by individual retirement savings plans - looming pension fund deficits; dismantling of sectoral preferential status; liberalisation of labour markets; and labour mobility to meet restructuring demands from trade liberalisation – carry direct implications for workers' political influence (James, 1997). This is confirmed by worker opposition to pension reforms (Kay, 1999).

Pension reforms reversed the involvement of labour organisations in the management and implementation of social protection. With individual retirement savings plans, this is embedded the very nature of their design. Individual retirement savings plans actively excluded labour organisations from the management of the plans, contributing to restrict the political influence of organised labour and its ability to organise and formulate relevant policy. In the new individual savings retirement plans, workers need not belong to a particular type of employment, occupation, sector, or a particular employer to shape their pension entitlements. Individual retirement savings plans generate few incentives for workers to organise around social protection provision. The management and implementation of workers savings is transferred to private pension managers (Borzutzky, 2019; Dorlach, 2020).[11]

Other features embedded in the design of individual retirement savings plans also carried implications for worker's organisation around social protection as a form of incorporation. Individual retirement savings plans offer a single modality of participation to all workers, with a close correspondence between contributions and benefits. Pensions depend solely on individual saving capacity and on the returns secured by investment fund managers. Retirement plans are fully portable across employers and occupations. Whereas in pay-as-you-go occupational pensions group membership is essential for participation and access to entitlements, in individual retirement savings plans, worker's capacity to save is the basis of participation and entitlements (Godoy & Valdés-Prieto, 1997). In sum, causality running from social protection to a reversal of worker incorporation.

7.2.2 'Frozen Landscapes' and Asset Theory

Insights from neo institutional theories of the politics of welfare appear can be deployed to explain the resilience of occupational insurance funds in the region, but only up to a point. Institutional theories of welfare state resilience emphasise the extent to which welfare institutions once in place are capable of exercising influence on policy making as relatively

[11] Bolivia's 2010 reform included a single public pension manager.

autonomous actors, for example through creating constituencies of support and through feedback mechanisms (Pierson, 2001).

Institutional approaches have been deployed to explain the influence of occupational pension funds to survive government attempts to centralise their governance structure through successive waves of pension reforms. Some public sector occupational pension funds, like the *Regimes Próprios de Previdência Social* in Brazil, have successfully resisted reforms and continue to absorb large public subsidies. Government efforts to consolidate and harmonise fragmented occupational insurance funds in the 1960s and 1970s failed to overcome concerted opposition from the constituencies served by these funds. Mesa-Lago (2020) notes in passing that in Mexico there are today more than a thousand special pension regimes (estates, municipalities, universities, etc.). A similar situation can be observed in Argentina and other countries in the region (Bertranou et al., 2018). The survival and expansion of special pension regimes remains a significant factor explaining the large inequalities in pension provision in the region (Barrientos, 2021).

However, it is change, as opposed to continuity, that characterises occupational insurance funds in Latin America. Their current design, scope, and generosity are fundamentally different to that of their early 1960s and 1970s counterparts, in terms of the range of transfers and services they offer and in terms of their membership. They have undergone substantive and regular reforms (Arenas de Mesa, 2019; IMF, 2018). Occupational insurance funds were originally set out to provide comprehensive security to their members and their dependants. By 1980 they had become unfunded pension schemes. Neo institutionalist approaches fail to account for the large scale changes to occupational pension funds over time.

The introduction of individual retirement saving accounts towards the end of the twentieth century further served to demonstrate the limitations of institutionalist explanations of the resilience of occupational insurance funds in the region. Individual retirement savings plans represent a wholly different paradigm for social protection, one that excluded labour organisations and other forms of group membership who roundly opposed radical pension reform proposals. In fact, the extent of resistance to the reforms resulted in the three main implementation models. In

Chile, Mexico, El Salvador, Bolivia, Panama, and the Dominican Republic, individual retirement saving plans fully replace existing occupational insurance funds. In Colombia and Peru opposition to the reforms secured the retention of occupational insurance funds in parallel to the new individual retirement saving plans.[12] In Costa Rica, and Uruguay, individual retirement plans were introduced as a complementary pillar to occupational insurance funds. Mesa-Lago and Müller (2002) and (Mesa-Lago, 2020) argue that in broad terms the depth of the reforms - hard/substitutive; moderate/parallel; soft/complementary - is inversely related to the health of democratic and political rights in the countries concerned.[13] This suggests that the retrenchment of workers incorporation associated with structural pension reforms came against well defined limits imposed by resistance to the reforms.

A further demonstration of the limits of institutionalist explanations of the resilience of occupational insurance funds, and a demonstration of the limits of disincorporation associated with structural pension reforms, is the path of individual retirement savings plans after their introduction. To date, several countries have subjected their individual retirement saving plans to substantive reforms (Mesa-Lago, 2020). Argentina switched back to a consolidated pay-as-you-go pension in 2008 (Bertranou et al., 2011). Bolivia legislated to retain a single publicly managed individual retirement savings plan in 2010 (Mesa-Lago, 2018).[14] Chile's individual retirement savings plans have undergone reforms aimed at improving the efficiency of private pension managers and reducing costs. The focus of the 2008 reform of individual retirement savings plans in Chile reforms was the implementation of a tax-financed old age transfer scheme as a first pillar. This is intended to secure minimum income support for older people without adequate retirement savings. The 2008 financial crisis

[12] In Argentina, the reforms also included a first pillar.

[13] They code the design features of reformed pension schemes to construct a 'privateness' index and find that the 'intensity' of the reformed outcomes is inversely related to countries' Freedom House democracy scores (Mesa-Lago & Müller, 2002). The 'hardest' reform, Chile's, was imposed while political process were suspended by a military dictatorship. The military leaders agreed to fully replace occupational insurance funds as long the armed forces and police retained their own occupational pension fund.

[14] Bolivia has a categorical old age transfer scheme, the main source of income security for older people in the country.

and COVID-19 have undermined individual retirement saving plans and strengthened social assistance transfers to older people (Arenas de Mesa, 2020; Kay & Borzutzky, 2022).

Individual retirement savings plans were not an instrument for disincorporation in every case. Introduced as a complement to occupational insurance funds, as in Uruguay, they are restricted to better paid workers able to save for a higher level of retirement income. They have contributed to further stratify workers but have had moderate effects on disincorporation. In countries where they were introduced as a competitor to occupational insurance funds, as in Colombia and Peru, disincorporation effects were stronger for participants in the latter. In countries transitioning to dominant individual retirement savings plans, disincorporation effects are strongest. In Chile, Mexico, and Bolivia, disincorporation has been mitigated by tax-financed old age transfers, to be discussed in the next section. To sum up, the explanatory power of institutionalist approaches is limited in the region, no 'frozen landscapes' in Latin American welfare institutions (Palier & Martin, 2007).

Iversen and Soskice's asset theory (2001, 2015a) could throw light on the disincorporation effects of pension reform. They argue that in a dual economy, with a modern high-tech sector requiring investment in firm specific skills and a vulnerable sector dominated by low skill employment, governments will aim to provide social protection for workers in the skilled sector but will have few incentives to offer social protection to workers in the vulnerable sector. Governments place economic growth at the top of their priorities. This is maximised by protecting and incentivising the accumulation of human capital among workers in the high-tech sector. Whether social protection is extended to workers in the vulnerable sector depends solely on whether they have representation and influence on the governing coalition. This is more likely in countries with proportional representation as the political representatives of workers in the vulnerable sector have a higher probability of participating in proportional representation coalition governments than in than in 'first-past-the-post' majoritarian political regimes. Iversen and Soskice predict that workers in the modern sector will be offered insurance instruments, whereas workers in the vulnerable sector would need to rely in redistribution (Iversen & Soskice, 2015b).

Their model was designed to explain conditions in welfare states, but it has interesting implications when applied to the Latin American context. In the asset model, truncated or dual social protection institutions follow from the duality present in the economy and labour market, complemented and reinforced by the type of political regime. Disincorporation is the norm, mitigated only by favourable conditions under proportional representation. In Latin America, proportional representation was adopted in all countries under authoritarian regimes. Proportional representation political regimes were in place during the expansion of occupational insurance funds in the 1960s and 1970s. Government support for import-substitution-industrialisation and the spread of occupational insurance funds is consistent with the outcomes predicted by the asset theory. Until the new century, Latin American governments remained uninterested in adopting social protection for workers in the vulnerable sector. Social assistance was non-existent, as predicted by the asset approach. The second incorporation contains the conditions needed for the expansion of redistribution to vulnerable sectors, namely the participation of political parties or movements in governing coalitions. However, the change in the offer to skilled workers from occupational insurance to individual savings retirement plans is an anomaly in the asset theory. Individual retirement savings plans lack design features protecting investment in human capital.

7.3 Second Incorporation

Beginning from the middle of the 1990s, Latin American countries expanded the provision of social assistance transfers to low-income families through conditional income transfers and old age transfers. Social assistance has transformed social protection system in the region, by targeting low-income groups often dependent on informal employment (Carnes & Mares, 2014). Conditional income transfers were eventually established in all countries in the region to provide income supplements to households in poverty and to facilitate social investment. (Barrientos, 2013a; Cecchini & Atuesta, 2017). Tax-financed transfers to older people are the second most important social assistance instrument in terms of reach, but the most important instrument in terms of budgetary allocations. Old age transfers have been in existence in some countries in the region since the middle of the last century, but their expansion since the mid-1990s is remarkable (Rofman et al., 2013). Old age transfers have rapidly closed the gap in income support in late age (Barrientos, 2021). By 2017, social assistance institutions reached around a third of the population of the region as direct or indirect beneficiaries. Are there any incorporation effects from social assistance expansion?

7.3.1 A second Incorporation?

The restoration of democracy in the 1980s and the rejection of neoliberal policies created the conditions for a third political realignment. Popular mobilisation intensified with the return to democracy. Left of centre coalition governments spread in the 2000s, a trend described as the 'pink tide' or the 'left turn' (Levitsky & Roberts, 2012). Global economic trends encouraged economic growth. Surging commodity prices following the entry of China into the global economy helped generate fiscal space for expansive social policy. Researchers have described this period as a 'second incorporation' phase (Kapiszewski et al., 2021; Silva & Rossi, 2017) underlining the prominence of social movements and grassroots organisations representing low income groups dependent on informal employment. Consensus is lacking on this point. Issues relating to the strength and resilience of social movements have led some researchers to question whether a 'second incorporation' did materialise, and whether recent changes are comparable to the first incorporation as regards their potential impact on the political regime (Collier, 2021; Roberts, 2021).

This debate raises interesting questions regarding potential incorporation effects of social assistance expansion. The expansion of social assistance is aimed at groups excluded from occupational insurance funds and largely outside individual retirement savings plans. The question is whether social assistance influences the political incorporation of these groups. Establishing the direction of causality is again central to this assessment.

To date, research into the politics of social assistance expansion has emphasised the role of incumbents facing electoral competition or the potential influence of ideological affinity as factors in the emergence of social assistance. From the perspective of identifying the incorporation effects of social assistance expansion, the central question is whether social assistance participation encourages the political inclusion of low income groups. These hypotheses are explored below.

7.3.2 Incumbent Electoral Advantage?

Most studies take it for granted that social assistance transfers are an instrument available to incumbent willing to push for electoral advantage. They hypothesise that governing coalitions implement social assistance programmes to collect political support among disadvantaged groups. This hypothesis echoes longstanding concerns with clientelism in the region where the volatility of party systems (Mainwaring, 2018) might encourage elites to 'buy votes' through the provision of discretionary transfers (Stokes, 2004). Some studies test this hypothesis by considering the incentives for incumbents (Borges, 2019). Studies relying on programme evaluation or attitudinal data test this hypothesis by measuring support for incumbents among actual or potential beneficiaries of social assistance transfer (Manacorda et al., 2011; Zucco & Power, 2013). Positive pro-incumbent findings are interpreted as confirming the presence of some form of vote buying strategy on the part of politicians. It is uncertain whether the pro-incumbent effect reflects retrospective reward flowing to the politicians who originally introduced the programme, a prospective concern with preventing reforms to the programme, or name recognition (Corrêa, 2010).[15]

The incumbent hypothesis has several contestable assumptions. Incumbents hoping to instrumentalise social assistance transfers would be best served by discretionary, reversible and excludable transfers, and would be well advised to stay clear of non-discretionary, non-excludable, and non-reversible conditional income transfers (Díaz-Cayeros & Magaloni, 2009). Clientelistic vote buying requires some mechanism to monitor transfer recipients' actual voting behaviour as well as a plausible

[15] Lopez Obrador's ending of Mexico's conditional income transfer programme has not led to a decline in electoral support to date.

threat of retribution if beneficiaries fail to fulfil their end of the bargain (Stokes et al., 2013). Yet as Stokes (2009) notes in the context of Brazil, "... ccts [conditional income transfers] allow us to ask how voters behave in the presence of tangible, identifiable and quantifiable benefits...but in the absence of a requirement to vote in a certain way, or to be part of specific networks" (p. 8). It is also unclear why would political elites opt for rules-based social assistance transfers in preference to public goods and unconditional discretionary transfers?[16] In the context of conditional income transfers, it is also unclear why would political elites favour social investment instruments with medium- and long-term returns to secure short-term support?[17]

Social assistance transfers cannot guarantee electoral success on their own. Sanches Corrêa and Cheibub (2016) argue the incumbent effect should be interpreted a net effect combining mobilisation of apathetic voters and repelling of programme detractors. Social assistance transfers likely add and subtract political support. The scale of social assistance transfers in Latin America is insufficient to turn national elections in favour of particular parties or candidates.[18] Assessing the contribution of *Bolsa Família* in the re-election of President Lula in Brazil, the largest conditional income transfer programme in the region, studies fail to confirm it had a deciding role (Bohn, 2011; Hunter & Power, 2007; Shikida et al., 2009; Zucco, 2013; Zucco & Power, 2013).

Relying on social assistance as an electoral strategy would also leave a footprint of strategic allocation of budgets or coverage. Matching electoral and *Bolsa Família* administrative data, Fried (2012) fails to find a correlation between the distribution of *Bolsa Família* budgets and population coverage on the one hand and indicators of potential core voter or swing voter strategies on the other. The absence of strategic allocation of conditional income transfers is also confirmed for Colombia's *Familias en Acción* by Nupia (2011).

---

[16] De la O (2015) suggests that if the opposition is entrenched in parliament, they may force presidents to adopt rules-based non-discretionary programmes.

[17] Zucco (2019) suggests that conditions in conditional income transfers help to get support from better off groups.

[18] Electoral effects might be more potent at the local level (Linos, 2013).

Garay (2016) puts forward an alternative perspective on the incumbent explanation for the expansion of social assistance. She argues that tight electoral competition pushes incumbents to instrumentalise social assistance. Garay's argument was developed in a comparative context, as a means of explaining cross-country differences in the depth of engagement with social assistance. It works as an additional modification to the incumbent hypothesis, but it is less compelling as the main explanation for social assistance expansion (Barrientos, 2022b). The proposition that Latin American politicians only discovered the electoral potential of social assistance transfers or old age transfers in the 21st century is not compelling.

7.3.3 Ideological Affinity?

An alternative hypothesis explains the expansion of social assistance in terms of the ideological affinity existing between left governing coalitions and low-income groups. The 'pink tide' which brought left coalitions to power in several countries in the region seems to offer a potential explanation. On closer examination this explanation is less compelling. Social assistance programmes were adopted, or expanded, both by left governing coalitions (e.g., Lula's *Bolsa Família*) and by right governing coalitions (e.g. Fox's *OPORTUNIDADES*). Borges (2019) finds that it took some persuading for left parties and leaders to eventually lend their support to the expansion of conditional income transfers.[19] This was due, in no small part, to the left's longstanding support for occupational insurance funds. Left coalitions' support for social assistance expansion was something they learned to do <u>after</u> coming to power. And some left governments have dismantled successful conditional income transfer programmes, as in Nicaragua under Ortega or Mexico under Lopez Obrador. The ideological affinity argument lacks general applicability, at best.

[19] Lula's government re-focused on *Bolsa Família* only after his *Fome Zero*, a set of disparate interventions, proved difficult to roll out successfully (Barrientos, 2013b).

7.3.4 Political Participation

An alternative to focusing on the motivations of incumbents or political elites is to consider the effects of social assistance expansion on the political incorporation of participant groups. This involves exploring the causal effects of social assistance on political participation of disadvantaged groups.

Hunter and Borges Sugiyama (2014) investigate whether *Bolsa Família* participation enhance citizenship in the Northeast of Brazil. Their main hypothesis is described as follows: "Social benefits, acquired through procedures that are judged to be reasonable, fair and transparent can only deepen poor people's appreciation of their newfound political rights" (Hunter & Borges Sugiyama, 2014, p. 829). They explore two main pathways to improved citizenship: (i) whether transfers signal to recipients that governments "recognise all members of the national community as worthy enough to have their basic needs met and life chances lifted" (Hunter & Borges Sugiyama, 2014, p. 830); and (ii) whether transfers strengthens the agency of recipient households in as far as they "foster a sense of recognition, fairness, and rights [that] facilitate the exercise of 'voice', which helps citizens hold their government accountable for meeting basic needs (Hunter & Borges Sugiyama, 2014, p. 830). Their research findings confirm that transfer receipt has positive effects on participants preparedness to engage in political activity.

Programme evaluation data offers some evidence of social assistance participation effects on registration and turnout at elections. Baez et al. (2012) find a 1.5 to 2.5 percentage points higher probability of registration and 7-9 percentage points higher probability of voting among Colombia's *Familias en Acción* participants.

Schober (2019) is interested in the question whether conditional income transfer receipt leads to increasing political participation. Using a dedicated survey of a representative sample of adults in three municipalities in Mexico with high levels of poverty, he explores political participation outcomes and pathways, which will be interpreted as causal mechanisms. His study contrasts political participation effects of conditional and unconditional income transfers.

He finds that conditional income transfer recipients are more likely to engage in a greater number of political activities (voting, contact public officials, community activism, and civil society engagement) compared with unconditional transfer recipients in the sample who are only likely to engage in a single activity (voting).[20] He then extends his analysis to other Latin American countries participating in LAPOP in 2014.[21] Analysis of LAPOP cross-country data for 2014 confirms that for conditional income transfer "participation is positively and significantly associated with several modes of political participation, including campaign activism, contacting public officials, civil society engagement, and protest" (Schober, 2019, p. 602).

Layton and Smith (2011) study the electoral outcomes associated with conditional income transfer recipients using 2012 LAPOP data for 23 countries. They start with a basic rational choice model in which transfers influence the balance of costs and benefits associated with political activity. As they put it, "… by altering beneficiaries' pocketbook calculations and directly linking recipients' well-being with state actors and policies, social assistance has the obvious potential to alter voting behaviour" (Layton & Smith, 2011, p. 855). They find partial support for their hypothesis.

Layton et al. (2017) examine whether the observed political effects of participation in *Bolsa Família* can be construed as reciprocal support for incumbents (transfers for votes) or reflect broader positive attitudes to state legitimacy. The study relies on LAPOP data for Brazil for the period 2007–2014. They finds that "…across all survey years, Bolsa Família recipients report significantly higher levels of support for core political institutions, trust in local government, and support for political actors than their matched nonrecipient peers. (Layton et al., 2017, p. 109).

[20] "In line with my expectations, there is a positive and statistically significant relationship between CCTs [*conditional income transfers*, AB] and several modes of political participation. CCTs are positively associated with contacting public officials, community activism, civil society engagement, and voting. For the average respondent, the estimated effect of CCT [*conditional income transfers*, AB] participation corresponds to an increase of 26 percent in contacting public officials, an increase of 28 percent in community activism, an increase of 21 percent in civil society engagement, and an increase of 6 percent in voting" (Schober, 2019, p. 597).

[21] LAPOP is a project collecting attitudinal data from Latin American countries. These data will be described in detail in later sections.

Barrientos (2022a) explores the mechanisms through which the incorporation effects might operate. A review of the literature drew attention to four main potential mechanisms structuring recipients' political responses to transfer receipt: (i) a support for redistribution mechanism encouraging electoral participation in support for incumbent redistributive policies; (ii) a bureaucratic mechanism encouraging political engagement by transfer recipients through the implementation features of the transfer programmes, e.g. birth and electoral registration, compliance with programme conditions, interactions with programme agencies; and (iii) a cognitive change causal mechanism in which transfers facilitate a cognitive change in recipients as regards their societal and political inclusion.[22] Exploring attitudinal data from LAPOP, the study finds support for all three mechanisms associated with social assistance beneficiary incorporation. Barrientos (2022b) argues that political inclusion associated with social assistance receipt can also manifest itself in stronger support for the political system. Using LAPOP attitudinal data enabling the identification of conditional income transfer recipients, the study finds that participants are more likely to support the political system than a respondent taken at random. This was interpreted as a political inclusion effect of social assistance.[23]

In sum, the findings from this literature indicate the presence of incorporation effects from social assistance participation. The expansion of social assistance in Latin America has influenced positively the political inclusion of disadvantaged groups, in line with a 'second incorporation'.

[22] A case could be made to consider a fifth potential causal mechanism in which transfers encourage recipients' engagement in local or community politics. Unfortunately, data restrictions preclude empirical investigation of a mechanism along these lines. However this is studied in Schober (2019) using a dedicated survey of three Mexican municipalities. He finds supporting evidence that participants in the *Prospera* programme engage in community politics to a greater extent than recipients of unconditional income transfers in Mexico.

[23] Rawls argued that polities in which inequality is endemic generate 'strains of commitment' among groups in the population who are repeatedly, and intergenerationally, disadvantaged (Rawls, 1999). He argued that social policies and institutions able to improve the life course of disadvantaged groups are essential to prevent the 'strains of commitment' from becoming impossible to bear.

7.4 Conclusions

This chapter offered an examination of the incorporation effects of social protection in Latin America. The materials covered in the chapter can also be described as part of an investigation into the politics of social protection in the region. The chapter broke new ground by framing the analysis in causal terms, by explicitly considering the incorporation effects of social protection institutions. It adopted an 'effects of causes' approach.

The analysis focused two intertwined elements in the analysis of the incorporation effects of social protection institutions and change: (i) the features of the 'critical realignments' shaping the incorporation effects of the emergent institutions; and (ii) the theories that can be brought to bear to explain change. The discussion of social protection incorporation effects was grounded on 'critical realignments' associated with the three most significant changes in social protection in the region: the 'first incorporation' or worker organisations and the emergence of occupational insurance funds; the neoliberal shift, retrenchment in incorporation and individual retirement savings plans; and the 'second incorporation' and the expansion of social assistance. The discussion approached these three 'critical realignments' separately and identify the patterns of incorporation and disincorporation that resulted from changes in the institutions of social protection. The discussion also considered the explanatory power of the theoretical frameworks and covered their main strengths and weaknesses. The intention was to assess these theoretical frameworks 'inductively' in the context if the region (Barrientos, 2024), especially where these frameworks had been development originally in the context of early industrialisers.

What are the main points to take away from this chapter?

First, developments in social protection in the region are primarily explained as processes of incorporation and disincorporation of wage earners. This makes sense as wage earners are the object of social protection. Occupational insurance funds emerged from the twin processes of industrialisation and democratisation in the region in the middle of the twentieth century. They facilitated the incorporation of sections of the wage earner class, principally urban industrial and public sector workers. The incorporation was partial, deeper in the more industrialised countries of the Southern cone and Mexico and superficial in the Central American and Andean countries. Their Bismarckian nature is explained by the largely 'top down' nature of the political incorporation of selected groups of workers and by the fact that industrial development took root in preferred sectors. A significant threat to occupational insurance funds came with trade and labour market liberalisation and from authoritarian governments in the last quarter of the twentieth century. Pension reforms, Individual retirement savings plans especially, expelled labour organisations from social protection institutions and replaced them with private financial institutions. A deepening of democracy in the new century, including a 'pink tide' of left coalitions, accompanied rapid growth of social assistance, hitherto missing from the region's social protection institutions. The new social protection institutions facilitated a 'second incorporation' this time focused on low-income groups, the popular sectors.

Second, in Latin America studying the incorporation and disincorporation effects of social protection institutions confirm that intra-class (wage earners) fragmentation and aggregation is far more productive than a focus on inter-class coalitions for an understanding of the politics of welfare institutions.

Third, identifying and studying critical realignments is essential to explaining changes in social protection institutions and the resulting processes of incorporation and disincorporation.

Fourth, theoretical frameworks developed to explain the emergence of welfare states enhance our conceptual and methodological toolbox, but there are few gains in extrapolating them to the Latin American context. Power resources theories can help explain the emergence of occupational insurance funds in the region, but not their limitations. There is significant fluidity in Latin American welfare institutions at the macro institutional level, as demonstrated by almost permanent pension reform, limiting the explanatory power of institutionalist approaches. Rational decision making and market approaches applied to the expansion for social assistance have limited explanatory power once their highly restrictive assumptions are considered.[24] It makes sense to seek to develop theoretical frameworks from an understanding of the Latin American context.

[24] A critical point here is that welfare institutions in the region are not simply the product of political elites' 'retail offer' and voter preferences but are intrinsically linked to issues of political inclusion and state legitimacy.

Fifth, the literature on the politics of social protection appears to have an in-built bias towards granting a primary role to the incentives of rulers/politicians. Research on the 'first incorporation' privileged elites as they set the terms of incorporation.[25] This also applies to the spread of individual retirement savings plans given the influence of authoritarian and populist governments. Incumbent-led explanations of the expansion of social assistance also privilege elites. A common factor in these approaches is a focus on elite incentives. This is unduly restrictive. Social protection is about wage earners and their families. Understanding the incorporation and disincorporation effects of social protection in Latin America necessitates closer attention to wage earners. If the gateway to more inclusive and egalitarian social protection in Latin America is dependent on broader wage earner coalitions, more research is needed to assess their likelihood. Focusing on the incorporation effects of social protection institutions shifts attention to wage earners, the primary actors of social protection.

References

Aidt, T. S., & Eterovic, D. S. (2011). Political competition, electoral participation and public finance in 20th century Latin America. *European Journal of Political Economy, 27*, 181–200.

Altimir, O. (1997). Desigualdad, Empleo y Pobreza en America Latina: Efectos del ajuste y del cambio en el estilo de desarrollo. *Desarrollo Económico, 37*(145), 3–29.

Arenas de Mesa, A. (2019). *Los sistemas de pensiones en la encrucijada. Desafíos para la sostenibilidad en América Latina* (159, Libros de La CEPAL). Comisión Económica para América Latina y el Caribe.

Arenas de Mesa, A. (2020). *Los sistemas de pensiones en América Latina. Institucionalidad, gasto público y sostenibilidad financiera en tiempos de*

[25] 'First incorporation' studies set the direction of the bias. See for example Collier and Collier: "If one wishes to explain why the incorporation periods occurred to begin with, it was obviously because a working class emerged, constituted itself as a labor movement, and often decided to challenge, rather than cooperate with, the state. On the other hand, if one wishes to explain why the incorporation periods took the specific form they did in each country, the answer will focus more centrally on the dynamics of intra-elite politics and choices by actors within the state" (Collier & Collier, 1991, p. 50).

COVID-19 (Documento 212; Macroeconomía Del Desarrollo). Economic Commission for Latin America.

Baez, J. E., Camacho, A., Conover, E., & Zárate, R. A. (2012). *Conditional cash transfers, political participation, and voting behavior* [Policy Research Working Paper]. The World Bank. http://documents1.worldbank.org/curated/en/859831468018048176/pdf/wps6215.pdf

Barrientos, A. (1998). *Pension reform in Latin America*. Ashgate.

Barrientos, A. (2013a). *Social assistance in developing countries*. Cambridge University Press.

Barrientos, A. (2013b). The rise of social assistance in Brazil. *Development and Change, 44*(4), 887–910.

Barrientos, A. (2021). Inequalities in income security in later age in Latin America. *Pan American Journal of Public Health, 45*. https://doi.org/10.26633/RPSP.2021.85

Barrientos, A. (2022). Political responses of conditional income transfer recipients: A mechanism approach. In J. Kuhlmann & F. Nullmeier (Eds.), *Causal mechanisms in the global development of social policies* (pp. 403–429). Palgrave. https://link.springer.com/chapter/10.1007/978-3-030-91088-4_13

Barrientos, A. (2023). Social assistance expansion and political inclusion in Latin America. *Journal of Politics in Latin America*, 15(1), 5–46.

Barrientos, A. (2024). The politics of social protection in Latin America. In D. B. Sattwick, C. Sambo, & S. Pellissery (Eds.), *The politics of welfare in the global south*. Oxford University Press.

Bénétrix, A. S., O'Rourke, K. H., & Williamson, J. G. (2012). *The spread of manufacturing to the periphery 19870-2007: Eight stylized facts* (Working Paper 617; Department of Economics Oxford University). University of Oxford.

Bertranou, F., Casalí, P., & Cetràngolo, O. (2018). *A mitad de camino entre Bismarck y Beveridge? La persistencia de los dilemas en el sistema previsional argentino* (OIT Cono Sur - Informes Técnicos 9). OIT.

Bertranou, F., Cetràngolo, O., Grushka, C., & Casanova, L. (2011). *Encrucijadas en la seguridad social argentina: Reformas, cobertura y desafíos para el sistema de pensiones*. CEPAL/OIT.

Bielchowsky, R., Castro, M. C., & Beteta, H. E. (Eds.). (2022). *Patrones de desarrollo económico en los seis países de centroamerica (1950-2018)*. Comisión Económica para America Latina y el Caribe.

Bohn, S. (2011). Social policy and vote in Brazil: Bolsa Família and the shifts in Lula's electoral base. *Latin American Research Review, 46*(1), 54–79.

Borges, F. A. (2019). Adoption and evolution of cash transfer programs in Latin America. In *Oxford Research Encyclopedia*. Oxford University Press. https://doi.org/10.1093/acrefore/9780190228637.013.1521

Borzutzky, S. (2002). *Vital connections. Politics, social security, and inequality in Chile*. University of Notre Dame Press.

Borzutzky, S. (2019). You win some, you lose some: Pension reform in Bachelet's first and second administrations. *Journal of Politics in Latin America, 11*(2), 204–230.

Carnes, M. (2009). *Institutionalizing inequality: The political origins of labor codes in Latin America* (Working Paper 363). Kellogg Institute, University of Notre Dame.

Carnes, M., & Mares, I. (2014). Coalitional realignment and the adoption of non-contributory social insurance programmes in Latin America. *Socio-Economic Review, 12*, 695–722.

Cecchini, S., & Atuesta, B. (2017). *Programas de transferencias condicionadas en América Latina y el Caribe* (Report 224; Series Politicas Sociales). CEPAL, División Desarrollo Social.

Collier, R. B. (2021). Prologue: Reflections on two episodes of popular inclusion. Structuring and restructuring arenas of participation. In D. Kapiszewski, S. Levitsky, & D. J. Yashar (Eds.), *The inclusionary turn in Latin American democracies* (pp. xxv–xlviii). Cambridge University Press.

Collier, R. B., & Collier, D. (1991). *Shaping the political arena. Princeton University Press*. https://muse.jhu.edu/book/45473

Coppedge, M. (1989). The evolution of Latin American party systems. In S. Mainwaring & A. Valenzuela (Eds.), *Politics, society and democracy: Latin America* (pp. 171–206). Westview Press.

Coppedge, M. (2001). Political Darwinism in Latin America's lost decade. In L. Diamond & R. Gunther (Eds.), *Political parties and democracy* (pp. 173–205). John Hopkins University Press.

Corrêa, D. S. (2010). *Conditional cash transfer programmes and their electoral effects* [Mimeo]. University of Illinois.

Corrêa, D. S., & Cheibub, J. A. (2016). The anti-incumbent effect of conditional cash transfer programs. *Latin American Politics and Society, 58*(1), 49–71.

De la O, A. L. (2015). *Crafting policies to end poverty in Latin America. The quiet transformation*. Cambridge University Press.

Díaz-Cayeros, A., & Magaloni, B. (2009). Aiding Latin America's Poor. *Journal of Democracy, 20*(4), 36–49.

Dion, M. L. (2010). *Workers and Welfare. Comparative institutional change in twentieth-century Mexico*. University of Pittsburgh Press.

Dix, R. H. (1989). Cleavage structures and party systems in Latin America. *Comparative Politics, 22*(1), 23–37.
Dorlach, T. (2020). Business interests, conservative economists, and the expansion of non-contributory pensions in Latin America. *Politics and Society, Online*, 1–24.
Esping-Andersen, G. (1990). *The three worlds of welfare capitalism*. Polity Press.
Esping-Andersen, G. (2014). Welfare regimes and social stratification. *Journal of European Social Policy*, 1–11.
Fried, B. J. (2012). Distributive politics and conditional cash transfers: The case of Brazil's Bolsa Família. *World Development, 40*(5), 1042–1053.
Garay, C. (2016). *Social policy expansion in Latin America*. Cambridge University Press.
Gill, I. S., Packard, T., & Yermo, J. (2004). *Keeping the promise of social security in Latin America*. Stanford University Press and the World Bank.
Godoy, O., & Valdés-Prieto, S. (1997). Democracy and pensions in Chile: Experience with two systems. In S. Valdés-Prieto (Ed.), *The economics of pensions. Principles, policy and international experience* (pp. 58–91). Cambridge University Press.
Gómez Galvarriato, A., & Williamson, J. G. (2008). *Was it prices, productivity or policy? The timing and pace of Latin American industrialization after 1870* (NBER Working Paper 13990). National Bureau of Economic Research.
Haggard, S., & Kaufman, R. R. (2008). *Development, democracy, and welfare states. Latin America, Asia and Eastern Europe*. Princeton University Press.
Huber, E., & Stephens, J. D. (2012). *Democracy and the left in Latin America. Social policy and inequality in Latin America*. University of Chicago Press.
Hunter, W., & Borges Sugiyama, N. (2014). Transforming subjects into citizens: Insights from Brazil's Bolsa Família. *Perspectives on Politics, 12*(4), 829–845.
Hunter, W., & Power, T. (2007). Rewarding Lula: Executive power, social policy, and the Brazilian elections of 2006. *Latin American Politics and Society, 49*, 1–30.
IBGE. (1951). *Anuário Estatístico do Brasil—1950* (Yaerbook 11; Anuário Estatístico Do Brasil). Instituto Brasileiro de Geografia e Estaística.
IDEA. (2022). *Voter turnout database*. International Institute for Democracy and Electoral Assistance. https://www.idea.int/es/data-tools/data/voter-turnout
IMF. (2018). *Growing pains. Is Latin America prepared for population aging?* (Report 18/05). International Monetary Fund. https://www.imf.org/en/Publications/Departmental-Papers-Policy-Papers/Issues/2018/04/16/Growing-Pains-Is-Latin-American-Prepared-for-Population-Aging-45382
Iversen, T., & Soskice, D. (2001). An asset theory of social policy preferences. *American Political Science Review, 95*(4), 875–893.

Iversen, T., & Soskice, D. (2015a). Democratic limits to redistribution. Inclusionary versus exclusionary coalitions in the knowledge economy. *World Politics, 67*(2), 185–225.

Iversen, T., & Soskice, D. (2015b). Politics for markets. *Journal of European Social Policy, 25*(1), 76–93.

James, E. (1997). Public pensions in international perspective: Problems, reforms, and research issues. In S. Valdés-Prieto (Ed.), *The economics of pensions. Principles, problems, and international experience* (pp. 350–370). Cambridge University Press.

Kapiszewski, D., Levitsky, S., & Yashar, D. J. (Eds.). (2021). Inequality, democracy, and the inclusionary turn in Latin America. In *The inclusionary turn in Latin American Democracies*. Cambridge University Press.

Kay, S. J. (1999). Unexpected privatizations. Politics and social security reform in the southern cone. *Comparative Politics, 31*(4), 403–422.

Kay, S. J., & Borzutzky, S. (2022). Can defined contribution pensions survive the pandemic? The Chilean case. *International Social Security Review, 75*, 31–50.

Korpi, W. (1980). Social policy and the distributional conflict in the capitalist democracies: A preliminary comparative framework. *West European Politics, 3*, 296–316.

Korpi, W., & Palme, J. (1998). The paradox of redistribution and strategies for equality: Welfare state institutions, inequality and poverty in the western countries. *American Sociological Review, 63*(5), 661–687.

Layton, M. L., Donaghy, M., & Rennó, L. (2017). Does welfare provision promote democratic state legitimacy? Evidence from Brazil's Bolsa Família Program. *Latin American Politics and Society, 59*(4), 99–120.

Layton, M. L., & Smith, A. E. (2011). *Social assistance policies and the presidential vote in Latin America* (Americas Barometer Insights: 2011 66). LAPOP Vanderbilt University. https://www.vanderbilt.edu/lapop/insights/IO866en.pdf

Levitsky, S., & Roberts, K. M. (2012). *The resurgence of the Latin American left*. The John Hopkins University Press.

Linos, E. (2013). Do conditional cash transfer programmes shift votes? Evidence from the Honduran PRAF. *Electoral Studies, 32*(4), 864–874.

Mainwaring, S. (Ed.). (2018). *Party systems in Latin America. Institutionalization, decay and collapse*. Cambridge University Press.

Malloy, J. M. (1979). *The politics of social security in Brazil*. University of Pittsburgh Press.

Manacorda, M., Miguel, E., & Vigorito, A. (2011). Government transfers and political support. *American Economic Journal: Applied Economics, 3*, 1–28.

Mesa-Lago, C. (1978). *Social security in Latin America: Pressure groups, stratification, and inequality*. University of Pittsburgh Press.
Mesa-Lago, C. (1989). *Ascent to Bankruptcy: Financing social security in Latin America*. University of Pittsburgh Press.
Mesa-Lago, C. (2007). *Reassembling social security. A survey of pensions and healthcare reforms in Latin America*. Oxford University Press.
Mesa-Lago, C. (2018). *Reversing pension privatization in Bolivia* (Extension of Social Security) [Working Paper]. International Labour Office.
Mesa-Lago, C. (2020). *Evaluación de cuatro décadas de privatización de pensiones en América Latina (1980-2020): Promesas y realidades* [Report]. Fundación Friedrich Ebert en México.
Mesa-Lago, C., & Müller, K. (2002). The politics of pension reform in Latin America. *Journal of Latin American Studies, 34*(3), 687–715.
Negretto, G. L., & Visconti, G. (2018). Electoral reform under limited party competition: The adoption of proportional representation in Latin America. *Latin American Politics and Society, 60*(1), 27–51.
Nupia, O. (2011). *Anti-poverty programs and presidential election outcomes: Familias en Acciòn in Colombia* [Documentos CEDE]. Universidad de los Andes Facultad de Economìa. https://papers.ssrn.com/sol3/papers.cfm?abstract_id=1864064
Palier, B., & Martin, C. (2007). Editorial introduction from 'a Frozen Landscape' to structural reforms: The sequential transformation of Bismarckian Welfare Systems. *Social Policy and Administration, 41*(6), 535–554.
Pérez-Liñan, A., & Mainwaring, S. (2013). Regime legacies and levels of democracy: Evidence from Latin America. *Comparative Politics, 45*(4), 379–397.
Pierson, P. (2001). *The new politics of the welfare state*. Oxford University Press.
Rawls, J. (1999). *A theory of justice. Revised edition* (Revised edition). Belknap Press.
Roberts, K. M. (2021). The inclusionary turn and its political limitations. In D. Kapiszewski, S. Levitsky, & D. J. Yashar (Eds.), *The inclusionary turn in Latin American democracies*. Cambridge University Press.
Rofman, R., Apella, I., & Vezza, E. (2013). *Mas alla de las pensiones contributivas. Catorce experiencias en America Latina* [Report]. The World Bank.
Schober, G. (2019). Conditional cash transfers, resources and political participation in Latin America. *Latin American Research Review, 54*(3), 591–607. https://doi.org/10.25222/larr.143
Segovia, A. (2022). *Las relaciones entre modelos y tipos de capitalismo: La experiencia de centroamérica* (Working Paper 198; Estudios y Perspectivas). CEPAL-Mexico.

Segura-Ubiergo, A. (2007). *The political economy of the Welfare State in Latin America*. Cambridge University Press.
Shikida, C. D., Monasterio, L. M., de Araujo, A. F., Jr., Carraro, A., & Damé, O. M. (2009). "It is the economy companheiro!": An empirical analysis of Lula's re-lection based on municipal data. *Economics Bulletin, 29*(2), 976–991.
Silva, E., & Rossi, F. M. (2017). *Reshaping the political arena in Latin America. From resisting Neoliberalism to the Second Incorporation*. University of Pittsburgh Press.
Stephens, J. D. (1979). *The transition from capitalism to socialism*. Macmillan.
Stokes, S. C. (2004). *Is vote buying undemocratic?* [Conference paper]. University of Chicago, Department of Political Science.
Stokes, S. C. (2009). *Globalization and the left in Latin America* [Mimeo]. Yale University.
Stokes, S. C., Dunning, T., Nazareno, M., & Brusco, V. (2013). *Brokers, voters, and Clientelism. The puzzle of distributive politics*. Cambridge University Press.
Zucco, C. (2013). When payouts pay off: Conditional transfers and voting behavior in Brazil 2002-2010. *American Journal of Political Science, 57*(4), 810–822.
Zucco, C., Luna, J. P., & Ozgen Baykal, G. (2019). Do conditionalities increase support for government transfers? *Journal of Development Studies, Online*.
Zucco, C., & Power, T. (2013). Bolsa Família and the shift in Lula's Electoral Base, 2002–2006: A reply to Bohn. *Latin American Research Review, 48*(2), 3–24.

8

Clusters

The materials and literature discussed so far in this book have referenced significant differences in social protection institutions across the countries in the region, but the nature and extent of these differences have not been addressed. They are the focus of this chapter. The chapter studies cross-country and sub-regional differences in a more systematic fashion.[1]

Cross-country differences in social protection institutions are interesting for their own sake in so far as they reveal country heterogeneity helping to confirm or falsify the hypotheses developed for the region. Studying whether countries can be grouped by their social protection institutions would add another dimension to our research, by indicating stable differentiation in institutions across countries and over time. Identifying clusters helps reduce the heterogeneity in country social protection institutions to a few configurations that can support theoretical generalisations. The suggestion is that the study of institutional differences and similarities will, in addition to facilitating a better understanding of institutions at the country level, sharpen the search for a theory of social protection institutions in Latin America.

[1] Extending this analysis to the sub-national is beyond the scope of this book. Recent studies have demonstrated the gains from it (Niedzwiecki, 2018).

A. Barrientos, *Social Protection in Latin America*, Global Dynamics of Social Policy,
https://doi.org/10.1007/978-3-031-49795-7_8

The comparative study of social protection institutions in the region and possible sub-regional groupings developed in the paper engages with a valuable comparative literature on social policy regimes in Latin America. Inspired by the literature on welfare regimes and welfare states, this literature seeks to arrange countries with similar institutions and outcomes in the expectation that the clusters will provide pointers to the existence of varieties of capitalism in the region.

The materials in the chapter are arranged as follows. Section 8.1 reviews the literature on social policy clusters in the region, including a review of concepts and methods. This review will provide the springboard for the analysis in the chapter. Section 8.2 groups countries based on their social protection effects on employment, protection, and incorporation. The clusters are repeated for different periods in the development of social protection institutions. Section 8.3 offers a perspective on the findings from the cluster analysis, focusing on continuity, disruption, and outliers. Section 8.4 discusses the implications from this analysis for the identification of varieties of capitalism in the region. A final section summarises the main findings from the chapter.

8.1 Social Policy Clusters

This section reviews the literature grouping countries in Latin America.

8.1.1 A First Approximation

It might be useful to begin by drawing a rough approximation to the presence of country clusters, based on the materials discussed in the book so far. Mesa-Lago (1978) offered an early example, by distinguishing three groups of countries by the timing of the emergence of social protection institutions: 'pioneer' counties were the first to establish social insurance funds for selected workers at scale in the 1920s and 1930s; 'intermediate' countries followed in the 1940s and 1950s encouraged by the ILO; 'delayed' countries were the last ones to do so in the 1950s and 1960s. Mesa-Lago was particularly interested in the timing of the emergent institutions. He sought to explain the emergent institutions in terms of the influence of pressure groups and the political incorporation of urban industrial workers.

Argentina, Uruguay, Costa Rica, and Cuba can be argued represent the 'old' model of social protection. Argentina, Uruguay, and Cuba are occupational insurance funds 'pioneers" in Mesa-Lago's description. Chile is a 'pioneer' in this respect but eventually led the region in replacing occupational pensions with individual retirement saving plans. And Costa Rica is in fact a newcomer. It is interesting that the countries in this group now provide contrasting sets of social protection institutions. Uruguay and Costa Rica have complementary pension schemes (occupational insurance and individual retirement accounts). Argentina has moved back to a pay-as-you go public pension scheme that Cuba retained throughout. Cuba's social assistance is residual (Mesa-Lago, 2012).

Brazil, Panama, and Mexico can be argued describe 'new' (alternative) models. In different ways, Brazil and Mexico have taken diverse pathways. Brazil did not introduce individual retirement plans, while Mexico and Panama replaced existing occupational insurance funds with individual retirement savings plans. Subsequently, reforms to individual retirement plans in Chile and Mexico have strengthened a public component in what is fundamentally a private saving scheme. Social assistance reaches a large proportion of the population in these countries.

The Andean countries and Central America are characterised by extractive economies and ethnic diversity. In Andean countries, occupational insurance funds emerged durins the import substitution period but failed to reach beyond a small minority of urban white-collar workers and workers in extractive industries. Ecuador might be an exception. In Central American countries, aside from Costa Rica, a dominant agro-exporting model restricted the reach of occupational insurance funds to public white-collar workers. In both Andean countries and Central America social assistance is now a significant component of their social protection institutions.

This rough first approximation and associated anomalies suggest a more systematic approach to cluster definitions and evidential support is needed.

8.1.2 Clustering Social Policy Regimes

A strand of the literature on social policy in Latin America has considered whether countries cluster around their social policy institutions and whether this matters for our understanding of their evolution. The brief discussion here is intended as an introduction to the range of perspectives on country groupings and as a useful reminder of the conceptual and methodological issues underlying them. They are foundational to the analysis that follows.

The approach to country clusters after 1990 has been heavily influenced by the work of Esping-Andersen (Esping-Andersen, 1990, 1999). His *Three Worlds of Welfare Capitalism* encouraged a large and still growing literature.[2] Its attraction resided in the linkages it established between configurations of welfare provision (welfare regimes) and forms of capitalism. In short time, Esping-Andersen's approach overcame functional and ideational theories of welfare state development. It has encouraged research seeking to apply this approach to Latin America. Antía (2018), Usabart-González and Minteguiaga (2017) and Sátyro et al. (2021) provide comprehensive reviews of the Latin American literature.[3]

Filgueira and Filgueira (2002), Filgueira (2005) developed a three-fold differentiation of Latin American countries' social policy provision grounded on top-down forms of worker incorporation. The three social policy regimes are: stratified universalism; dual; and exclusionary social policy regimes. 'Stratified universalism' describes social policy regimes in countries where intra-elite competition ensured workers incorporation led to extensive but stratified social policy provision. 'Dual' social policy regimes emerged in countries where the two strategies of worker incorporation – co-optation and repression – remained in play and led to segmented social policy provision. Finally, 'exclusionary' social policy

[2] See the Special Issues in the Journal of European Social Policy (25(1), 2015) and Social Policy and Society (12(1) ,2015) marking the twenty-five-year anniversary of the publication of the *Three Worlds*.

[3] My own contribution to this literature (2004, 2009) and with Martin Powell (2021) apply the welfare regime approach to characterise Latin American social policies as a region. These papers trace an evolution from conservative-informal to liberal-informal to *sui-generis* liberal. They will be discussed briefly below.

institutions emerged in countries where elites made very limited efforts to incorporate workers. Country clusters have a basis in social conflict, as argued by Esping-Andersen for welfare states, but with a dominant role bestowed on elites.

Martínez Franzoni (2008) follows closely Esping-Andersen's conceptual and normative framework and applies it empirically in the context of Latin America (Usabart-González & Minteguiaga, 2017). She argues that welfare states can be assessed in terms of two key indicators: de-commodification and de-familialism. The former measures the extent to which citizens' wellbeing is independent of what they can sell in the market. The latter measures the extent to which an individual wellbeing is independent from their position within the family, a dimension neglected in the *Three Worlds*. One of Martínez-Franzoni's achievements is to have brought the family and social reproduction dimension into the assessment of social policy provision. Having collected data on a broad range of indicators capturing the contribution of markets, government and families, cluster analysis was applied to identify three main clusters: *state productivist* include countries that made relatively larger investments in human capital; *state protectionist* covers countries that invested relatively more in employment related protection; while *state familialist* countries relied to a larger extent on families to ensure wellbeing.

Pribble (2011) eschews the Esping-Andersen approach in favour of a focus on elite's relative preferences for risk prevention and risk coping. Countries in which elites have strong preferences for both risk pooling and risk prevention form the *mobilizing-incorporation industrialist* cluster. At the other extreme are countries in which elites have low preferences for both risk pooling and risk prevention, they are in the *exclusionary agrarian* cluster. Countries in which elites show weak preferences for risk prevention and average preferences for risk prevention form the *interrupted incorporation agrarian* cluster. Countries in which elites have average preferences for risk prevention and high preferences for risk prevention compose the *corporatist-incorporation industrialist* cluster. As can be ascertained from the cluster titles, industrialisation, the mode of incorporation, and partisan competition are the main discriminating factors underpinning cluster differentiation.

Cruz-Martínez (2014, 2017) is interested in measuring the level of welfare state development in Latin American countries. He collects data on indicators of spending, coverage, and outcomes and relies on principal components analysis to collapse the indicators into three separate indexes. The latter are then combined into a multidimensional welfare index. Countries are then ranked based on their scores on the index and grouped to identify clusters (Table 8.1).

As can be seen from the Table, there is a large measure of agreement around the rankings, even though the three studies adopt different indicators, data points, and methodologies. This serves to underline the marked differences in social indicators existing between countries in the region. Roughly Andean and Central American countries, except Costa Rica, are clustered together in the bottom rankings. Pribble's rankings distinguish within this groups between Andean and Central American countries, again except Costa Rica. Some individual country rankings merit discussion, especially compared to the rough groupings in the earlier section of the chapter. Chile appears in the top cluster in all three studies. Uruguay and Costa Rica's membership in the top cluster varies across the studies.

The studies reviewed so far group countries using cross-section data (Martínez Franzoni & Sánchez-Ancochea, 2016). An interesting recent development in this literature extends the analysis to a matrix structure, where differentiation across countries is mapped onto a periodisation of social policies in Latin America's over time. The time periods include: an industrialisation period up to the 1980s; a neoliberal period in the last two decades of the century; and a post-liberal period in the new century. This extension of the approach opens the possibility that countries mapped onto one cluster in one period could be mapped into another cluster in a different period. The normative dimension of the analysis could now indicate potential progression and regression over time. In the main, the clusters identified in the discussion above were mapped with data from the neoliberal period (Martínez Franzoni & Sánchez-Ancochea, 2016). Recent literature has examined the extent of potential changes in country groupings in the post-liberal period (Sátyro et al., 2021).

Table 8.1 Country groupings in selected social policy regime studies

	Martínez Franzoni (2008)	Pribble (2011)	Cruz-Martínez (2014)
Argentina	A	A	A1
Chile	A	A	A3
Costa Rica	B	A	B1
Uruguay	B	A	A2
Brazil	B	B	B2
Mexico	B	B	B5
Panama	B	B	B3
Peru	Ca	C	C3
Colombia	Ca	C	C1
Ecuador	Ca	C	C2
Bolivia	Cb	*	C7
Paraguay	Cb	C	C6
Dominican Rep.	Ca	D	C4
El Salvador	Ca	D	C5
Guatemala	Ca	D	C8
Nicaragua	Cb	D	*
Venezuela	Ca	*	B4
Data points	c2000	Late 1990/ early2000	1970–2000
Method	Hierarchical cluster analysis.	Hierarchical cluster analysis.	PCA derived welfare index.
Indicators	28 indicators on commodification, decommodification, de-familialism.	8 indicators on schooling, health, coverage.	3 indices: spending coverage and outcomes.
Clusters descriptions	A State productionist B State protectionist C Familialist. (a and b are subgroups)	A Mobilizing industrial/ B Corporatist industrial/ C interrupted agrarian/ D Exclusionary agrarian.	A High Welfare B Intermediate C Low. (all countries ordered by numbers)

Data source: Clusters extracted from selected studies (Martínez Franzoni, 2008; Pribble, 2011; Cruz-Martínez, 2014). (*) Indicates ranking left out due to data gaps

8.1.3 Revisiting Concepts and Methods

The contributions summarised in the previous sub-section have collectively carved out a very fertile research agenda capable of providing insights into the character of social policies taken as a whole, as well as of their change over time. An assessment of the literature would require revisiting some conceptual and methodological issues in need of clarification. The discussion below focuses on four such issues: the scope of regimes; measures of social protection; research motivations; and data reduction methods.

The first issue requiring further discussion is the nature and scope of the policies under study. Esping-Andersen focused on welfare regimes, understood as the combined contribution of markets, states, and families to the generation of wellbeing. Wellbeing does not fall from the sky, it needs to be produced (Gough & Wood, 2004). Families, markets, and governments combine to secure adequate levels of wellbeing in the population. In Esping-Andersen's approach, the relative significance of these institutions in particular societies define a particular configuration of their social arrangements and outcomes. Markets dominate in liberal welfare regimes, for example, and result in limited outcomes in terms of decommodification.

As Martínez Franzoni (2008) demonstrates, this approach throws a powerful light on the different sources of wellbeing production, including social reproduction. However, its ambitious scope can be a disadvantage, in that social policies are but a component in welfare regimes.[4] This helps explain why most studies restrict themselves to social policies

[4] I would argue Esping-Andersen's attempt to characterise 'welfare regimes' empirically was ambitious but not fully successful. The main issue is that in the process of taking a comprehensive view of welfare production the linkages to its underlying politics are downgraded. The *Three Worlds* (1990) attributes institutional development to class conflict, but in the *Social Foundations* (1999), which fully explores a welfare regime approach, the more technocratic changes in social risk become the determining factor. The European research that followed is predominantly focused on welfare states, one component of the regime. My own attempt to apply the welfare regime approach to the Latin America region was also unsuccessful in that respect (Barrientos, 2004). Arguably, setting aside the welfare regime approach in favour of a more limited focus on social policy would pose less of a problem in the Latin American context because we are dealing with only 'one world' of those proposed by Esping-Andersen, the liberal regime (Barrientos & Powell, 2021). We lack examples in Latin America of countries in which the state dominates (social democracy) or where families dominate (conservative regimes), although see Martínez Franzoni (2008).

and set aside market and family institutions.[5] Transfers in cash and in kind provide the bases for most, if not all, the variables considered in the literature. The focus of this book on social protection is in line with the focus of the studies reviewed.[6]

A second issue in need of further clarification is associated with how best to measure social protection institutions. It is feasible to measure institutions in terms of their inputs, outputs, or outcomes. In practice, decisions made by researchers in this respect are heavily influenced by data availability and are often ad hoc. As we know from the findings in Chap. 6 with reference to pension schemes, there is no guarantee that measuring inputs, outputs, or outcomes independently of each other will deliver the same country rankings. Social spending levels taken as a social protection input might not be a good indicator of income security in later age (Barrientos, 2021). Along the same lines, high pension participation among salaried workers, an output of social protection institutions, might not result in high levels of pension receipt among future older groups or on adequate benefit levels for the lucky ones to be able to access their entitlements (Altamirano Montoya et al., 2018). Ideally, an assessment of social protection regimes should focus on outcomes.[7]

This raises an interesting issue: what is the motivation behind researchers' construction of country rankings and groupings? There are at least two motivations present in the literature on social policy clusters. One motivation is to differentiate countries according to their social protection regimes in ways that could throw light on the factors underlying their particular social protection institutional configuration. Countries are classified into clusters in the expectation that their similarities and dissimilarities will point to the factors explaining their respective

[5] Some studies focus on 'welfare states' which is taken to mean social policies (transfers in cash and in kind). From my perspective, the term welfare states should be reserved for welfare institutions in early industrialisers.

[6] The justification for the narrower approach adopted in this book were explained in the Introduction.

[7] The literature often focuses on social spending which is taken to act as a proxy for 'welfare effort'. Given the large inequalities which characterise social protection in Latin America, a focus on spending without accounting for its distribution can be misleading. A focus on outputs, like pension coverage of the labour force, or more precisely worker participation in pension schemes at a point in time, can also be an imperfect measure of social protection.

institutions. An alternative motivation is essentially normative. It is to do with assessing the relative effectiveness or success of the institutional configuration of different clusters. Pribble (2011), for example, classifies countries as a means to find supportive evidence for the hypothesis that elite approaches to risk prevention and risk coping actually shape their countries' social protection institutions. It provides an example of the first motivation. Martínez Franzoni (2008), on the other hand, is concerned with assessing the extent to which country clusters achieve decommodification and defamilialism. In this case the dominant motivation is principally a normative one, although with an expectation that the findings will provide both fruit and light.

In the analysis of country social protection regimes which follows, the notions of decommodification and familialism are less appropriate. Arguably, the very notion of decommodification is problematic. Take pensions for example. They sustain living standards in retirement by replacing labour earnings with pension income. But pension income is earned income if it simply represents backloaded labour earnings, as in individual retirement savings plans for example. Alternatively, if retirement income is a transfer from those in work to those in retirement, as in pay-as-you-go- occupational insurance funds, it is unearned income. In both cases accessing entitlements require a history of payroll contributions which imply longstanding commodification. It is problematic in this context that decommodification as dependent on prior commodification.[8] Defamilialism is a more well-defined normative concept to assess the effectiveness of social protection, as Martínez Franzoni (2008) demonstrates, but in Latin America it is a by-product of social protection institutions rather than their primary motivation (Rossel, 2013).

The fourth issue has to do with methods to cluster countries. Data reduction techniques are the most common methods employed in the literature. They include amalgamation of cases as in cluster analysis (Hierarchical cluster analysis, K-means cluster analysis) (Farragina & Seeleib-Kaiser, 2011; Gough, 2001; Powell & Barrientos, 2004); or analysis of variance as in principal components analysis (Cruz-Martínez, 2014, 2017).

[8] Of course, this is true at the aggregate level, as the resources accessed by retirees and others not in work must be produced somehow.

8.2 Clustering Causal Outcomes

This section will cluster countries in Latin America focusing on the three main causal outcomes identified in previous chapters: employment stratification, protection of living standards of workers and their dependents; and political incorporation. The justification, and motivation, for focusing on these outcomes is analytical as opposed to normative. The expectation is that identifying similarities and dissimilarities across countries in the region will provide information on the factors that shape the causal effects of social protection, including potential mechanisms. It is important to keep in mind that here the focus is on social protection institutions, as opposed to social policy regimes. The justification for restricting the analysis to income transfers was explained in the introduction. There are important distinctions between the 'logic' of service provision and that of income transfers.

The analysis below will rely on hierarchical cluster methods, essentially a technique for grouping countries successively by the means of their cluster scores until all countries are in a single group. Centroid linkage merges the groups whose means, the centre of gravity of the group, are similar. It focuses on the distances of the means of the groups. This is a nonparametric data reduction technique and a standard method employed in the literature. It is more likely to provide useful information if it is bookended by causal analysis.

In the analysis below, clusters will be identified separately for the three main periods: industrialisation and the spread of occupational insurance funds, neoliberal retrenchment and individual retirement savings plans, and the expansion of social assistance. The objective is to track changes in cluster memberships over time, if any. This will provide some information on possible convergence or divergence in social protection outcomes.

The choice of measures of social protection outcomes capable of helping cluster countries in the region is restricted by available data. The further back in time the analysis is attempted, the more binding these restrictions are. Available data and changes in social protection institutions over time makes it unavoidable that the indicators used in the clustering will have to change to some extent from one period to another.

Social assistance was residual prior to the mid-1990s for example. Measures of industrialisation are an exception because they track both the rise and its relative decline or stagnation. To mitigate data gaps and data volatility, all the indicators are averaged within decades (denoted by the letter d).[9]

Table 8.2 describes all the variables employed in the cluster analysis below. Their relevance will be explained when reporting on each of the three periods.

Table 8.2 Variables employed in the cluster analysis, description, and data sources

Variable name	Description	Source
dindus	Ratio of manufacturing to agriculture value added—continuous	MOxLAD
Employment		
dinformal	Share of employment of workers in small firms, own account, and zero income—percentage	CEDLAS
dlarge	Share of employment in large firms—percentage	CEDLAS
dtu	Share of population engaged with trade unions v2catrauni_mean—percentage	Vdem
Protection		
datk	Atkinson inequality index	WIID
dfgt0	Poverty headcount—percentage	CEDLAS
dfgt1	Poverty gap—percentage of poverty line	CEDLAS
dlaby_all	Gini of monthly labour earnings—percentage	CEDLAS
ds80s20	Ratio of top quintile to bottom two quintiles share of income	WIID
dtransacc	Social assistance transfers concentration coefficient	CEQ
dpensioncc	Pension income concentration coefficient	CEQ

(*continued*)

[9] In a couple of cases, values for the end of one decade are repeated at the start of the new decade.

Table 8.2 (continued)

Variable name	Description	Source
Incorporation		
dleft	Share of left parties in parliament—percentage	Huber & Stephens Latin America and Caribbean Political Dataset, 1945–2012
dpolineq	Power distributed by socio-economic position categorical v2pepwrses_mean	Vdem
drepress	v2csreprss_mean	Vdem
dturnout	Turnout parliamentary elections—percentage of population legally entitled to vote	IDEA

Data sources: MOxLAD is the Montevideo-Oxford Latin American Economic History Dataset (MOxLAD, n.d.); CEDLAS is the Center of Distributive, Labor and Social Studies (CEDLAS)(CEDLAS & World Bank, 2022); Vdem is Vdem Institute Database, (Coppedge, Michael, John Gerring, Carl Henrik Knutsen, Staffan I. Lindberg, Jan Teorell, David Altman, Michael Bernhard, Agnes Cornell, M. Steven Fish, Lisa Gastaldi, Haakon Gjerløw, Adam Glynn, Ana Good God, Sandra Grahn, Allen Hicken, Katrin Kinzelbach, Joshua Krusell, Kyle L. Marquardt, Kelly McMann, Valeriya Mechkova, Juraj Medzihorsky, Natalia Natsika, Anja Neundorf, Pamela Paxton, Daniel Pemstein, Josefine Pernes, Oskar Ryden, Johannes von Römer, Brigitte Seim, Rachel Sigman, Svend-Erik Skaaning, Jeffrey Staton, Aksel Sundström, Eitan Tzelgov, Yi-ting Wang, Tore Wig, Steven Wilson, and Daniel Ziblatt. 2023. "V-Dem [Country-Year/Country-Date] Dataset v13" Varieties of Democracy (V-Dem) Project. https://doi.org/10.23696/vdemds23.); WIID is the UNU World Income Inequality Database (UNU-WIDER, 2022); CEQ is the Commitment for Equity Database (CEQ Institute, 2022); Huber and Stephens Latin American and Caribbean Political Dataset 1945–2012 (Huber et al., 2012); IDEA is the Voter Turnout Dataset (IDEA, 2022)

Focusing first on the 1970s decade, Fig. 8.1 below shows the relevant country clusters.

The Figure shows country groupings using 1970s outcomes.

The clusters are based the *dindus* variable which measures the ratio of manufacturing to agriculture value added; the share of left members of the lower legislative chamber *dleft*, the share of the population experts estimated to be engaged with trade unions *dtu*, and expert measures of repression against civil society organizations *drepress*. The variables cover employment and incorporation outcomes. It was not possible to find

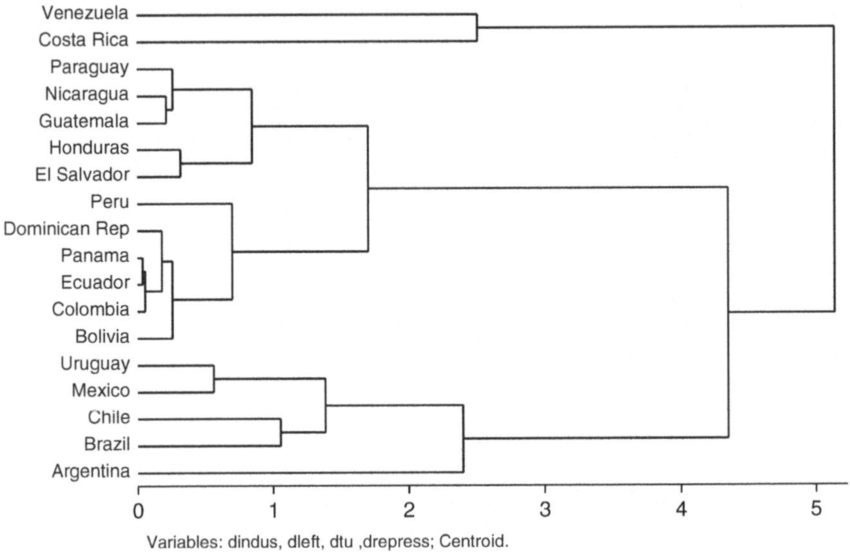

Fig. 8.1 Country clusters using 1970s outcomes

reliable and comparable measures of the protection outcome, because of the absence of regular household surveys or administrative data.

Starting from the left hand of the agglomeration of countries, the clusters have a straightforward explanation in terms of the country classifications proposed at the beginning of the chapter. There is a group of countries, Uruguay, Mexico, Chile, Brazil, and Argentina that industrialised relative earlier and more intensely. This is strongly reflected in the incorporation and employment outcomes. Then there are two middle groups of countries, including a group of Andean countries plus the Dominican Republic and Panama separated from a group of Central American countries plus Paraguay. Finally, Venezuela and Costa Rica are in a separate group joining the other groups at the end. The clusters are roughly in line with predicted effects of diverse experiences with industrialisation.

The next Fig. 8.2. shows the clusters formed when using average data for the 1990s. In this period, reforms to social protection associated with

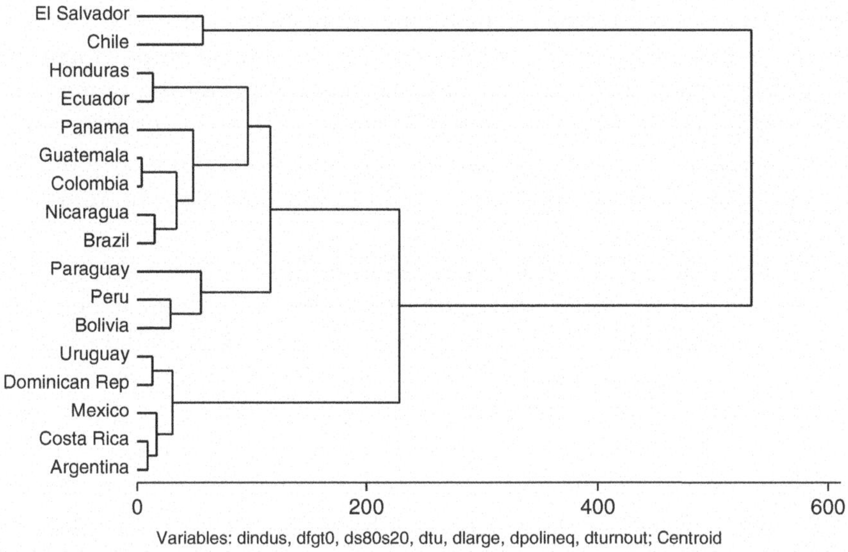

Fig. 8.2 Country clusters using 1990s outcomes

pension reform, both parametric and structural, are beginning to show their effects on social protection outcomes.

The Figure shows the country groupings based on 1990s outcomes.

Two variables are retained from the 1970s clusters, *dindus* and *dtu*. Both variables are likely to show some reversals form the 1970s, the stagnation or decline of industrialisation and industrial employment and the decline in trade union engagement. The same variables now represent a trend change. Two additional incorporation variables are now included, *dpolineq* and *dturnout*. The former comes from expert assessments of the extent to which economic interests dominate politics, while the latter captures the share of the population of voting age that participates in parliamentary elections. There is also an additional employment variable, *dlarge* captures the share of employment in large firms[10] constructed from household survey data. The expectation is that the gradual removal of ISI

[10] There are differences across individual countries, but most of them identify large firms with firms employing 5 workers or more. In a Latin American context, this makes sense as a significant plurality of workers are employed in firms below 5 employees or are own account workers. See the Employment chapter above.

preferential sector treatment, including occupational insurance funds, and trade liberalisation will have resulted in a decline in employment in large firms. Then there are two variables now capturing the protection effects of economic liberalisation: *dfgt0* measures the poverty headcount at the moderate international poverty line; and *ds80s20* the ratio of the income share of the top quintile to the share of income of the bottom two quintiles.

There is a loosening of the clusters identified in the 1970s. Argentina, Costa Rica and Mexico form a group that joins with Uruguay and the Dominican Republic. The middle group collecting most of the Central American and Andean countries now includes Brazil. Finally, El Salvador and Chile are now the outliers joining the rest of the countries at the end. The clusters are now looser than in the 1970s, keeping in mind that the variables selected are different in as much as they now include measures of poverty and inequality as well as political inequality. The pairing of countries at the base of the agglomeration raises interest questions, e.g., the pairing of Brazil and Nicaragua, or Guatemala and Colombia, or Ecuador and Honduras. This is a decade of considerable change not only in the developing model and in democratization, but also in terms of social protection. The focus on outcomes is informative. Inputs and outputs change only gradually, pension spending or the pension coverage of the labour force for example are sticky.[11] The focus on outcomes represents more accurately the effects of social protection changes.

Figure 8.3 clusters countries based on average data from the 2010s. Data availability forced some changes in the variables used in the cluster analysis. The sole employment variable now is *dinf*, the share of the employed labour force in small firms plus own account workers and zero wage workers. Changes in social protection provision, especially with the expansion of social assistance, meant it now reaches workers in informal employment. Two variables capture incorporation, *dpolineq* and *dturnout*. Three variables stand for protection effects, *dlaby_all* measures the

[11] Kurtz and Brooks (2008) for example, examining the changes to the state in the neoliberal period note the existence of a compromise between promoting liberalization and maintaining social spending (with pensions as a significant share). This is also borne out by the debate on the effect of globalization on social spending (Avelino et al., 2005; Huber et al., 2008; Kaufman & Segura-Ubiergo, 2001).

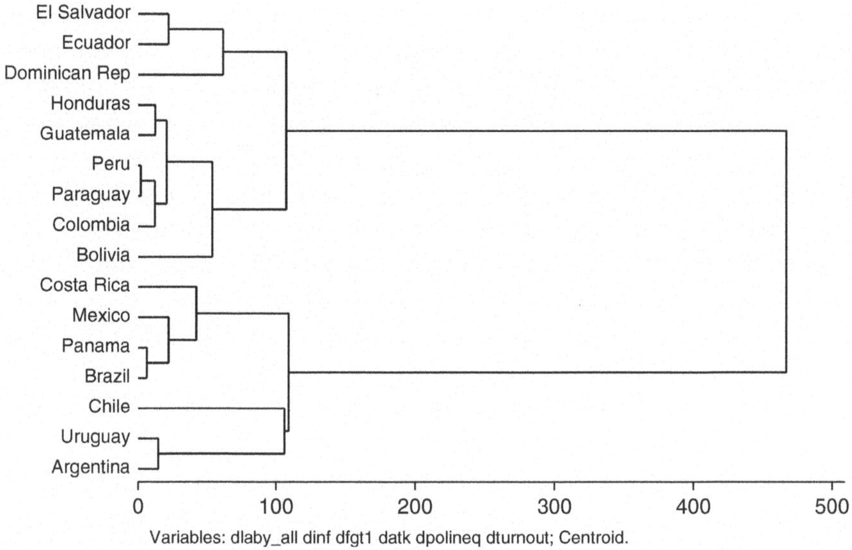

Fig. 8.3 Country cluster using 2010s outcomes

gini coefficient of monthly wages for all workers and *dakt* stands for the Atkinson measure of income inequality. The poverty gap dfgt1 measures the average poverty gap in the economy as a share of the poverty line (using the moderate international poverty line for comparability). Nicaragua and Venezuela drop out of the exercise due to lack of comparable data.

The Figure shows country groupings using 2010s outcomes.

There appears to be a return to the country groupings from before the disruption of the neoliberal period. Starting from the bottom left-hand side there are two groups of countries Chile, Argentina, and Uruguay showing similar outcomes. They are joined by Costa Rica, Mexico, Panama, and Brazil at the next stage in the agglomeration. The next cluster contains the Andean and the remaining Central American countries. The initial clusters for these two groups retain some of the disruption observed for the 1990s in the basic pairings, e.g., Peru and Paraguay, or El Salvador and Ecuador.

Figure 8.4 shows the clusters obtained by extending the range of data employed to include a measure of the distribution of social protection transfers, pension benefits and social assistance transfers. The variable set now includes the concentration coefficients for social assistance and pension transfers as calculated by the Commitment for Equity initiative (CEQ Institute, 2022). Concentration coefficients capture inequality in the distribution of transfer income. Because the data points are year-specific, as opposed to an average of the observations from a decade for the other variables, they may contain an idiosyncratic component. The justification for their inclusion is that they provide information on the contribution of the social protection transfers to overall income inequality. They are a more precise proxy for the protection effects of social protection, than overall income inequality.

The Figure shows country groupings using post mid-2010s data points.

These two variables are combined with the variables used in the clustering for the 2010s datapoints. Therefore, the differences in the clusters shown by Figs. 8.3 and 8.4 are primarily associated with the inclusion of the two transfer concentration coefficient variables. The differences in clusters are interesting. There is continuity in the three main clusters:

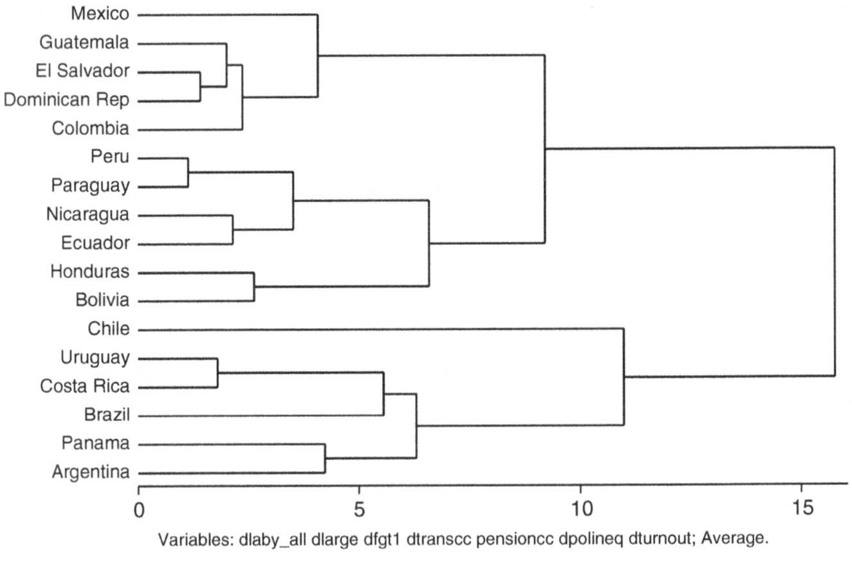

Fig. 8.4 Country clusters using post mid-2010s data points

early industrialisers plus Costa Rica and Panama; Andean group plus Paraguay and Nicaragua; and remaining Central American countries plus Colombia. Mexico is now aligned with the Central American group. Chile is now in a group of its own eventually joined to the early industrialisers.

8.3 Continuity, Disruption, and Outliers

It is now time to consolidate the findings from the country groupings. It is important to keep in mind that the variables employed to group countries were selected to capture the three main causal effects of social protection, on employment, protection, and incorporation.

The main finding is that countries in Latin America group into three main clusters based on their social protection effects. One cluster collects the countries in the Southern cone which industrialised earlier and more intensely. A second cluster includes the Andean countries. A third cluster contains Central American countries. There appears to be a strong continuity in this basic structure for the region since the 1970s. The three cluster structure also comes through in the findings in the associated literature, with a weaker focus on outcomes and a broader focus on social spending. There are three main social protection clusters in the region since the 1970s.

While there is a strong continuity in membership of the country clusters, there are observable changes in time. The neoliberal period had a disruptive effect on the country groupings. During this period, the three worlds of social protection in Latin America threatened to become four worlds, as Chile and El Salvador separated from their respective groupings. The Andean and Central American groupings became more mixed in their membership. The shift to neoliberal policies clearly had a highly disruptive effect on social protection institutions and on their effects. The finding suggest that the three worlds of Latin American welfare are not set in stone and can be disrupted by shifts in the political-economy model.

Several variables employed in the analysis measured country decadal averages, like employment and turnout, that are likely to be sticky and therefore dampen change over time. Including distributional variables like income inequality measures could prove more sensitive to change over time. Focusing on decadal data points mitigated data gaps and idiosyncratic volatility but also had the effect of dampening change over time. Even so, disruption to established groupings is observable. Entering distributional variables into the cluster analysis also proved disruptive for the country clusters, as the last Figure show.

The potential findings on convergence and divergence tell a partial story. The cluster analysis is designed to identify full convergence, when previously different groups now are joined together; or divergence, when a single group splits into two or more groups. Gradual convergence or gradual divergence is harder to observe with cluster analysis. An interesting finding in this respect is that there is more fluidity across the Central American and Andean groups of countries than between these and the early industrialised countries. Country memberships in the Central American and Andean clusters are less stable in time.

Observed changes in the membership of individual countries might provide information on outliers. Chile, Brazil, and Mexico merit a brief discussion. Chile's membership varies a great deal after the 1970s. This is due to the disruption associated with neoliberal policies. Chile made structural changes to its social protection institutions in 1981, earlier than other countries in the early industrialiser group. The 1990s data points cluster places Chile in a separate group with El Salvador. This is replicated with the 2010s data points. Chile returns to the early industrialisers group in the last Fig. 8.4. but only joins the group at the end of that stage in the agglomeration. Mexico's initial membership in the early industrialisers group is retained in the 1990s and 2010s but in the last Fig. 8.4, including distributional effects of social assistance and pension transfers, it relocates to the Central American group. This suggests Mexico's membership of the early industrialisers loosens towards the end of the period, especially if the protection effects of social protection institutions are explicitly included. Brazil drifted away from the early industrialiser group in the 1990s, returning to this cluster in the later decades. The impact of neoliberal policies disrupted Brazil's group membership but in a different direction than Chile's. Acknowledging that tracking individual countries across clusters is not the most appropriate use of cluster analysis, it nonetheless helps identify countries with loose memberships. This will be considered further below.

8.4 Three Worlds of Latin American Social Protection/Welfare Capitalism?

One of the significant contributions of cluster analysis applied to social protection effects is to draw attention to systematic differences in these effects across countries. In the plurality of existing studies, differences in underlying economic relationships are believed to shape social protection institutions in the countries under investigation. Here the approach adopted reversed the implied causality. The argument is that social protection institutions help to shape underlying social and economic relationships, for example in terms of employment and its productivity; or the welfare of wage earners and their dependants; or political inclusion. Social protection institutions are understood to have causal effects in these three areas through facilitating specific stratification modalities of the wage earners.

Cluster analysis on outcome indicators of the three main social protection effects leads to the identification of country groupings. It is straightforward to extend this argument and suggest that country groupings reflect distinct types of social protection effects on economic relationships. This is important because the cluster findings reject the proposition that, as far as social protection institutions are concerned, all countries in the region can be located within a single institutional structure. Put differently, the findings from the cluster analysis are inconsistent with the proposition that the social protection dynamics for all countries in the region fit a unique development path.

Taking our cue from Esping-Andersen's three worlds of welfare capitalism, these findings suggest there are also three worlds of welfare, more precisely social protection, in Latin America. One 'world' contains an early industrialiser group of countries, including Argentina, Chile, Uruguay, Brazil, Venezuela, Mexico, and Costa Rica (not an early industrialiser). Another 'world' contains an Andean group of countries including Bolivia, Peru, Ecuador, Colombia, and Paraguay. A third 'world' contains a Central American group of countries including Dominican Republic, El Salvador, Guatemala, Honduras, and Nicaragua. They could be described by development economists as three types of capitalism: industrialising, extractive, and agro-exporting, respectively. It is important to keep in mind that there are significant differences across countries in each of these groups and similarities across countries in different groups. It is also the case, as the cluster analysis showed, that group memberships can be fluid in time.

8.5 Conclusions

The chapter studied differences and similarities in social protection institutions across countries in the region with the aim of identifying country groupings or clusters. The discussion in the book has noted country specific differences in the features of social protection institutions, in their reach and depth, and in their development paths. From a comparative perspective, studying institutional differences and similarities is an important step towards theory development. Reducing the heterogeneity of social protection institutions in the countries in the region to a few ideal types is a first step towards the identification of causal associations.

The methodological approach implemented in the paper was borrowed from the literature in social policy regimes seeking to identify country clusters in the region. This valuable literature provided the launching pad for the analysis in the chapter. This literature groups and ranks countries in the region based on selected social policy indicators. A review of research on social policy regimes raised some conceptual and methodological issues. They helped define an approach to grouping countries based on the causal outcomes of social protection institutions—employment, protection, and incorporation - and repeated for the periods associated with institutional development.

The results from this analysis reported in the chapter largely confirm the findings in the social policy regime literature. In broad terms, country groupings based on social protection outcomes indicate there are three main clusters of countries: Southern cone countries plus Costa Rica, Mexico, and Panama; Andean countries including Paraguay; and Central

American countries. This result is in line with the findings from the social policy regime literature and more generally the country groupings identified by early social protection research like those in Mesa-Lago (1978).

Repeating the cluster analysis for different periods characterised by social protection reforms provides additional insights. The temporal analysis suggests a large measure of continuity in the country groupings over time, but it also shows disruption in the membership of the clusters during the neoliberal period. Cluster memberships loosen up during this period, especially for countries like Chile and Mexico. Cluster analysis was performed on country decadal averages to forestall the influence of data gaps and idiosyncratic data. Paying attention to measures of the distribution of transfers introduces a measure of fluidity in the membership sets of Andean and Central American countries.

Cluster analysis is a data reduction technique and it makes sense not to overinterpret its results. The findings raise some intriguing issues for further research with appropriate methods. Considering the factors potentially explaining the continuity in the membership of the three clusters, historians are likely to underline the timing and spatial distribution of industrialisation; neo institutionalists will emphasise longer term institutional resilience; and social policy/economic development scholars will point to overlaps with the three varieties of capitalism in the region: industrialised; agro-exporting, and extractive.

References

Altamirano Montoya, A., Berstein, S., Bosch, M., & García Huitrón, M. (2018). *Presente y futuro de las pensiones en América Latina y el Caribe*. Inter-American Development Bank.

Antía, F. (2018). Regímenes de política social en América Latina: Una revisión crítica de la literatura. *Desafíos, 30*(2), 193–235.

Avelino, G., Brown, D. S., & Hunter, W. (2005). The effects of capital mobility, trade openness, and democracy on social spending in Latin America, 1980–1999. *American Journal of Political Science, 49*(3), 625–641.

Barrientos, A. (2004). Latin America: Towards a liberal-informal welfare regime. In I. Gough, G. Wood, A. Barrientos, P. Bevan, P. David, & G. Room (Eds.),

Insecurity and welfare regimes in Asia, Africa and Latin America (pp. 121–168). Cambridge University Press.

Barrientos, A. (2009). Labour markets and the (hyphenated) welfare regime in Latin America. *Economy and Society, 38*(1), 87–108.

Barrientos, A. (2021). Inequalities in income security in later age in Latin America. *Pan American Journal of Public Health, 45*. https://doi.org/10.26633/RPSP.2021.85

Barrientos, A., & Powell, M. (2021). How "Liberal" are Latin American Welfare Regimes? In *Latin American social policy developments in the twenty-first century* (pp. 135–160). Palgrave Macmillan. https://link.springer.com/chapter/10.1007/978-3-030-61270-2_5

CEDLAS, & World Bank. (2022). *Socio-economic database for Latin America and the Caribbean*. CEDLAS.

CEQ Institute. (2022). *CEQ Standard Indicators Web version 4.0*. Tulane University.

Cruz-Martínez, G. (2014). Welfare state development in Latin America and the Caribbean (1970s–2000s): Multidimensional Welfare Index, its methodology and results. *Social Indicators Research, 119*, 1295–1317. https://doi.org/10.1007/s11205-013-0549-7

Cruz-Martínez, G. (2017). Welfare state development, individual deprivations and income inequality: A cross-country Analysis in Latin America and the Caribbean. *Social Indicators Research, 134*, 955–979. https://doi.org/10.1007/s11205-016-1465-4

Esping-Andersen, G. (1990). *The three worlds of welfare capitalism*. Polity Press.

Esping-Andersen, G. (1999). *Social foundations of postindustrial economies*. Oxford University Press.

Farragina, E., & Seeleib-Kaiser, M. (2011). Welfare regime debate: Past, presents and futures? *Policy and Politics, 39*(4), 583–611. https://doi.org/10.1332/030557311X603592

Filgueira, C. H., & Filgueira, F. (2002). Models of welfare and models of capitalism: The limits of transferability. In E. Huber (Ed.), *Models of Capitalism: Lessons from Latin America* (pp. 127–158). University of Pennsylvania Press.

Filgueira, F. (2005). *Welfare and democracy in Latin America: The development, crises and aftermath of Universal, dual and exclusionary social states*. UNRISD.

Gough, I. (2001). Social assistance regimes: A cluster analysis. *Journal of European Social Policy, 11*(2), 165–170.

Gough, I., & Wood, G. (2004). *Insecurity and welfare regimes in Asia*. Cambridge University Press.

Huber, E., Mustillo, T., & Stephens, J. D. (2008). Politics and social spending in Latin America. *Journal of Politics, 70*(2), 420–436. http://www.jstor.com/stable/10.1017/s0022381608080407

Huber, E., Stephens, J. D., Mustillo, T., & Pribble, J. (2012). *Latin America and the Caribbean political dataset 1945-2008 [Dataset]*. University of North Carolina.

IDEA. (2022). *Voter turnout database*. International Institute for Democracy and Electoral Assistance. https://www.idea.int/es/data-tools/data/voter-turnout

Kaufman, R. R., & Segura-Ubiergo, A. (2001). Globalization, domestic politics, and social spending in Latin America: A time-series cross-section analysis, 1973-97. *World Politics, 53*(4), 553–587. https://www.jstor.org/stable/25054165

Kurtz, M. J., & Brooks, S. (2008). Embedding neoliberal reform in Latin America. *World Politics, 69*, 231–280. https://doi.org/10.1353/wp.0.0015

Martínez Franzoni, J. (2008). Welfare regimes in Latin America: Capturing constellations of markets, families, and policies. *Latin American Politics and Society, 50*(2), 67–100.

Martínez Franzoni, J., & Sánchez-Ancochea, D. (2016). Regímenes de bienestar en América Latina: Tensiones entre universalización y segmentación. In E. del Pino & M. J. Rubio Lara (Eds.), *Los estados de bienestar en la encrucijada. Politicas sociales en perspectiva comparada* (pp. 200–220). Tecnos.

Mesa-Lago, C. (1978). *Social security in Latin America: Pressure groups, stratification, and inequality*. University of Pittsburgh Press.

Mesa-Lago, C. (2012). *Sistemas de Protección Social en AmericaLatina y el Caribe: Cuba* (Report LC/W.510). CEPAL.

MOxLAD. (n.d.). *Montevideo-Oxford Latin American Economic History Data Base* [Database]. Montevideo-Oxford Latin American Economic History Data Base. http://moxlad.cienciassociales.edu.uy/en#

Niedzwiecki, S. (2018). *Uneven social policies. The politics of subnational variation in Latin America*. Cambridge University Press.

Powell, M., & Barrientos, A. (2004). Welfare regimes and the welfare mix. *European Journal of Political Research, 43*(1), 83–105.

Pribble, J. (2011). Worlds apart: Social policy regimes in Latin America. *Studies in Comparative International Development, 46*(1), 191–216.

Rossel, C. (2013). *Politicas para las familias en America Latina: Panorama de políticas de reduccion de pobreza y reconciliacion entre trabajo-familia* [Mimeo]. Universidad Catolica del Uruguay.

Sátyro, N., del Pino, E., & Midaglia, C. (2021). *Latin America social policy developments in the Twenty-first Century*. Palgrave Macmillan.
UNU-WIDER. (2022). *World Income Inequality Database WIID*. UNU World Institute for Development Economic Research. https://www.wider.unu.edu/project/world-income-inequality-database-wiid
Usabart-González, G., & Minteguiaga, A. (2017). Esping-Andersen in América Latina. El estudio de los regímenes de bienestar. *Política y Gobierno, 24*(1), 213–236.

9

Conclusion

This Conclusion aims to bring together the main strands of the argumentation in the book. It will perform two main functions.

First, it will draw out some pointers from the discussion in the book for the construction of a theory of social protection institutions in Latin America. The motivation for the book was to advance towards a general theory of social protection institutions. Researching Latin America's social protection institutions is an important step in this direction because of its leadership among late industrialisers in the spread of occupational pension funds, individual retirement savings plans and social assistance. The confluence of diachronic, synchronic, and analytical dimensions of social protection institutions in the Latin American context support theory development. The study of social protection institutions in Latin America offers a range or insights into the parameters of a general theory of welfare institutions.

Second, this Conclusion contains a summary of the main findings emerging from the analysis reported in the book and, on that basis, speculates on implications for policy. Latin American researchers and policy makers are well provided with proposals for the reform of social protection institutions addressing their perceived shortcomings. The chapter

A. Barrientos, *Social Protection in Latin America*, Global Dynamics of Social Policy ,
https://doi.org/10.1007/978-3-031-49795-7_9

ends with a discussion of potential insights from the research reported in this book that could inform reform proposals.

9.1 Pointers for a General Theory of Welfare Institutions

The analysis in the book offers some pointers for the development of a general theory of welfare institutions.

9.1.1 Causal Inference

A general theory of social protection institutions should explain their existence, configuration, and causal effects. Causal inference is at the core of the development of a theory of social protection in Latin America.

The discussion in the book distinguished between 'causes of effects' and 'effects of causes' as two distinct modalities of causal inquiry (Gelman & Imbens, 2013). A 'causes of effects' enquiry starts from a given phenomenon and seeks to find explanations for its existence. In the Latin American context, 'causes of effects' type enquiries would attempt to find answers for why did Bismarckian occupational insurance funds emerged in Latin American countries in the middle of the 20th century? Or why did conditional income transfers emerged and spread in Latin American countries in the new century? These are interesting and valuable enquiries to pursue, but they are unlikely to secure unique and precise answers.[1] This does not mean that 'causes of effects' enquiries are meaningless, on the contrary. Reducing the number of potentially valid explanations by excluding those that could be shown not to be valid, greatly improves our understanding of the issue. This recommends that, as researchers, we maintain an 'ecumenical' approach to 'causes of effects' enquiries and their findings. It is likely that competing enquiries might come to

[1] For an alternative view see Yamamoto (2012).

conclusions that overlap imperfectly, even after harmonising their methods and data (Flechtner & Sánchez-Ancochea, 2022).[2]

'Effects of causes' inquiries study the effects of interventions, understood broadly as changes in policies or institutions. 'Effects of causes' enquiries have come to the fore in social protection with the spread of (quasi-)experimental research, for example research on the effects of conditional income transfer programmes. Experimental studies aim to control for sample selection and omitted variables by random allocation of the intervention to a homogeneous sample. There are considerable challenges to extending this approach in the context of dynamic processes and observational data (Acharya et al., 2016; Blackwell, 2013; Blackwell & Glynn, 2018) that characterising most of the topics studied in this book. This is a tall order for studies of social protection institutions because the effects of institutions are often diffused in time and across the population groups affected. This implies that great care must be exercised in addressing potential methodological issues, especially confounders and mediators. Implementing 'effects of causes' enquiries will rest on stronger grounds if a potential outcomes methodology is adopted. The potential outcomes assumption acknowledges explicitly the role of counterfactuals. Attention to the underlying causal model is essential. Graphical causal models offer an accessible tool to refine the causal associations hypothesised and offer guidance on empirical counterparts (Elwert, 2013).

Constructing a theory of social protection institutions requires engaging with both 'causes of effects' and with 'effects of causes' enquiries. 'Causes of effects' studies help identify the range of variables that can, or cannot, explain the emergence and configuration of social protection institutions. Research on the emergence of institutions in the region have significantly advanced our understanding of the political economy of social protection. 'Effects of causes' enquiries are becoming standard for the evaluation of the impact of social programmes, mainly through quasi-experimental studies. There are synergies here, 'causes of effects' studies often help identify up the issues which 'effects of causes' studies need to investigate.

[2] The discussion on globalisation and social spending in the neoliberal period is a good example of imperfectly overlapping conclusions (Avelino et al., 2005; Huber et al., 2008; Kaufman & Segura-Ubiergo, 2001). The discussion on the role of democratic political regimes and social protection institutions is another case in point (Mares & Carnes, 2009).

9.1.2 Diachronicity, Synchronicity, and Analysis

The analysis revealed a helpful confluence of diachronic and synchronic dimensions in the development of social protection institutions in Latin America. Critical realignments led to the emergence in time of occupational insurance funds, individual retirement savings plans, and social assistance programmes. They are also the core institutions in place currently. Complementary social protection institutions fail to add substantive analytical insights. Occupational insurance funds changed over time, eventually becoming occupational pension schemes by dismantling the 'cradle to the grave' set of entitlements included in their original versions. Individual retirement savings plans were introduced in three distinct modalities and have been the object of large scale reforms and refinements including their termination in Argentina. However, the confluence of diachronic and synchronic dimensions enabled the research on this book to focus on the three main sources of social protection entitlements: membership (of occupational insurance funds), savings capacity (individual retirement savings plans), and citizenship (social assistance). It would be interesting to check whether the same confluence of dimensions applies in the development of social protection institutions in other late industrialisers.

Critical realignments are a critical tool to research the diachronic dimension of social protection institutions (Haggard & Kaufman, 2008).

9.1.3 Wage Earner Stratification

Wage earners are the object of social protection institutions. The evolution of social protection in the long century identified specific groups of workers as the primary object of social protection institutions, manufacturing workers in the early expansion of industry, workers in the public sector and in import substituting sectors in the middle of the twentieth century, and high skilled cognitive and manual non-routine workers since the turn of the century. Social protection institutions contribute to the stratification of groups of wage earners. The timing and speed of stratification varies across countries in the region, and by clusters of countries.

In the discussion above, two dominant dimensions of stratification were identified: sectoral and skill stratification. Factor stratification led to the emergence of an urban working class and preceded the emergence of government-supported social insurance funds. Sectoral stratification was associated with import substitution industrialisation policies and the political coalitions underpinning them. Skill stratification was associated with neoliberal policies and their aftermath. The suggestion, currently contested, is that social protection institutions support a degree of polarization in the labour force, with growth in cognitive non-routine and in manual non-routine jobs. Polarization is relatively more marked for female workers, in part because of rising labour force participation among them.

The main point is that social protection institutions influence the stratification of wage earners into distinct groups. The design and implementation of social protection institutions help define strata among wage earners. Identifying the effects of social protection necessitates paying attention to the intra-class differentiation of wage earners.[3]

9.1.4 Actors

Research on social protection in Latin America suffers from an elite bias.[4] Studies on the first phase of social protection development in the region rightly focused on the primary role played by elites in the incorporation of selected groups of organised workers (Collier & Collier, 1991; Malloy, 1979). The fact that incorporation was top down in most countries in the

[3] Welfare state theory assumes a three-class model: blue-collar or working class, white-collar or middle class, and employers (Esping-Andersen, 1990; Korpi, 1980; Moene & Wallerstein, 2001). The middle class is pivotal in defining the type of welfare state capitalism that takes root in a country (van Kersbergen & Vis, 2014). The three-class model generates standard findings, on targeting for example, even if applied, in theory, to late industrialisers (Gelbach & Pritchett, 1995).

[4] Perhaps this applies more widely. "The dominant framework used in theoretical and comparative accounts, then, has not only adopted an actor-based perspective rather than a structural one but also tends to privilege certain kinds of actors: individual elites rather than collective actors, strategically defined actors rather than class-defined actors, and state actors over societal actors." (Collier 1999:8). "For too long, scholars of party politics in Latin America have ignored individual voters. Instead they focused on charismatic leaders, interest groups, and elite coalitions" (Lupu, 2017, p. 184).

region justified an initial focus on elites, but wage earners and their organisations grew in strength and influence over the following period. The neoliberal period involved disincorporation in terms of the exclusion of worker organisations from the design and management of social protection institutions. A wave of authoritarian government, many of which implemented pension reforms, again placed elites at the centre of decision making (O'Donnell, 1975). The second incorporation has challenged this elite bias in paying attention to the emergence of popular movements ad sectors and the stagnation and decline of traditional parties, but this is contested in the literature (Kapiszewski et al., 2021; Levitsky & Roberts, 2012; Lupu, 2017; Silva & Rossi, 2017). Research on social assistance has given disproportionate consideration to the view that the expansion of conditional income transfers and old age transfers was primarily an electoral strategy designed and orchestrated by governing elites and international organisations (Barrientos, 2020; Borges, 2019).

Broadening the range of actors under investigation will contribute to a more comprehensive theory of social protection institutions. The need to pay closer attention to wage earners and their stratification was covered above. Understanding social protection in Latin America where occupational and savings modalities dominate requires that attention is paid to the role of business, firms, and employers (Dorlach, 2020; Fairfield & Garay, 2017).

9.1.5 Stratification Effects

The analysis in the book focused on three main stratification effects: on employment; on protection; and on incorporation. As the relevant discussion noted, the effects of social protection institutions on employment and protection are well understood and have been extensively covered in the literature. The critical issue raised in the discussion was that the assumed direction of causality was often fuzzy or reversed. Studies on the relationship existing between employment and social protection often take it for granted that changes in the structure of employment or changes in demand for will effect a change in social protection institutions.[5] The argument developed in the book demonstrates it makes sense to study the effects of social protection institutions on employment and skills. The protection effects of social protection are also well understood and extensively covered in the literature, but the direction of causality is often uncertain, especially in the policy arena. The spread of impact evaluation studies in social assistance has improved our understanding of the effects of conditional income transfers and old age transfers. However, discussions on the features of social assistance, targeting for example, often offer contrasting teleological and deontological understandings of social assistance (Barrientos & Villa, 2015). Teleological approaches focus on the poverty and vulnerability reduction effectiveness of transfers. Deontological approaches, on the other hand, take transfers are confirmation of rights, independent of any effects. The discussion on old age income security demonstrated that prevalent understandings of the protection effects of pension schemes are defective. The protection effects of pension scheme participation for less advantaged workers are exaggerated.

The effects of social protection institutions on incorporation have not received the attention they deserve. Researching the incorporation effects of social protection is an essential component of the work needed to construct a general theory of social protection.

9.2 Prospects for Change

The limitations of social protection institutions in Latin America are well understood (Abramo et al., 2019; Mesa-Lago, 2007). From their origins in mid twentieth century, social protection institutions have evolved into dual structures, with insurance/savings institutions aimed at protecting skilled workers in large firms and the public sector, military and police; and assistance institutions supporting less skilled own account workers and workers in small firms and (Barrientos, 2019). Even within these two sets of institutions, protection is segmented meaning that conditions of access and entitlements are themselves stratified (Arza et al., 2022). What are the prospects for change?

[5] For an example of this fuzziness see Barrientos (2009).

9.2.1 Universalism?

Proposals for reforms are a constant in social protection research and policy debates, usually under the banner of universalism. The reference point in global debates is Nordic universalism, describing social programmes provided to all citizens under the same institutional structures (Brady & Bostic, 2010). Esping-Andersen's description applies to programmes in which all " …citizens are endowed with similar rights, irrespective of class or market position" (Esping-Andersen, 1990, p. 69). The influential *Cepalista* approach to social policy borrowed much of its original universalism from the Nordic approach. Retrenchment in the neoliberal period, the stagnation of occupational insurance, and the expansion of social assistance, have led to more nuanced versions of universalism. Filgueira et al. (2005) advocate a 'basic universalism' with a focus on ensuring a scaled down form of public protection for all, but maintaining selective social protection institutions supporting the better off. Huber and Stephens (2012) reluctantly support this 'basic universalism' as a way forward. Martínez-Franzoni and Sánchez-Ancochea (2017) have moved further by advocating for a form of universalism which incorporates stratified protection. Their universalism has as its central objective to make sure that some form of protection reaches all workers and their dependents even if this is achieved through multiple programmes with stratified institutional structures, access, and benefits.

It is hard to disagree with the intention behind universalism, especially the Nordic version. In the context of social protection however, one of the central arguments developed in the book was that social protection institutions are mechanisms for stratification of wage earners.[6] This argument does not run counter the ideal of universalism, but suggests there is no underlying process leading to it in Latin America. It challenges the view that, however imperfect, social protection institutions are designed and implemented with the objective of achieving universalism. It also challenges the Polanyi assumption that social protection institutions follow a solidaristic logic in direct contradiction to the commercial logic

[6] Prospects for basic services, health and education for example, may be different because they are not intrinsically mechanisms for stratification.

under capitalism.[7] The main argument developed in this book is that an understanding of social protection institutions could only be achieves by paying close attention to their stratification effects.

In recent work Garcia-Fuente (2021) argues that the starting point matters for the success of universalistic policies. In his view, countries that began to develop social policies starting from institutions supporting low income groups, as in European welfare states, have a good chance to build upwards by integrating better off groups in social insurance schemes. On the other hand, countries that developed their social policy institutions starting from better off, privileged, groups of workers will find it hard to grow by integrating low income groups. Universalism from below, he argues, generate synergies by expanding the pool of the insured with groups with higher income and lower social risks. Universalism from above is a zero sum game for privileged groups of workers who are asked to agree to higher contributions and less generous services. Whether this applies more generally, Gracia-Fuente assumes an insurance model at work, the fact of the matter is that resistance to the expansion of social protection in Latin America has been strong among insured workers (Garay, 2016). It is also the case that weak preferences for redistribution among non-insured workers could be explained by their low expectations they would benefit from it (Holland, 2018). In the Latin American context, there are significant practical and financial barriers to the expansion of occupational insurance (Barrientos, 2014).

9.2.2 Continued Change and Resilient Dualism?

The discussion in the book underlined the fact that large changes in social protection institutions have taken place since the middle of the last century. Far from social protection institutions in the region representing 'frozen landscapes', their main feature is change—although not always in a positive direction. The last three decades are a case in point. Since the return to democracy in the 1990s, Latin American countries have

[7] Barry (1989, p. 395) cites James Meade wry comment on this: "In my view, the ideal society would be one in which each citizen developed a real split personality, acting selfishly in the market place and altruistically at the ballot box…[I]t is for example, only by such 'altruistic' political action that there can be any alleviation of 'poverty' in a society in which the poor are in a minority".

embraced remarkable policy activism and innovation in social protection. The implementation of individual retirement savings plans and the emergence of large-scale social assistance programmes are the most salient changes. Institutional change is far reaching. Whereas at the beginning of the 1980s occupational insurance funds monopolised social protection, by the second decade of the new century, they have become just one of its components. Perhaps most significantly, whereas at the beginning of the 1980s the sole gateway to social protection was membership of an insurance fund, today there are three sources of social protection entitlements: group membership, savings, and citizenship.

There are firm signs that institutional change in social protection will continue in the region. Occupational insurance pensions are under secular pressure from demographic trends, volatile labour markets, shallow financial markets, and fiscal policy (Arenas de Mesa, 2019; Bosch et al., 2013; CAF, 2020; IMF, 2018). Parametric reforms will continue to be deployed to address these challenges and fine-tune institutional capacities. Individual retirement savings plans were acutely affected by COVID19 due to the suspension of economic activity and the demands to release savings to support participant households (Arenas de Mesa, 2020; Kay & Borzutzky, 2022). Before that, the 2008 financial crisis seriously undermined their rationale and credibility. Demands for reforms to individual retirement savings plans, in countries where they are expected to transition to full institutional supremacy, have become stronger.[8] Further reforms to individual retirement savings plans in Chile, for example, have been recently advocated by an ex-President who already reformed them when in power.[9] Social assistance, especially conditional income transfers, have been successfully transformed into child transfers and schooling subsidies in Argentina and Mexico. Improved institutional infrastructure will continue to facilitate gradual reforms and fine-tuning. Old age transfers are expected to become a basic pension provision institutions in several countries in the region, and perhaps the only reliable means of addressing demographic change and the selectivity of pension

[8] Tuesta and Bhardwaj (2023) explore retirement savings plans for informal workers.

[9] Michelle Bachelet 2023 Reforma previsional en Chile: la necesidad de un acuerdo político, El País 16/07/2023.

benefits. Change will continue to be a feature of social protection in the region.

Dual social protection institutions in the region are likely to stay (Barrientos, 2009, 2012, 2014, 2016, 2019). There are strong barriers to a downward integration of social insurance and assistance. In countries where individual retirement savings plans replaced social insurance schemes, as in Chile, public old age support has greatly expanded.[10] In countries that retained occupational insurance pensions, marked inequality in the generosity of old age pensions they provide will strengthen opposition to integration. Brazil offers a telling example. Public subsidies to the civil service social insurance fund accounted for between 2 and 2.5 percent of GDP in 2008–2009 helping finance one million pensions (Barrientos, 2014). Extending the same deal to the rest of the labour force and population, around 16 million pensioners at the time, is unfeasible. Downward integration requires diluting the generosity of social insurance transfers, but will be strongly challenged by powerful insiders.

The emergence of social assistance as an independent component has led to institutional building and innovation. Dual institutional structures are the norm. Most governments in the region have a Ministry of Labour and Social Security alongside a Ministry/Agency charged with Social Development (Cecchini & Martínez, 2011). Social development agencies have contributed essential capacities within governments, including social registers and programme evaluation, development and implementation. COVID19 has amply demonstrated their effectiveness. The new institutional structures will reinforce growing dualism in social protection institutions in the region.

Perhaps consideration of granular change could work as a Plan B. This would involve the intensification of current trends, sustaining efforts to reduce gender and age bias in social protection, for example. Pace the growth of old age transfers contributing to improving women's income support in later age. Or reaching children through conditional income transfers, child benefits, and scholarships. A further expansion in the

[10] Arenas de Mesa notes that 10 years after the 2008 Reform to individual retirement savings plans in Chile which introduced a basic pension provision for those retirement age without pension entitlements, and contribution subsidies for workers with low earnings, 55 percent of those retired were in receipt of public support (1.5 million) (Arenas de Mesa, 2019, p. 70).

reach old age transfers, and the associated rise in public spending, will continue to exert political pressure towards the gradual withdrawal of public subsidies to occupational and private pensions. Greater transparency in the substantive share of resource revenues in current government financing will continue highlight their origins in the commonwealth and support redistributive policies.

References

Abramo, L., Cecchini, S., & Morales, B. (2019). *Programas sociales, superación de la pobreza e inclusión laboral.* CEPAL.

Acharya, A., Blackwell, M., & Sen, M. (2016). Explaining causal findings without bias: Detecting and assessing direct effects. *American Political Science Review, 110*(3), 512–529. https://doi.org/10.1017/S0003055416000216

Arenas de Mesa, A. (2019). *Los sistemas de pensiones en la encrucijada. Desafíos para la sostenibilidad en América Latina* (159; Libros de La CEPAL). Comisión Económica para América Latina y el Caribe.

Arenas de Mesa, A. (2020). *Los sistemas de pensiones en América Latina. Institucionalidad, gasto público y sostenibilidad financiera en tiempos de COVID-19* (Documento 212; Macroeconomía Del Desarrollo). Economic Commission for Latin America.

Arza, C., Castiglioni, R., Martínez Franzoni, J., Niedzwiecki, S., Pribble, J., & Sánchez-Ancochea, D. (2022). *The political economy of segmented expansion. Latin American Social Policy in the 2000s.* Cambridge University Press. https://doi.org/10.1017/9781009344135

Avelino, G., Brown, D. S., & Hunter, W. (2005). The effects of capital mobility, trade openness, and democracy on social spending in Latin America, 1980–1999. *American Journal of Political Science, 49*(3), 625–641.

Barrientos, A. (2009). Labour markets and the (hyphenated) welfare regime in Latin America. *Economy and Society, 38*(1), 87–108.

Barrientos, A. (2012). Dilemas de las políticas sociales latinoamericanas ¿Hacia una protección social fragmentada? *Nueva Sociedad, 239*, 65–78.

Barrientos, A. (2013). *Human Development Income Transfers in the Longer Term.* (Working Paper 116, International Policy Centre for Inclusive Growth (IPC-PG)). http://www.ipc-undp.org/pub/IPCWorkingPaper116.pdf

Barrientos, A. (2014). On the distributional implications of social protection reforms in Latin America. In G. A. Cornia (Ed.), *Falling inequality in Latin America: Policy changes and lessons* (pp. 340–360). Oxford University Press.

Barrientos, A. (2019). Social protection in Latin America: One region, two systems. In G. Cruz-Martínez (Ed.), *Welfare and social protection in contemporary Latin America* (pp. 59–71). Routledge.

Barrientos, A. (2020). Transnational actors and institutionalization of social protection in the global south. In C. Schmitt (Ed.), *From colonialism to international aid: The influence of external, national, and transnational actors* (pp. 333–356). Palgrave Macmillan.

Barrientos, A., & Villa, J. M. (2015). Evaluating antipoverty transfer programmes in Latin America and Sub-Saharan Africa Better Policies? Better Politics? *Journal of Globalization and Development, 6*(1), 147–179.

Barry, B. (1989). *Theories of justice*. Harvester Wheatsheaf.

Blackwell, M. (2013). A framework for dynamic causal inference in political science. *American Journal of Political Science, 57*(2), 504–520.

Blackwell, M., & Glynn, A. N. (2018). How to make causal inferences with time-series cross-sectional data under selection on observables. *American Political Science Review, 112*(4), 1067–1082.

Borges, F. A. (2019). Adoption and evolution of cash transfer programs in Latin America. In *Oxford Research Encyclopedia*. Oxford University Press. https://doi.org/10.1093/acrefore/9780190228637.013.1521

Bosch, M., Melguizo, A., & Pages, C. (2013). *Mejores pensiones, mejores trabajos*. Inter-American Development Bank.

Brady, D., & Bostic. (2010). Paradoxes of social policy: Welfare transfers, relative poverty, and redistribution preferences. *American Sociological Review, 80*(2), 268–298.

CAF. (2020). *Los sistemas de pensiones y salud en América Latina. Los desafíos del envejecimiento, el cambio tecnológico y la informalidad.* Corporación Andina de Fomento.

Cecchini, S., & Martínez, R. (2011). *Protección social inclusiva en América Latina: Una mirada integral, un enfoque de derechos*. CEPAL.

Collier, R. B., & Collier, D. (1991). *Shaping the political Arena*. Princeton University Press.

Dorlach, T. (2020). Business interests, Conservative economists, and the expansion of non-contributory pensions in Latin America. *Politics and Society, online*, 1–24.

Elwert, F. (2013). Graphical causal models. In *Handbook of causal analysis for social research*. Springer. https://doi.org/10.1007/978-94-007-6094-3_13

Esping-Andersen, G. (1990). *The three worlds of welfare capitalism*. Polity Press.

Fairfield, T., & Garay, C. (2017). Redistribution under the right in Latin America: Electoral competition and organized actors in policy making. *Comparative Political Studies, 50*(14), 1871–1906.

Filgueira, F., Molina, C. G., Papadopulos, J., & Tobar, F. (2005). *Universalismo básico: Una alternativa posible y necesaria para mejorar las condiciones de vida en América Latina* [CIESU Documento de Trabajo]. Centro de Informaciones y Estudies del Uruguay.

Flechtner, S., & Sánchez-Ancochea, D. (2022). Why is the accumulation of knowledge so hard? Exploring econometric research on the determinants of public social spending in Latin America. *Latin American Research Review, 57*, 258–277. https://doi.org/10.1017/lar.2022.21

Garay, C. (2016). *Social policy expansion in Latin America.* Cambridge University Press.

Garcia-Fuente, X. (2021). *The paradox of redistribution in time. Social spending in 53 countries, 1967-2018.* (Working Paper 815; LIS Working Papers). Luxembourg Income Study.

Gelbach, J. B., & Pritchett, L. (1995). *Does more for the poor mean less for the poor? The politics of targeting* (Policy Research Working Papers 1799). The World Bank.

Gelman, A., & Imbens, G. (2013). *Why ask why? Forward causal inference and reverse causal questions* (Working Paper 19614; NBER). National Bureau of Economic Research.

Haggard, S., & Kaufman, R. R. (2008). *Development, democracy, and welfare states. Latin America, Asia, and Eastern Europe.* Princeton University Press.

Holland, A. C. (2018). Diminished expectations. Redistributive preferences in truncated welfare states. *World Politics, 70*(4), 555–594.

Huber, E., Mustillo, T., & Stephens, J. D. (2008). Politics and social spending in Latin America. *Journal of Politics, 70*(2), 420–436. http://www.jstor.com/stable/10.1017/s0022381608080407

Huber, E., & Stephens, J. D. (2012). *Democracy and the left in Latin America. Social policy and inequality in Latin America.* University of Chicago Press.

IMF. (2018). *Growing pains. Is Latin America prepared for population aging?* (Report 18/05). International Monetary Fund. https://www.imf.org/en/Publications/Departmental-Papers-Policy-Papers/Issues/2018/04/16/Growing-Pains-Is-Latin-American-Prepared-for-Population-Aging-45382

Kapiszewski, D., Levitsky, S., & Yashar, D. J. (Eds.). (2021). *The inclusionary turn in Latin American democracies.* Cambridge University Press.

Kaufman, R. R., & Segura-Ubiergo, A. (2001). Globalization, domestic politics, and social spending in Latin America: A time-series cross-section analysis, 1973-97. *World Politics, 53*(4), 553–587. https://www.jstor.org/stable/25054165

Kay, S. J., & Borzutzky, S. (2022). Can defined contribution pensions survive the pandemic? The Chilean case. *International Social Security Review, 75*, 31–50.

Korpi, W. (1980). Social policy and the distributional conflict in the capitalist democracies: A preliminary comparative framework. *West European Politics, 3*, 296–316.

Levitsky, S., & Roberts, K. M. (2012). *The resurgence of the Latin American left.* The John Hopkins University Press.

Lupu, N. (2017). Explaining party breakdown across Latin Am. In *Party brands in crisis.* https://doi.org/10.1017/CBO9781139683562.003

Malloy, J. M. (1979). *The politics of social security in Brazil.* University of Pittsburgh Press.

Mares, I., & Carnes, M. (2009). Social policy in developing countries. *Annual Review of Political Science, 12*, 93–113.

Martínez-Franzoni, J., & Sánchez-Ancochea, D. (2017). *The quest for universal social policies in the south.* Cambridge University Press.

Mesa-Lago, C. (2007). *Reassembling social security. A survey of pensions and healthcare reforms in Latin America.* Oxford University Press.

Moene, K. O., & Wallerstein, M. (2001). Inequality, social insurance, and redistribution. *American Political Science Review, 95*(4), 859–874.

O'Donnell, G. (1975). *Reflexiones sobre las tendencias de cambio en el estado burocrático-autoritario* (Working Paper 1). CEDES/CLACSO.

Silva, E., & Rossi, F. M. (2017). *Reshaping the political arena in Latin America. From resisting neoliberalism to the second incorporation.*

Tuesta, D., & Bhardwaj, G. (2023). *Pensiones para todos. Propuestas para sistemas de pensiones más inclusivos en Latinoamérica.* PinboxAmericaLatina.

van Kersbergen, K., & Vis, B. (2014). *Comparative welfare state politics: Development, opportunities, and reform.* Cambridge University Press.

Yamamoto, T. (2012). Understanding the past: Statistical analysis of causal attribution. *American Journal of Political Science, 56*, 237–256. https://doi.org/10.1111/j.1540-5907.2011.00539.x

Index[1]

[1] Note: Page numbers followed by 'n' refer to notes.

A. Barrientos, *Social Protection in Latin America*, Global Dynamics of Social Policy ,
https://doi.org/10.1007/978-3-031-49795-7

Q

R

S

T

U

V

W

SPRINGER NATURE

GPSR Compliance

The European Union's (EU) General Product Safety Regulation (GPSR) is a set of rules that requires consumer products to be safe and our obligations to ensure this.

If you have any concerns about our products, you can contact us on ProductSafety@springernature.com

In case Publisher is established outside the EU, the EU authorized representative is:

Springer Nature Customer Service Center GmbH
Europaplatz 3
69115 Heidelberg, Germany

The manufacturer's authorised representative in the EU is Springer Nature Customer Service Centre GmbH, Europaplatz 3, 69115 Heidelberg, Germany. If you have any concerns regarding our products, please contact ProductSafety@springernature.com

Printed and bound by CPI Group (UK) Ltd, Croydon, CR0 4YY
01/10/2026
02225894-0011